Contents

1 Were the peace treaties of 1919–23 fair? 10

Background: the peace treaties of 1919–23 1

What were the motives and aims of the "Big Three" at Versailles? 10

What were the main terms of the Treaty of Versailles? 12

Why did all the victors not get everything they wanted? 13

What was the impact of the Treaty of Versailles on Germany up to 1923? 16

How were Germany's allies affected by the other peace treaties? 18

Could the treaties be justified at the time? 19

Review 23

Raise your grade 24

2 To what extent was the League of Nations a success? **29**

Background: the League of Nations' aims, organisation, and power 29

How successful was the League in the 1920s? 31

What were League's failures in the 1920s? 32

How far did weaknesses in the League's organisation make failure inevitable? 33

The impact of the Great Depression on the League 34

How successful was the League in the 1930s? 35

Review 38

Raise your grade 39

3 Why had international peace collapsed by 1939? **43**

Background: international peace in the 1920s and 1930s 43

What were the long-term consequences of the peace treaties of 1919–23? 43

What were the consequences of the failure of the League of Nations in the 1930s? 44

How far was Hitler's foreign policy to blame for the outbreak of war in 1939? 45

What foreign policy actions were taken by Hitler from 1933–6? 46

What happened from 1936–9? 47

Was the policy of appeasement justified? 53

Review 54

Raise your grade 55

4 Who was to blame for the Cold War? **59**

Background: tensions between the Soviet Union and the United States in 1945 59

Why did the United States–Soviet Union alliance begin to break down in 1945? 59

How did the United States react to Soviet expansion? 62

What was the Berlin Blockade? 64

The consequences of the blockade 66

Who was the most to blame for starting the Cold War: the United States or the Soviet Union? 67

Review 68

Raise your grade 69

5	**How effectively did the United States contain the spread of communism?**	**73**
	Background: American concerns about communism	73
	Korea	73
	The United States and events in Cuba, 1959–62	77
	American involvement in Vietnam	83
	Why did the United States become involved in Vietnam?	83
	Review	88
	Raise your grade	89
6	**How secure was the Soviet Union's control over Eastern Europe?**	**93**
	Background: Soviet control over Eastern Europe, 1945–53	93
	Why was there opposition to Soviet control in Hungary in 1956?	93
	How did the Soviet Union react to this opposition?	94
	Why was there opposition to Soviet control in Czechoslovakia in 1968?	94
	How did the Soviet Union react to this opposition?	95
	Events in Hungary in 1956 and in Czechoslovakia in 1968—similarities and differences	96
	Why was the Berlin Wall built in 1961?	97
	What was the significance of "Solidarity" in Poland for the decline of Soviet influence in Eastern Europe?	99
	How far was Gorbachev personally responsible for the collapse of Soviet control over Eastern Europe?	101
	Review	102
	Raise your grade	103
7	**Why did events in the Gulf matter, c.1970–2000?**	**107**
	Background: the importance of events in the Gulf	107
	Why was Saddam Hussein able to come to power in Iraq?	107
	What was the nature of Saddam Hussein's rule in Iraq?	109
	Why was there a revolution in Iran in 1979?	110
	What were the causes and consequences of the Iran–Iraq War, 1980–8?	111
	Why did the First Gulf War take place?	114
	Review	116
	Raise your grade	117
8	**The First World War 1914–18**	**121**
	Background: events immediately before the First World War	121
	Why was the war not over by December 1914?	121
	How successful was the British Expeditionary Force (BEF)?	122
	Why was there stalemate on the Western Front?	124
	How important were new developments such as tanks, machine guns, aircraft, and gas?	125
	What was the significance of the Battles of Verdun and the Somme?	126
	How important were other fronts?	127

Why did the Gallipoli campaign of 1915 fail? 128
Why did Russia leave the war in 1918? 129
What was the impact of war on civilian populations? 130
Why did Germany ask for an armistice in 1918? 131
Why was the German offensive of 1918 unsuccessful? 132
Why did revolution break out in Germany in October 1918? 133
Why was the armistice signed? 133
Review 134
Raise your grade 135

9 Germany, 1918–45 **142**
Background: the formation of the Weimar Republic 142
Was the Weimar Republic doomed from the start? 142
What was the impact of the Treaty of Versailles on the Weimar Republic? 144
To what extent did the Republic recover after 1923 under Stresemann? 146
Why was Hitler able to dominate Germany by 1934? 147
Why was Hitler able to become Chancellor by 1933? 149
How did Hitler consolidate his power in 1933–4? 151
How effectively did the Nazis control Germany, 1933–45? 152
What was it like to live in Nazi Germany? 154
Review 159
Raise your grade 160

10 The United States, 1919–41 **164**
Background: the build-up to the 1920s boom 164
How far did the American economy boom in the 1920s? 164
How far did American society change in the 1920s? 167
How widespread was intolerance in American society? 168
Why was Prohibition introduced and later repealed? 170
How far did the roles of women change during the 1920s? 172
What were the causes and consequences of the Wall Street Crash? 173
What did Hoover do to try to combat the Great Depression? 175
Why did Roosevelt win the election of 1932? 176
How successful was the New Deal? 176
How far did the character of the New Deal change after 1933? 178
Why did the New Deal encounter opposition? 178
Why did unemployment persist despite the New Deal? 180
Review 181
Raise your grade 182

11 Israelis and Palestinians since 1945 **185**

Background: history of the conflict between the Israelis and Palestinians 185

How was the Jewish state of Israel established? 185

How was Israel able to survive despite the hostility of its Arab neighbours? 190

What was the impact of the Palestinian refugee issue? 197

Why has it proved impossible to resolve the Arab–Israeli issue? 200

Review 204

Raise your grade 205

Glossary **208**

Please go to **www.oxfordsecondary.com/esg-for-caie-igcse** for the answers to the 'Apply' tasks.

Introduction

Matched to the latest Cambridge assessment criteria, this in-depth Exam Success Guide brings clarity and focus to exam preparation with detailed and practical guidance on raising attainment in IGCSE® & O Level 20th Century History.

This Exam Success Guide can be used alongside the Student Book *Complete 20th Century History for Cambridge IGCSE® & O Level* and contains links to it where necessary.

This Exam Success Guide:

- Is **fully matched** to the latest Cambridge IGCSE® & O Level syllabuses
- Includes comprehensive **recap** and **review features** which focus on key course content
- Equips you to **raise your grade** with sample responses and examiner commentary
- Will help you to **understand exam expectations** and avoid common mistakes with **examiner tips**
- **Apply knowledge** and test understanding via **exam-style questions**, with answers available online
- Is perfect for use alongside the *Complete 20th Century History for Cambridge IGCSE® and O Level Student Book* or as a standalone resource for independent revision

Key revision points are included as follows:

- **Key ideas:** at the start of every section. This summarises key things you need to know for each topic.
- **Recap:** each chapter recaps key content and theory through easy-to-digest chunks and visual stimulus. Key terms appear in bold and are defined in the Glossary.

- **Apply:** targeted revision activities are written specifically for these guides, which will help you to apply your knowledge in the exam paper. These provide a variety of transferrable exam skills and techniques. By using a variety of revision styles you'll be able to cement your revision.

- **Review:** throughout each section, you can review and reflect on the work you have done, and find advice on how to further refresh your knowledge. This will include references back to the Student Book or link synoptically to other sections in your Exam Success Guide.

- **Analysis:** Strengthen exam performance through analysis of sample student answers and examiner responses.
- **Exam tips:** include particular emphasis on content and skills where students commonly struggle. The tips give details on how to maximise marks in the exam.

Exam tip

- **Raise your grade:** can be found at the end of each chapter. This section includes answers from candidates who didn't achieve maximum marks and advice on how to improve answers.

You are also encouraged to build a record of essential key terms, and either track your revision progress or use the guidelines to indicate topics you are more or less confident about.

Create a revision planner like the one below to plan your revision timetable.

Monday	Tuesday	Wednesday	Thursday	Friday	Saturday	Sunday

Please go to **www.oxfordsecondary.com/esg-for-caie-igcse** for the answers to the 'Apply' tasks.

How will you be assessed?

Candidates for Cambridge IGCSE® History take three components: Paper 1 and Paper 2, and *either* Component 3 or Paper 4.

Candidates for Cambridge O Level History are required to take two papers: Paper 1 and Paper 2.

Paper 1 (2 hours)

There are a total of 60 marks available. Section A consists of four structured essay questions from the Core Content for 20th Century History. You must answer **two** questions.

Section B contains two structured essay questions on each of the Depth Studies. You must answer **one** question.

For IGCSE, Paper 1 is worth 40% of your total marks.

For O Level, Paper 1 is worth 55% of your total marks.

Paper 2 (2 hours)

There are a total of 50 marks available. You are required to answer **six** questions on one topic from the Core Content - your teacher will guide you on which option you will be taking. The six questions are based on source material provided in the paper.

For IGCSE, Paper 2 is worth 33% of your total marks.

For O Level, Paper 2 is worth 45% of your total marks.

And for **Cambridge IGCSE®** candidates, *either*:

Component 3 Coursework

There are a total of 40 marks available. You are required to produce one piece of extended writing based on Depth Study, either from the syllabus or devised by your centre. The investigation will be marked by your teachers and moderated by Cambridge. For IGCSE®, Component 3 is worth 27% of your total marks.

Or:

Paper 4 (1 hour)

There are a total of 40 marks available. You must choose **one** question to answer, based on the Depth Studies that you have covered. There will be a choice of two questions for each Depth Study.

For IGCSE, Paper 4 is worth 27% of your total marks.

1 Were the peace treaties of 1919–23 fair?

You need to know:

- the motives and aims of the "Big Three" at Versailles
- the main terms of the Treaty of Versailles and the other peace treaties
- how far each of the "Big Three" was satisfied with the peace settlement
- the impact of the peace treaties on Germany and other defeated countries up to 1923
- attitudes at the time towards the treaties

Background: the peace treaties of 1919–23

The First World War resulted in the deaths of almost 10 million people, cost more than any previous war in history and destroyed 4 empires. It led to the creation of several new nations in Europe and the Middle East, triggered a revolution in Russia and, perhaps indirectly, led to the rise of the Fascist government in Italy in 1922, and then the Nazi regime in Germany in 1933. In January 1919 delegates from 32 countries were invited to meet in Paris at the palace of Versailles. Each nation present wanted a settlement that would last. The defeated nations and Soviet Russia were not invited to attend.

At the Paris Peace Conference, which began in January 1919, five treaties were drawn up and referred to collectively as the Versailles Settlement. The main one was the Treaty of Versailles, which dealt with Germany; the other treaties dealt with Germany's allies Austria, Hungary, Bulgaria, and Turkey.

Clemenceau's priorities were the defence of France, and the return of land previously lost to Germany; he wanted action regarding the territories of Alsace-Lorraine, the Saarland, and the Rhineland. He also wanted Germany harshly punished and prevented from waging war again.

While representatives from 27 nations participated in the peace conference, proceedings were dominated by 3 men: Prime Minister Georges Clemenceau of France, Prime Minister Lloyd-George of Great Britain, and US President Woodrow Wilson.

What were the motives and aims of the "Big Three" at Versailles?

Clemenceau, Lloyd-George, and Wilson approached the peace conference determined to prevent the recurrence of a major conflict; however, they differed over the methods they believed would successfully achieve this goal.

Clemenceau's priority was to secure the defence of France, and the return of land lost to Germany in 1871. He believed the best way to achieve these goals was to punish Germany harshly and make it impossible for Germany to wage war again.

The Fourteen Points addressed the key areas to be settled after the war, including disarmament, self-determination, the League of Nations, and territorial disputes. (See the Student Book, page 5.)

Lloyd-George believed that a "just and firm" peace that did not create a desire for revenge in Germany, along with the economic revival of Europe and Germany, would be the best way to prevent war. However, he also wanted a share of Germany's colonies to strengthen Britain's global position.

Wilson wanted a fair and lasting peace, with the Fourteen Points as the basis (see the Student Book, page 5), that would increase future international cooperation and encourage nations to negotiate rather than use violence as a tool to settle their differences.

Worked example

What did Lloyd-George hope to achieve from the peace settlement of 1919–20? (4)

Lloyd-George hoped to make Germany pay for starting the war and therefore thought the Germans should pay compensation to the Allies. He therefore insisted that he chair a committee at Versailles to investigate how much Germany should pay.

He also hoped to maintain the dominant position of Britain's navy, which was essential to the protection of Britain's colonies and for trade within the British Empire, and therefore supported restricting Germany's navy to 36 ships.

Worked example

Why did Clemenceau and Wilson disagree over how to treat Germany? (6)
(See the Student Book, pages 3–5.)

Wilson and Clemenceau disagreed over the issue of reparations. Clemenceau wanted to impose a very high level of reparations that would not only compensate the invaded countries for the destruction caused by the war, but would also prevent Germany being able to wage war in the future. Wilson objected to reparations and only accepted that Belgium should be compensated for war damage because, he argued, the invasion of neutral Belgium was illegal.

They also disagreed over disarmament: in his "Fourteen Points", Wilson stated that he wished to see nations' armaments reduced to a level only necessary for national defence but Clemenceau disagreed, arguing instead for the permanent disarmament of Germany. He believed this was essential to protect France from future German attacks.

Exam tip

To answer a question like this you should provide two of Lloyd-George's aims for the peace settlement, with a supporting detail for each.

Recap

As well as their desire to prevent a future conflict, the leaders were heavily influenced by public opinion in their own countries. In France and Britain, the strongest feeling was that Germany should be made to pay for starting the war, while many people in the United States were very reluctant to see their country become involved in the affairs of European states again.

Key fact

The Peace Settlement 1919–20 refers to all five of the peace treaties signed with the defeated powers after the First World War. They were the treaties of:

- Versailles (with Germany)
- St Germain (with Austria)
- Trianon (with Hungary)
- Sèvres (with Turkey)
- Neuilly (with Bulgaria).

Exam tip

The key to success with this type of question is to provide two fully explained reasons.

What were the main terms of the Treaty of Versailles?

The treaty was not negotiated with Germany, and its terms were presented to the German delegation at the peace conference in May 1919. The following points were included in the main terms.

- Germany must take full responsibility for starting the war (the "War Guilt" clause).
- Germany must accept liability for the damage caused by the war and therefore pay reparations to the countries directly by the war (a figure later set at £6600 million).
- The Rhineland must be demilitarised.
- Anschluss was forbidden.
- Disarmament: the German army was limited to 100 000 men, conscription was banned, the navy was limited to 36 warships, and Germany was forbidden from possessing any tanks or air force.
- Loss of territories in Europe was addressed. Land was given to France (Alsace-Lorraine), Belgium (Eupen and Malmedy), Denmark (North Schleswig), to new states: Poland (West Prussia, Posen, and parts of Upper Silesia) and Lithuania (Memel). The Saarland would temporarily be administered by the new League of Nations for 15 years when a plebiscite would be held to decide its future. Danzig became a free city administered by the League of Nations.
- Germany's colonies became mandates of the League of Nations.

Key term

Anschluss—the term given to the unification of Germany with its neighbour, Austria.

Worked example

Describe the military restrictions placed on Germany as a result of the Treaty of Versailles. (4)

The size of the German army was limited to 100 000 men as a result of the Treaty of Versailles, and the army was not allowed to possess any tanks or heavy artillery.

Restrictions were also placed on Germany's navy. No submarines were allowed, while the number of warships was limited to 36. In addition, Germany was not allowed either a military or naval air force.

Exam tip

You only need to describe the main restrictions, with supporting details. You are not being asked to analyse whether they were fair or not.

Apply

Prepare a table with three columns, one for each of the "Big Three" leaders at Versailles. List each leader's main ideas about how to prevent the recurrence of a major conflict.

Why did all the victors not get everything they wanted?

Given the differences between the aims of the "Big Three" and the complexity of devising a peace settlement that sought to both identify and punish the country responsible for starting the conflict, and put in place features to prevent the outbreak of a similar war in the future, it is perhaps understandable that each of Clemenceau, Lloyd-George, and Wilson were pleased with some aspects of the Treaty of Versailles, but were significantly unhappy with other aspects.

In summary, Clemenceau was most pleased with:

- the return of Alsace-Lorraine to France
- the imposition of reparations on Germany
- the weakening of Germany's military
- the increased security for France as a result of the demilitarisation of the Rhineland.

However, he was less pleased with:

- the United States' refusal to create an Anglo-American Treaty of Guarantee to deal with Germany if it became aggressive again
- the Saarland coming under the control of the League of Nations and not been given to France.

Lloyd-George was most pleased with:

- the extension of the British empire through the transfer of Germany's colonies to the League of Nations; several would be mandated to Britain to manage
- the fact that Germany wasn't completely destroyed economically by the Treaty of Versailles, meaning it could play a part in the economic future of Europe.

He was less pleased that many German-speaking people were not ruled by Germany and found themselves in other countries, for example in Poland or Czechoslovakia.

Wilson was most pleased that:

- the creation of a new League of Nations was included in the treaties
- the principle of self-determination resulted in the creation of new countries out of the defeated old empires of Europe
- some degree of disarmament took place after the war.

However, he was less pleased that:

- self-determination did not apply across the whole of Europe
- the treaty was much harsher on Germany than Wilson envisaged in his Fourteen Points
- ultimately, the United States never approved the treaty as Congress did not ratify it when Congress voted on it in November 1919, and again in March 1920—as a result, the United States did not join the League of Nations.

Key term

Mandated territories—the former colonies of defeated countries of the Ottoman Empire, such as Palestine, Syria and Mesopotamia, which were taken over by the League of Nations and legally transferred to other countries in the aftermath of the First World War.

Recap

While the US President has the constitutional power to make and sign treaties, the president cannot ratify a treaty until two-thirds of the US Senate has voted to approve it. This is why Wilson had to carry out an intensive lobbying campaign in the autumn of 1919 to ensure that public opinion would force the Senate to approve the Treaty of Versailles.

Source 1

▲ **Fig. 1.1** *An American cartoon from March 1920*

Exam tip

It is very important to refer to the context in which this cartoon was published, and how it will affect both the message and purpose of the source.

Worked example

Why was this cartoon published in March 1920? Explain your answer using details of the source and your own knowledge. (7)

This cartoon was published in March 1920 because the cartoonist wished to criticise the refusal of the US Senate to approve the Treaty of Versailles in a vote taken that month. The US Constitution requires the Senate to approve any foreign treaty with a two-thirds majority before the President can ratify it. The Senate had failed to approve it in November 1919, and had again failed to do so in March 1920. The cartoonist appears to be suggesting that by "killing off" the treaty, the Senate is effectively endangering the rest of humanity and future world peace: should a future conflict occur then humanity would be able to accuse the US Senate of being partially to blame, hence the title of the cartoon: "The Accuser". By rejecting the treaty, the Senate prevented the United States from joining the new League of Nations, undermining President Wilson's attempt to develop international cooperation and create a lasting peace.

Worked example

"Prime Minister Clemenceau of France was the most satisfied of the 'Big Three' with the Treaty of Versailles." How far do you agree with this statement? Explain your answer. (10)

Clemenceau was probably the most satisfied of all the "Big Three" with the Treaty of Versailles. He would have been highly satisfied that Germany was harshly punished and that France's security seemed to have been assured. Germany had to accept the War Guilt clause and pay a large amount of reparations, most of which went to France. Germany was also punished by losing its colonies, some to France, such as Togoland, and by losing a considerable amount of land in Europe, such as Danzig, which became a Free City. France's security seemed assured because of the extent of disarmament Germany had to accept, with an army of 100 000 volunteers and no air force or tanks. Furthermore, the west bank of the Rhineland had to be completely demilitarised.

Clemenceau was also highly satisfied because both Lloyd-George and Wilson were unhappy with key elements of the treaty. For example, both objected to the scale of reparations. Lloyd-George was keen to see Germany develop as a trading partner for Britain. Wilson believed the Germans would resent the reparations, possibly leading to future conflict.

However, Clemenceau was not satisfied that France's permanent protection from German aggression wasn't guaranteed: the United States would not agree to a Treaty of Guarantee against German aggression. Certain territories taken from Germany could be returned in the future, such as the Saarland, and Allied occupation of the Rhineland would end after 15 years.

It could also be argued that Lloyd-George was the most satisfied as he wanted a moderate peace to allow the European economy to thrive, and that was essentially achieved at Versailles. While Germany was punished, it was not broken up or de-industrialised, as Clemenceau wanted. In addition, Britain's interests were largely enhanced by gaining new colonies, such as Palestine, and by the removal of the German navy as a threat to British naval interests.

Many historians would disagree that Clemenceau was the most satisfied of the "Big Three". The treaty was closest to Lloyd-George's aims before the peace conference, and considerably strengthened Britain's position in the world.

Exam tip

It is important that you provide arguments and evidence to support the view presented in the statement, and then present arguments and evidence that challenge this view. Your conclusion should then comment on the extent to which you believe the statement is correct.

What was the impact of the Treaty of Versailles on Germany up to 1923?

German reaction to the Treaty of Versailles was hostile almost from the point it was presented to Germany. These were the Germans' main criticisms.

- They did not believe the War Guilt clause was fair as they disputed that they were solely to blame for starting the conflict in 1914.
- The extent of disarmament was a severe blow to national pride: for decades the German military had been a symbol of German strength and prestige.
- The Germans claimed to have agreed to an armistice in November 1918 on the basis that the peace would be based on the Fourteen Points. However, the eventual treaty appeared to be much harsher than Wilson's original plan.
- The peace settlement appeared to be inconsistent. For example, self-determination was provided for some nations' people, such as Poles, but not for many Germans.
- Furthermore, the peace settlement was imposed on Germany.
- Germany claimed that it was unable to pay the amount of reparations demanded and refused to pay any more at the end of 1922.

The Treaty of Versailles, and the wider effects of the war, had a significant effect on Germany, with political, economic, and social unrest plunging the country into chaos by 1923.

Exam tip

To score highly on this question you need to provide two fully explained reasons why many Germans believed that this treaty was unfair.

Worked example

Why did many Germans believe that the Treaty of Versailles was unfair? (6)

Many Germans believed that the Treaty of Versailles was unfair because they felt it wrongly blamed them for starting the war. As a result, they strongly objected to the War Guilt clause. They argued that Serbia and Russia contributed greatly to the start of the conflict through their provocation of Austria, and that Germany was merely coming to the assistance of its neighbour and ally in the summer of June 1914.

They also believed it was unfair because they were not given the opportunity to discuss or negotiate the terms of the treaty. They argued that their agreement to an armistice in November 1918 was on the basis that the war would be brought to an end and negotiations would follow; especially considering Germany had agreed to Wilson's conditions to remove the Kaiser from his throne and Germany had not itself been invaded. However, the treaty was a dictated peace, which was decided upon by the victors at Versailles and presented to the German delegates as something that they would have to accept.

Worked example

How far would you agree that the Treaty of Versailles was an unfair treaty? (10)

On the one hand, there is a strong argument that the Treaty of Versailles was unfair. First, it appeared that Germany was being punished twice over for the damage that was caused during the war. The Treaty stated that Germany would have to pay reparations to the victorious powers for war damage, for example the rebuilding of Ypres in Belgium, which had been virtually destroyed during four years of fighting. When the final amount of reparations was agreed upon—£6.6 billion—Germany argued that it was not able to pay this amount, especially when the very resources that Germany would need to pay for the reparations (coal, iron ore) were not available to the Germans as the Saarland was under the control of the League of Nations and Upper Silesia was given to Poland.

The treaty was also thought to be unfair because Germany appeared to have been treated differently from other nations. While the principle of self-determination was used to create new nations for Poles and Czechs, many Germans were left under the control of foreign governments, for example in the Sudetenland in Czechoslovakia. The principle of disarmament was applied to the defeated nations, but this was not applied to the other nations at Versailles.

However, one could suggest it was not unfair because the experience of Russia at the hands of Germany in March 1918 indicated that Germany would have imposed a treaty that was harsh, if not more harsh, on the Allies if it had won the war. The Treaty of Brest-Litovsk required Russia to give up approximately 1 million square miles of its territory to Germany, Austria, and Turkey, losing around 30 per cent of its population in the process, and 90 per cent of its coal mines.

Furthermore, one of the more controversial aspects of the Versailles Treaty, the War Guilt clause, was fair because German militarism and support for Austria in the summer of 1914 were the main cause of the war: if Germany had not given Austria a "blank cheque" in its dispute with Serbia and then implemented the Schlieffen Plan, there would not have been a war in Europe.

Exam tip

You should provide a balanced response, ideally providing two arguments for each side and a conclusion evaluating how far you agree with the statement.

Apply

Some believed that the Paris peace treaties were unfair. Others believed that the treaties were not harsh enough. Consider both views. For both viewpoints, write three bullet points, giving a supporting example for each point.

How were Germany's allies affected by the other peace treaties?

The peace treaties with Austria, Bulgaria, Turkey, and Hungary followed similar principles to the treaty with Germany.

- The countries had to disarm.
- They had to pay reparations.
- They lost territory.
- New countries were created out of the land the defeated countries lost.

	Treaty of St Germain, with Austria (September 1919)	**Treaty of Trianon, with Hungary** (June 1920)	**Treaty of Neuilly, with Bulgaria** (November 1919)	**Treaty of Sèvres, with Turkey** (August 1920)
Disarmament	Troops were limited to 30 000 men There was to be no conscription There was to be no navy	Troops were limited to 35 000 men There was to be no conscription 3 patrol boats only were allowed	Troops were limited to 20 000 men There was to be no conscription 4 torpedo boats only were allowed There was to be no air force	Troops were limited to 30 000 men 6 torpedo boats only were allowed
Reparations	Reparations were agreed, but they were never set due to Austrian bankruptcy	Reparations were set at 200 million gold crowns	Reparations were set at £90 million	No reparations were imposed as the Allies did not believe Turkey would be able to repay them However, the Allies did take control of Turkey's finances
Loss of territory	The Austro-Hungarian Empire was to be broken up Anschluss was forbidden	Fiume to Italy	Territory was lost to: Greece Romania Yugoslavia	Smyrna and East Thrace were given to Greece Rhodes was given to Italy
New countries created from their land	Czechoslovakia Romania Poland Yugoslavia	Czechoslovakia Yugoslavia Romania	None	Syria Iraq Palestine Kurdistan Armenia

Worked example

Describe how Austria and Hungary were treated in the Paris peace settlements. (4)

Both Austria and Hungary were forced to disarm as a result of the peace settlement in 1919. Both countries were forbidden from conscripting men to their armies, and while Austria could have an army consisting of 30 000 men, Hungary was allowed an army of 35 000 men.

New countries were also created from land taken from Austria and Hungary. Czechoslovakia, Romania, and Yugoslavia were all created using land taken from Austria and Hungary.

Exam tip

The 4-mark description question is an introductory question. The answer needs to present two points, each with a supporting detail or example.

Could the treaties be justified at the time?

Opinions in the years immediately following the peace treaties broadly divided into three viewpoints.

- The treaties were too harsh. Some, like Lloyd-George, feared that the treaties would stir up such resentment in the defeated countries, especially Germany, that Europe would be plunged back into war. Others, such as British economist John Maynard Keynes, argued that the scale of punishment would prevent Germany's economy recovering, which would impact on the prosperity of the rest of Europe.
- The treaties were not harsh enough. Many people in France feared that the Treaty of Versailles merely brought France a temporary respite from German aggression, and thought that Germany should have also been broken into smaller states and had its industrial capacity completely destroyed. In Italy, Prime Minister Orlando was heavily criticised for not demanding that extra territory should be taken from Austria and given to Italy.
- The treaties were fair. President Wilson argued that the treatment of the defeated nations was appropriate for their roles in starting and sustaining the war. Edward M House, one of the American diplomats at Versailles, acknowledged that it was not a perfect peace settlement, but probably the best that could have been achieved given the circumstances.

Source 2

"Wilson's principles survived the eclipse of the Versailles system and they still guide European politics today: self-determination, democratic government, collective security, international law, and a League of Nations. Wilson may not have gotten everything he wanted at Versailles, and his treaty was never ratified by the Senate, but his vision and his diplomacy, for better or worse, set the tone for the twentieth century. France, Germany, Italy, and Britain may have sneered at Wilson, but every one of these powers today conducts its European policy along Wilsonian lines."

▲ *A historian writing about President Wilson in 2001.*

Source 3

At the Peace Table

—*From Hvepsen, Christiania.*

CLEMENCEAU (to the German delegates): "Take your seats, gentlemen!"

▲ **Fig. 1.2** *A view of the peace talks from an American newspaper*

Source 4

"To those who are saying that the treaty is bad... I feel like admitting it. But I would also say that empires cannot be shattered and new states raised upon their ruins without disturbance. To create new boundaries is always to create new troubles. While I should have preferred a different peace, I doubt whether it could have been made."

▲ *Extract from the diary of Edward M House, an American diplomat, June 1919.*

Worked example

Look at sources 3 and 4 (on the previous page). How far do these sources disagree? Explain your answer using details of the sources. (7)

Sources 3 and 4 disagree in their main message. Source 3 suggests that the peace settlement is extremely harsh on the defeated powers, as represented by the spikes on the chairs and handcuffs on the table. Source 4, in contrast, suggests that the "Big Three" came up with as good and fair a peace as was possible given the impact of the war on Europe.

However, the sources do agree that the treaties were not essentially fair. Source 4 implies that the author acknowledges that he would have preferred a better treaty, and even suggest he agrees with those who say it was a "bad" treaty, which agrees with the main message and details of source 3.

In conclusion, the sources mostly agree that the peace treaties were not fair, although source 3 states this more explicitly and does not consider the context in which the peacemakers found themselves.

Exam tip

You should explain how the two sources agree and disagree on either the details or main message, and provide a judgment on the extent of agreement.

Source 5

"The Treaty contains no provisions for the economic rehabilitation of Europe; nothing to make the defeated Central empires into good neighbours, nothing to stabilise the new states of Europe, nothing to reclaim Russia; not does it promote in any way a compact of economic solidarity amongst the Allies themselves; no arrangement was reached at Paris for restoring the disordered finances of France and Italy or to adjust the systems of the Old World and the New."

▲ *Extract from* The Economic Consequences of the Peace, *by JM Keynes, 1919. Keynes participated at the peace conference as part of the British delegation.*

Exam tip

Base your response on the specific content of the source and relate it to what you know of the event being described.

Worked example

Study source 5 (on the previous page). Are you surprised by this source? Explain your answer using details of the source and your own knowledge. (8)

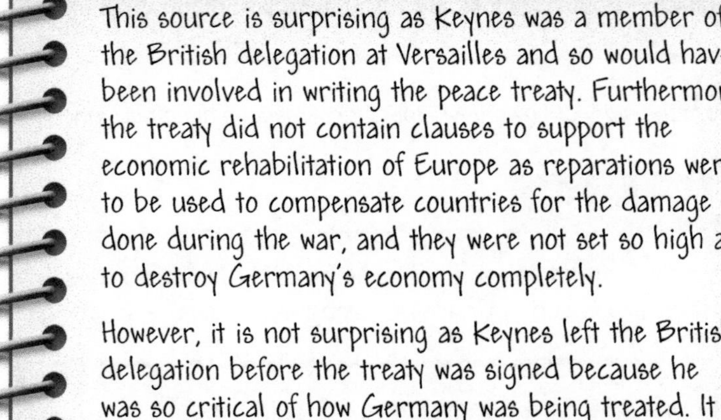

This source is surprising as Keynes was a member of the British delegation at Versailles and so would have been involved in writing the peace treaty. Furthermore, the treaty did not contain clauses to support the economic rehabilitation of Europe as reparations were to be used to compensate countries for the damage done during the war, and they were not set so high as to destroy Germany's economy completely.

However, it is not surprising as Keynes left the British delegation before the treaty was signed because he was so critical of how Germany was being treated. It is also not surprising because the peacemakers intended to punish the defeated Central Powers and were not concerned with rehabilitating them. The loss of land and extent of disarmament are good examples of this.

On balance, the message of the source is not surprising considering the harsh way in which the treaties dealt with the Central Powers after the war.

Source 6

"The criminal madness of this peace will drain Germany's national life-blood. It is a shameless blow in the face of common sense. It is inflicting the deepest wounds on us Germans as our world lies in wreckage about us."

▲ *Extract from a speech made by a member of the Reichstag, 1919.*

See "Raise your grade" for a question on this source.

Source 7

▲ **Fig. 1.3** *A cartoon from a British newspaper, May 1919*

See "Raise your grade" for a question on this source.

Review

1. What were the consequences of the Treaty of Sèvres for Turkey? [4]
2. Describe how the peacemakers at Versailles attempted to achieve disarmament of the defeated powers. [4]
3. Why would President Wilson have been pleased with the terms of the Treaty of Versailles? [6]
4. "German opposition to the Treaty of Versailles was unjustified." How far do you agree with this statement? Explain your answer. [10]
5. Who would have been happier with the Treaty of Versailles, Wilson or Lloyd-George? [10]
6. Study source 3. Are you surprised by this source? Explain your answer using details of the source and your knowledge. [8]
7. Study sources 4 and 7. How far do these two sources disagree? Explain your answer using details of the sources. [7]
8. Study all of the sources in the chapter. How far do they provide convincing evidence that the Paris peace treaties 1919–20 were unfair? Use the sources to explain your answer. [12]

For further information review this section in the Student Book.

1. Describe German territorial losses as a result of the Treaty of Versailles. **[4]**

Analysis

✓ This question is asking you to provide two features of German territorial losses as a result of the Treaty of Versailles.

✓ You must also give supporting examples for each point you make.

✓ Germany's territorial losses after the war were in Europe, such as east Prussia which was given to the new state of Poland, and also further afield because she lost her colonial territories, such as Togoland, as well.

Mark scheme

1 mark for each relevant point, additional mark for supporting detail, maximum 2 marks per point.

Student answer

Germany lost a lot of land as a result of the Treaty of Versailles and therefore became much smaller.

Examiner feedback

To answer question 1, the student only provides a single general comment. Two points with specific examples would improve the answer. For example: Germany lost land to France as a result of the Treaty of Versailles, including Alsace-Lorraine, which it had gained in 1871, and Eupen and Malmedy to Belgium. Land was also given to the League of Nations to administer, including Danzig and Germany's colonies. 1 mark awarded.

2. Why would Austria have been unhappy with the Treaty of St Germain? **[6]**

Analysis

✓ As this is a "Why" question, the answer needs to provide two reasons why Austria would have been unhappy with the treaty.

✓ Each of the two reasons you provide should be explained and illustrated with a relevant detail.

✓ Reasons why the Austrians may have been unhappy with the Treaty of St Germain include the loss of territory to new states such as Czechoslovakia, the ban on Anschluss, and restriction of military capabilities.

Mark scheme

Level 1:	general answer lacking specific contextual knowledge (1 mark)
Level 2:	identifies AND/OR describes reasons (2–3 marks)
Level 3:	explains ONE reason (4–5 marks)
Level 4:	explains TWO reasons (6 marks)

Student answer

Austria would have been very unhappy with the Treaty of St Germain because Austria lost a lot of territory. Land was taken from Austria to help create new countries. Galicia was given to the new state of Poland, most of Dalmatia went to Yugoslavia while much of Bohemia went to Czechoslovakia.

Examiner feedback

This question requires two explained reasons, and the student only provides one. Therefore, to achieve full marks the student would need to give a second explained reason, for example explaining why the military restrictions on Austria would have caused discontent. 3 marks awarded.

3. "The 'Big Three' set out to cripple Germany at Versailles."
How far do you agree with this statement? Explain your answer. **[10]**

Analysis

✓ This question requires a balanced response, with clearly laid out arguments for each side, and using relevant supporting information to support each argument.

✓ To get full marks, it is essential to provide a concluding judgment responding to the "how far" element of the question.

✓ For this particular question, you should analyse the motives of Clemenceau, Lloyd-George and Wilson, considering how far they wished to "cripple" Germany. While the positions of the French and American leaders were clear, you would be wise to identify those aspects of Lloyd-George's position that support the "cripple Germany" argument and those that challenge it.

Mark scheme

Level 1:	general answer lacking specific contextual knowledge (1 mark)
Level 2:	identifies AND/OR describes reasons (2–3 marks)
Level 3:	gives a one-sided explanation (4–5 marks) or one explanation of both sides (4–6 marks)
Level 4:	explains both sides (7–9 marks)
Level 5:	explains with evaluation (10 marks)

Student answer

On the one hand, this statement is correct. The French Prime Minister, Clemenceau, was intent on revenge on Germany for starting the war and inflicting terrible damage on France, and ensuring that Germany was in no position to ever wage war, and threaten France, again. He wanted to cripple Germany militarily by permanently disbanding most of its armed forces and economically by imposing extremely high reparations, with the figure specified in the treaty so Germany could not negotiate a lower amount later. He also wanted Germany's industrial base either given to the League of Nations or placed under French control, to prevent Germany from ever developing into a military power in the future.

British Prime Minister, Lloyd-George, was very aware of the British public's demand to make Germany pay for the war and so he started the peace talks arguing for a high level of reparations that would cripple Germany and act as a deterrent for future aggressors. He also wanted to cripple Germany's navy, ensuring British naval supremacy, so took possession of most of Germany's military and merchant ships.

President Wilson did not intend to cripple Germany, and instead hoped to create a fair and lasting peace. He wanted to make his Fourteen Points the basis of the Versailles settlement. These were more concerned with removing the issues he believed had contributed to the start of the war, such as secret treaties and naval rivalry, and introducing a new international association, The League of Nations, through which countries could resolve differences.

On balance, although Wilson had different intentions, as Clemenceau and Lloyd-George did set out to make Germany pay heavily at Versailles, it can be argued that most of the "Big Three" intended to cripple Germany.

Examiner feedback

This response stays focused on the question and provides a reasonably balanced argument with a clear judgment on how far the statement is correct. Relevant factual supporting detail is also provided. However, a further argument that the "Big Three" did not set out to cripple Germany is required. The student could perhaps point to Lloyd-George's shift in position closer towards Wilson's viewpoint once the conference had started; and the desire for a rebuilt Germany to act as a trading partner for Britain, and as a bulwark against Soviet communism. 9 marks awarded.

4. Study source 7. What is the message of the cartoonist? Explain your answer using details of the source and your own knowledge. **[8]**

Analysis

- ✓ This question requires you to identify and explain the main message and sub-message of a cartoonist.
- ✓ In the answer you need to state what the cartoonist thinks about the likely impact of the Treaty of Versailles.
- ✓ The cartoonist manages to suggest that the peacemakers are oblivious to the effects their actions may have on future generations of Europeans, represented by the child behind the pillar.

Mark scheme

Level 1:	describes or misinterprets the cartoon (1 mark)
Level 2:	identifies AND/OR explains valid sub-messages in the cartoon (2–4 marks)
Level 3:	identifies AND/OR explains the big message, but does not include the cartoonist's view (5–6 marks)
Level 4:	identifies AND/OR explains the the big message and the cartoonist's view (8 marks)

Student answer

The message of this source is that the peacemakers at Versailles do not appear to be concerned that future generations will be upset by the decisions made at Versailles. The peacemakers clearly believe that they have come up with a good peace treaty and Clemenceau only thinks it curious that someone who may be a child in 1919 would be upset by the treatment of the defeated powers at Versailles.

Examiner feedback

This type of question requires students to identify and explain the attitude of the cartoonist, something which this response does not fully do. A more developed answer would explain that the cartoonist is critical of the peace settlement and fears that the peacemakers have constructed treaties that may lead to a further conflict, possibly in 1940, as referenced by the use of "cannon fodder" in the title of the cartoon and the "class of 1940" weeping. 5 marks awarded.

5. Study sources 3 and 5. How far do these two sources disagree? Explain your answer using details of the sources. **[7]**

Analysis

- ✓ This question requires you not only to understand the sources but also compare the extent to which their main messages and sub-messages agree.
- ✓ Consider the views of the author and the cartoonist on the terms of the Treaty of Versailles: do they agree, and if so, why? (This is the big message of each source.)
- ✓ Think not only about the big message but also the sub-messages—which particular aspects of the treaty the author and the cartoonist believe are the most significant.

Mark scheme

Level 1:	writes about the sources but makes no valid comparison (1 mark)
Level 2:	identifies information that is in one source but not in the other OR states that the sources are about the same subject (2 marks)
Level 3:	agrees or disagrees with sub-messages or other details (3–4 marks)
Level 4:	agrees and disagrees with sub-messages or other details (5 marks)
Level 4:	compares what the sources suggest about the Treaty of Versailles (6–7 marks)

Student answer

Sources 3 and 5 fundamentally agree that the post-war peace treaties were deeply flawed and likely to create resentment among the defeated powers after the war. These sources agree that the treaties seek to punish the defeated powers: source 3 includes hand-cuffs on the table for the German delegation; source 5 suggests that there was nothing designed to make the defeated powers willing to work with the other nations after the war.

However, the sources also disagree: source 3 suggests that the victorious powers are united and working together as they are helping to "serve" the meal as a team. However, source 5 suggests that the peace treaties didn't promote unity among the victors or encourage cooperation to deal with economic problems faced by countries such as France and Italy.

Examiner feedback

This response focuses on the question and provides an assessment of how the two sources both agree and disagree, including reference to the details of each source and the main messages of both sources. 6 marks awarded.

You need to know:

- the successes and failures of the League of Nations in the 1920s
- how far the weaknesses in the League of Nation's organisation made failure inevitable
- the impact of the Great Depression on the League of Nations
- how successful the League of Nations was in the 1930s

Background: the League of Nations' aims, organisation, and power

The aims of the League of Nations were set out in the Covenant. They were to:

- achieve international peace and security
- promote international cooperation, especially in business and trade
- encourage nations to disarm
- improve living and working conditions for the people of all nations
- uphold and enforce the Treaty of Versailles.

The League of Nations was created through the peace treaties at the end of the First World War. It was based in Geneva, Switzerland. It started work in 1920.

At the League's inception there were 42 members. The League was originally made weaker by the absence of the United States, Germany, and Soviet Russia and by the withdrawal of certain countries, including Germany, Japan, and Italy, in the 1930s. Britain and France were the only major countries to remain members throughout the time of the League's existence.

Collective security was the intended means to maintain peace. There were three stages to this—moral disapproval, economic sanctions, and military sanctions. The League did not have an army of its own.

The 1920s proved to be a relatively successful period for the League, although even during this period it adopted the role of passive bystander. However, the League used agencies and commissions to address issues of disease, poverty, and exploitation and achieved a lot in the 1920s.

The 1930s saw the work of the League made more difficult by the World Depression. This decade also saw the League fail in its peacekeeping role in Manchuria and Abyssinia.

The organisation and structure of the League

The Assembly

- The Assembly met annually at the League's headquarters.
- All members of the League were represented.
- The Assembly considered matters of general policy and recommended action to the Council.
- The Assembly fixed the budget.
- Every member of the League had one vote.
- Decisions had to be unanimous.

The Council

- The Council met four times a year and for emergencies.
- There were both permanent and non-permanent members of the Council.
- In 1920 the permanent members were Britain, France, Italy, and Japan.
- The non-permanent members were elected by the Assembly for three-year periods.
- In 1926 Germany became a permanent member.
- The number of non-permanent members increased from 4 in 1920 to 9 in 1926 and 11 in 1936.
- Each member country had one vote.
- Decisions had to be unanimous.

The Secretariat

- All the administrative and financial work of the League was performed by the Secretariat.
- This work included organising conferences and meetings, keeping records, and preparing reports.

Agencies, committees, and commissions

- The Mandates Commission ensured that Britain and France acted in the interests of the people of the former colonies of Germany and its allies.
- The Refugees Committee assisted in the return of refugees to their original homes following the end of war.
- The Slavery Commission worked to abolish slavery around the world.
- The Health Committee began to educate people about health and sanitation and started to deal with dangerous diseases.

Using the information on the Assembly, Council and Secretariat above, draw a diagram that shows how the League worked.

The powers of the League

The League could take action in three ways to try to solve a dispute.

- Moral condemnation—the League could put pressure on a country guilty of failing to cooperate with the League's aims by bringing world opinion against that country.
- Economic and financial sanctions—members of the League could refuse to trade with the uncooperative country.
- Military force—armed forces from member countries could be used against an aggressor.

The power of the League lay in the idea it worked collectively—nations together applying pressure through economic, military, or moral methods.

How successful was the League in the 1920s?

Why was the League able to achieve some successes in the 1920s?

- **There was no appetite for conflict**—people and governments did not want a repeat of a the First World War and so there was a high level of goodwill towards the League.
- **Disputes were often between smaller countries**—they were willing to give the League a chance and readily accepted the League's decisions, an example of this being the dispute over the Aaland Islands.
- **Countries were rebuilding after the First World War**—they were in no position, economically or militarily, to enter into further conflict.
- **The League of Nations was new and countries were willing to give it a chance to be successful**—it was led by the victors of the First World War (except the United States). This gave the League some credibility.

Success in settling political disputes

Issue	Solution reached by the League
Sweden and Finland fought over the Aaland Islands (1921).	Territory was given to Finland.
There was a dispute between Germany and Poland over Upper Silesia (1921).	A plebiscite was held and the area was divided between the two.
There was a dispute between Turkey and Iraq over the province of Mosul (1924).	Agreement was reached, meaning that Iraq kept the territory and Turkey received 10 per cent royalty payment each year on oil deposits.
Greece and Bulgaria fought over their borders (1925).	Greece was ordered to withdraw and pay Bulgaria £45 000 compensation.

During the 1920s the League proved successful at settling disputes between smaller countries and finding peaceful solutions.

Success in dealing with humanitarian issues

- **Refugees**—after the war around 400 000 prisoners and refugees were successfully returned to their homelands from Russia and Greece.
- **Health organisation**—the League helped Soviet Russia to prevent a typhus epidemic in Siberia; worked hard to defeat leprosy; and started an international campaign to exterminate mosquitoes, reducing the spread of malaria and yellow fever.
- **Transport**—the League made recommendations for the marking of shipping lanes and produced an international highway code for road users.
- **Economic and financial**—to deal with Austria's economic problems, the League devised a plan that stabilised the currency; and devised similar plans for Hungary, Greece, and Bulgaria.
- **Social issues**—200 000 slaves in British-owned Sierra Leone were freed; and the League challenged the use of forced labour on the Tanganyika railway in Africa, reducing the death rate from 50 per cent to 4 cent. The League also blacklisted large international companies involved in illegal drug selling.

- **Working conditions**—the League banned poisonous white lead from paint, and recommended a limit on working hours for young children.

Recap

The League carried out humanitarian work at a hugely important time—the end of the First World War had created huge issues with shifting borders, scarcity of medical resources, and also lack of working relationships between governments.

Exam tip

With a question like this the aim is to identify specific actions the League took and add supporting detail. Aim to present three significant points.

Worked example

Describe how the League of Nations tried to improve living and working conditions around the world.

The League of Nations attempted to address working hours. Although it couldn't pass laws, the League recommended a reduction of the hours of work for children, for example.

The League also established a Health Committee that attempted to address major challenges faced by member states. It worked hard to defeat leprosy, including setting up leper colonies. The League also tried to eliminate malaria—its attempts failed but the League did reduce the number of cases.

What were League's failures in the 1920s?

Failure to deal with aggressors

- Poland and Lithuania fought over Vilna (1920). Poland was clearly the aggressor but did not withdraw. The French would not act against Poland as they saw the Polish as a possible future ally.
- Italy and Greece had a dispute over Corfu (1923). In this case Mussolini went behind the back of the League to the Conference of Ambassadors, persuading it to change the League ruling.

Failure to implement disarmament

- All attempts at international disarmament failed, despite the efforts of the Disarmament Commission. The French regarded disarmament as a threat to their security. This encouraged the Germans to argue that they had a right to rearm to protect themselves.

Agreements made outside the League

- There was limited faith in the League's ability to deal with any major challenge in the 1920s as the resolution of disputes was in relation to minor countries.
- France was the country most concerned about its security, making mutual assistance pacts with other countries, including Poland and Czechoslovakia.
- The Locarno Treaties of 1925 provided guarantees for the frontiers of north-eastern Europe.
- The Kellogg-Briand Pact had 65 signatories of countries renouncing war by 1928.

Failures with disarmament and also in dealings with major European powers such as France and Italy weakened the League and undermined its power. They also provided a hint of the problems it would face in the 1930s.

Worked example

Describe two successes of the League of Nations in the 1920s.

In 1919, Poland and Czechoslovakia fought over Teschen, an area rich in coal. In 1920 the League arbitrated on the dispute, splitting the area between the two countries. Although neither country was happy about the decision, they accepted it and stopped the fighting.

The League was also able to settle a dispute between Sweden and Finland. This also proved successful.

Exam tip

The answer starts well and gives a good explanation of one success in the 1920s. However, it needs to include more detail on: the dispute between Sweden and Finland over the Aaland islands; the investigation the League led, which resulted in the Islands staying with Finland.

Create a table with one column for the successes of the League in the 1920s and one for its failures. Can you argue that the League was functioning well up until 1929 or did it already seem flawed?

How far did weaknesses in the League's organisation make failure inevitable?

Membership

Three of the most powerful countries in the world were not initially members of the League.

- The United States refused to join.
- Germany was only allowed to join the League in 1926 after it had demonstrated its peaceful intentions.
- The Soviet Union was not invited to join the League because it was communist.

This reduced the ability of the League to take action against aggressive countries either militarily or by considering economic and trade sanctions. Britain and France were the only major powers that were members of the League throughout its existence but they were both greatly weakened by the First World War. Britain was trying to maintain its empire while France was primarily concerned with increasing security against Germany.

Also several countries left the League once it had begun.

- Japan left in 1933 following criticism for invading Manchuria.
- Italy left in 1937 following the imposition of sanctions over Abyssinia.

Unanimous decisions were in place to prevent the League from being dominated by stronger, more powerful, countries. This gave all members an equal say in the running of the League.

Collective security

The League did not have an army of its own and so relied heavily on collective security.

- If military sanctions were to be imposed, member countries would be asked to contribute towards a fighting force. This created uncertainty as an appropriate army would be difficult to assemble since member states would be reluctant to send their army to participate in a dispute in which they were not directly involved.
- In theory, collective security appeared to be a good idea for the preservation of peace but often nations looked to the League to take action when they were not willing to take action themselves.
- The absence of the United States reduced the League's effectiveness as it was deprived of a powerful army and strong financial backing in support of sanctions.
- The League's Covenant demanded unanimous decisions in both the Assembly and the Council. This made it difficult to take decisive action against any country acting in a war-like manner.

Collective security was the intended means by which the League aimed to maintain peace. However, it depended on the willingness of the members of the League to work together to deal with aggression.

Collective security represented an idealistic approach. It was unrealistic to expect a nation to obey the rules of the collective security system while at the same time failing to give the system the power to enforce the nation's will.

The impact of the Great Depression on the League

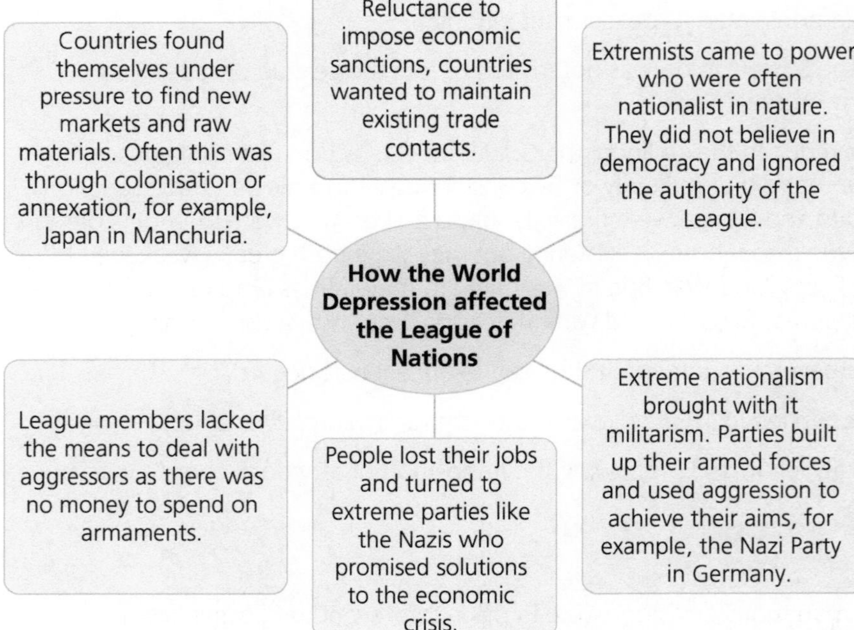

▲ **Fig. 2.1** *The effects of the World Depression on the League of Nations' effectiveness*

How successful was the League in the 1930s?

Faced with an economic slump from a declining export market for its silk, in part due to the global depression that had occurred, Japan invaded Manchuria in an attempt to find an answer to a need for food and raw materials.

Response of the League to Japan's invasion of Manchuria

Action

- The League instructed Japan to withdraw, but was ignored and the invasion continued.
- A commission of enquiry was set up, led by Lord Lytton. This concluded that the invasion was not justified. The commission did not present its report until 1932, a full year after the invasion. The findings were considered by the League in February 1933 and were accepted by a vote of 42 to 1.
- Japan responded by terminating its membership of the League.

Failure to introduce sanctions

- No European country wanted to cut back its trade with the Far East, especially as the United States would have taken over.
- Imposing military sanctions was less appealing as this would have involved the sending of a naval task force to the other side of the world with little chance of success.
- Britain and France feared attack on their Far East colonies if sanctions were imposed.
- The League was Eurocentric in nature and did not see Asia as vital for Europe.

Results

- Japan demonstrated blatant aggression as Hitler and Mussolini watched with interest.
- The League looked weak when faced with aggressive action taken by a strong country.
- To avoid taking action the League regarded Manchuria as a Japanese sphere of interest.
- As these events took place in East Asia the League was less damaged. Some League members believed that if the aggression had been in Europe the League would have taken appropriate action.

Source 1

"Manchuria showed that the League was toothless. The failure of the League to stop aggression in Manchuria had grave consequences in Europe too. The lesson was obvious; there was no power in the world to stop a determined aggressor."

▲ *Extract from* Essential Modern World History *by Steven Waugh, published in 2001.*

Recap

Japan's behaviour showed a flaw in the workings of the League—once Japan withdrew from the organisation the sanctions the League could apply were rendered useless.

Source 2

▲ *A cartoon published in Britain's* Evening Standard *newspaper, 19 January 1933.*

Exam tip

The sources seem largely in full agreement. It is important to use evidence from both sources to indicate this. Also make sure you place the sources in context—give detailed information about what they are discussing.

Worked example

Read source 1 and look at source 2. How far would the cartoonist have agreed with source 1?

I think the cartoonist would have largely agreed with the views expressed in source 1. The cartoonist shows Japan having walked over the figure representing the League of Nations, implying that it was not powerful enough to stand in the way of Japan. In a similar way this view is expressed by source 1, which states that "Manchuria showed the League was toothless" and that "there was no power in the world to stop a determined aggressor", supporting the view expressed by the cartoonist. Both of these sources are referencing the events surrounding the Manchuria crisis, where Japan's aggression could not be stopped by the attempted sanctions of the League once Japan withdrew. The only part of the source 1 the cartoonist might have disagreed with would be that source 1 indicates this was catastrophic for the League, while the cartoon does at least suggest that the League is attempting to save face and therefore implying the event may not be as serious.

Italy's invasion of Abyssinia

- In October 1935 Italy invaded Abyssinia.
- Mussolini was looking for ways to boost his popularity in Italy following a period of economic recession and unemployment.
- Abyssinia's defences were relatively primitive—they were no match for the modern Italian army and air force.

Action

The League immediately condemned the unprovoked aggression of Italy and imposed economic sanctions that immediately banned arms sales to Italy (but not Abyssinia), monetary loans to Italy, imports from Italy, and exports to Italy of rubber, tin, and metals.

Failures of the League

- The League failed to ban oil and coal exports to Italy as it was thought that the United States would not support this and that the economic interests of League members would be affected.
- The League did not close the Suez canal to Mussolini's supply ships for fear of reprisals against the British colonial possessions of Gibraltar and Malta.

Results

- On 9 May 1936 Mussolini formally annexed the whole of Abyssinia. The League watched helplessly.
- Britain and France showed self-interest—for example, it was reported that if coal had been included in the sanctions 30 000 British coal miners would have lost their jobs.
- The incident showed the League was powerless when its most important members failed to take effective action. They feared that Mussolini would ally with Hitler and so did not respond to the invasion.
- In November 1936 Mussolini and Hitler signed the Rome–Berlin Axis, showing that attempts by Britain and France to keep Italy on their side had failed despite their lack of action.

Collective security was now dead, as was the existence of the League as a peacekeeping organisation.

Source 3

"Economic sanctions against Italy were serious, but not a great problem. Banning the sale of weapons and rubber simply made Italy look for suppliers who were not members of the League. The biggest worry was a ban on selling oil. If that happened in 1935 the invasion of Abyssinia would have halted in a week."

▲ *Extract from* Mussolini *by Denis Mack Smith, published in 1983.*

Compare the Abyssinian and Manchuria Crises. Consider the following questions. What similarities are there in how the League reacts? Is one of these crises more important than the other in exposing the weaknesses of the League? For each question write a bullet list of information to use in your answer.

Source 4

"Could the League survive the failure of sanctions to rescue Abyssinia? Could it ever impose sanctions again? Probably there had never been a clear-cut case for sanctions. If the League had failed in this case there could probably be no confidence that it could succeed again in the future."

▲ *Anthony Eden, British Foreign Minister, speaking to members of the government about the crisis in Abyssinia, May 1936.*

Exam tip

To answer this question it is important to explain whether or not you are surprised based on the content of the sources, but you also must consider their provenance. Think about: who wrote each source? When was each source written? How does this impact on whether you are surprised?

Worked example

Read source 3 (on the previous page) and source 4. Having read source 4 are you surprised by source 3?

In one way I'm surprised by source 3, as Eden in source 4 seems to suggest that sanctions wouldn't have worked and that the failure of them may be the end of the League, whereas source 3 suggests that Italy would have been forced to pull out of Abyssinia if sanctions had been used to full effect.

However, I'm not completely surprised having considered the provenance of the source. It is written by the British Foreign Secretary who may be seeking to downplay the potential effectiveness of sanctions in the context of the crisis. He is explaining to the government a situation where ultimately Britain chose not to support action against Italy, in part due to the fear of Italy's reaction, thus undermining the credibility of the League. In contrast, source 3 is written after the event by a historian who will have had a chance to write about the incident with hindsight.

Review

1. Describe the methods available to the League to uphold its aims. **[4]**
2. Describe how the League of Nations tried to prevent future wars between nations. **[4]**
3. In what ways did the League of Nations lose credibility? **[6]**
4. Why was it difficult for the League to achieve its aims? **[6]**
5. Why did the League fail in Corfu? **[6]**
6. "The League of Nations was doomed to failure from the start." How far do you agree with this statement? Explain your answer. **[10]**
7. "The League of Nations failed because of Britain and France." How far do you agree with this statement? Explain your answer. **[10]**

For further information review this section in the Student Book.

1. What was collective security? **[4]**

Analysis

- ✓ The answer needs to have a clear focus on collective security and what it means.
- ✓ Once collective security is defined, a point is needed outlining how it works.
- ✓ The key to any question about collective security is the idea that its strength lay in all the members working together as a show of force.
- ✓ To answer this question, keep the focus on the League of Nations itself, don't talk in general terms.
- ✓ The question is not asking for specifics of how the League did or didn't act, so there is no need to give examples.

Mark scheme

1 mark for each relevant point, additional mark for supporting detail, maximum 2 marks per point made.

Student answer

Collective security is the idea that everyone works together to act as a deterrent against aggression. Its basis is that if everyone promises to act as one if someone else attacks, any form of conflict is less likely.

Examiner feedback

The answer is good in the way it attempts to explain two issues relating to collective security. First, it offers a brief explanation of what collective security is, then it attempts to put this explanation into context with further explanation.

Where the answer could be better is by attempting to focus more on the League itself, and offering less of a generalised answer. It doesn't speak of countries, or members, and doesn't explain how collective security is an effective deterrent by other countries working together. 2 marks awarded.

2. Why did the structure and membership weaken the League? **[6]**

Analysis

- ✓ There are two parts to address with this question—structure and membership.
- ✓ For a 6-mark question you need to identify and explain two reasons that help answer the question—so for this question one explanation is needed for structure and one for membership.
- ✓ In terms of membership it is important to think of who didn't join the League initially (Germany and Russia) and also consider who never was a member (the United States). These countries were major powers in Europe and would probably be at the heart of any conflict. Without them the League was weakened.

✓ In terms of structure the League also had problems. It often required a unanimous decision to be reached.

✓ The League only met once a year and this meant decisions could take a long time to be made and might come long after the event they were referring to. The League's decisions therefore lacked credibility.

Mark scheme

Level 1:	general answer lacking specific contextual knowledge (1 mark)
Level 2:	identifies AND/OR describes reasons (2–3 marks)
Level 3:	explains ONE reason (4–5 marks)
Level 4:	explains TWO reasons (6 marks)

Student answer

The membership of the League of Nations caused real problems for the organisation. After feeling drawn into the First World War, the United States opted out of joining the League and was never a member. Russia, which had become the world's first communist state, didn't join the League until 1934 and Germany wasn't allowed to join until 1926 due to its role in the First World War. Even though Germany did join, it left the League in 1933. Other countries also left, such as Japan in 1933, Italy in 1937, and Russia in 1939.

Examiner feedback

The answer gives a lot of relevant information about membership issues that the League faced and the details presented are correct. However, the student doesn't explain why these countries either joining late or leaving the League posed it a problem—there needs to be more focus on what this actually meant and how it weakened the organisation.

There is also no attempt to address structural weaknesses the League faced. The student could have mentioned that the structure as set out by the covenant meant that the power lay in who the members were, and so by not including some key countries the League was unable to act. 3 marks awarded.

3. How far was the League of Nations a success? **[10]**

Analysis

- ✓ While the question implies it is a one-sided statement, by asking "how far" it is asking for an evaluation of the level of success achieved by the League. The answer therefore needs to consider successes and failures.
- ✓ Specific examples of successes and failures need to be included.
- ✓ For the successes of the League the answer could include, for example, dealing with issues from the First World War, making recommendations regarding working hours, and establishing a health organisation that addressed the spread of disease.
- ✓ The League also solved some disputes, such as over the Aaland islands, as well as administering plebiscites in various territories to decide whether or not they wanted to stay in Germany.
- ✓ When it comes to the League's failures it is the events of the 1930s that need attention. Failures with Abyssinia and Manchuria showed the League to be weak, as did the lack of agreement on disarmament.
- ✓ To gain maximum marks you need to evaluate the evidence presented—so it is worth considering the significance of the material you choose to include. For example, does the fact that the League dealt with the issues post-war in the early 1920s mean it deserves credit, or did the failure to halt the aggressive actions in the 1930s encourage others such as Hitler to pursue their territorial aims?

Mark scheme

Level 1:	general answer lacking specific contextual knowledge (1 mark)
Level 2:	identifies AND/OR describes reasons (2–3 marks)
Level 3:	gives a one-sided explanation (4–5 marks) or one explanation of both sides (4–6 marks)
Level 4:	explains both sides (7–9 marks)
Level 5:	explains with evaluation (10 marks)

Student answer

The League of Nation's main successes came not from fighting but from helping to resolve the problems caused by the violence of the First World War. After the First World War many people were left homeless and the League helped to solve the large refugee problem. In the Treaty of Versailles, German and Turkish colonies were put under temporary control of Britain and France, and the Mandates Commission kept a close eye on them until it was felt that these countries were able to govern themselves.

Another success of the League was the work done to improve conditions for ordinary people. Workers were represented by actions such as the banning of poisonous white lead from paint and the limitations placed on the working hours for young children. A health organisation was also set up to help combat the spread of epidemic diseases. The League was also able to resolve disputes at times. When Finland and Sweden clashed over the Aaland Islands the League ruled that the territory belonged to Finland, but no weapons were to be kept there. Both sides agreed to this.

However, once the Great Depression occurred the League was unable to have the same impact as countries turned away from cooperation. As high unemployment and depression hit, self-preservation in countries led to the pursuit of selfish aims. In the face of emerging dictators in Italy, Germany and Russia the League was powerless due to inherent weakness.

Examiner feedback

The student addresses the "success" part of the question well, and in the first paragraph identifies and explains several different reasons why the League was a positive organisation in the 1920s. This is a good example of how to make points and then explain them—it shows the impact and the importance of the statements made.

However, the counter argument with focus on the failures is minimal. The second paragraph offers an explanation of the reasons why the League failed, and is quite an evaluative comment, but there isn't the same level of detail focusing on the League's weaknesses. Much more is needed on the failures of the League to make this less of a one-sided answer. 6 marks awarded.

You need to know:

- the long-term consequences of the peace treaties of 1919–23
- the consequences of the failures of the League of Nations in the 1930s
- Hitler's foreign policy and whether it led to the outbreak of war in 1939
- whether the policy of appeasement was justified

Background: international peace in the 1920s and 1930s

In the 1920s the existence of the League of Nations, as well as a series of international agreements such as Locarno, brought a period of relative calm and stability. Some people were even suggesting that it was an age of peace and tranquillity.

Despite this, few were surprised that war broke out again in 1939. The 1930s was an age of increasing tension and conflict in Europe, as the economic crisis that resulted from the Wall Street Crash brought a return to strong nationalism and aggression across Europe.

What had gone wrong?

The peace treaties had left many countries resentful and determined to reverse the terms. The most significant country affected was Germany. The people, encouraged by the "stab in the back" myth, turned to the Nazi Party. The Nazi Party led by Hitler followed a foreign policy designed to destroy the hated Treaty of Versailles. Additionally, Hitler made aggressive demands such as "lebensraum" and the destruction of communism.

The Great Depression brought militarist extremists to power. In Germany many people turned to the Nazi Party as the Nazis promised work and food. It was clear by the summer of 1936 that the League had failed and with it the idea of collective security. An alternative had to be found to preserve world peace. Britain and France turned to appeasement while at the same time rearming as a matter of urgency.

It was clear that appeasement had failed when Hitler occupied Czechoslovakia in March 1939. The next country to be invaded by Germany would be Poland. Britain and France promised assistance should Germany decide to attack. When Germany did, and refused to leave, Britain declared war on Germany.

Key fact

The **"stab in the back"** myth that Germany had been betrayed by a group of weak, unpatriotic politicians developed after the First World War. The myth gained popularity, giving rise to the thinking that if the war had not really been lost then the peace settlement was unnecessary and should be overturned.

What were the long-term consequences of the peace treaties of 1919–23?

Fig. 3.1 *The "stab in the back"*

Recap

The Paris Peace Settlement left many nations dissatisfied and wanting revisions to the treaties. Japan had wanted increased trading rights, for example, and Italy had expected to receive a greater share of the redistriblted territories. The most dissatisfied nation was Germany. Most Germans wanted to reject the Treaty of Versailles as they did not agree with the territorial provisions, disarmament, war guilt, and reparations. This dissatisfaction stemmed from the "stab in the back" myth.

Although the Treaty of Versailles was harsh on Germany, it failed to completely disable the country militarily and economically. This gave Germany the opportunity to rebuild when the time was right.

Hitler promised to destroy the treaty and this promise assisted his rise to power. To carry out this promise would require the rise of Germany as a strong military nation. This was forbidden by the treaty.

Britain and France disagreed about how to treat Germany. The British thought the Treaty of Versailles had been too harsh and were prepared to make concessions; the French were afraid of Germany becoming strong again.

What were the consequences of the failure of the League of Nations in the 1930s?

Issue	Actions	Consequences
Japan	Japan invaded Manchuria in 1931. A Special Assembly of the League was held and 40 nations voted that Japan should withdraw. Instead of withdrawing from Manchuria, Japan withdrew from the League.	• It showed that the League was weak in the face of aggression by a great power, encouraging further acts of aggression. • Having withdrawn from the League, Japan moved closer to Hitler and then to Mussolini through the Anti-Comintern Pact. • The invasion of Manchuria encouraged Italy and Germany to think that their territorial ambitions were achievable. • The League had no power to force countries to obey.
Italy	When Italy invaded Abyssinia in October 1935, Abyssinia appealed for help from the League. The League took action by imposing economic sanctions.	• The sanctions imposed failed to include essential commodities such as oil and coal and so were not hard-hitting. • Britain and France refused to support the action. Both countries needed Mussolini's friendship as they saw him as an ally against Hitler. • This showed countries were incapable of putting internationalism before national interests.
Disarmament	The League of Nations tried to persuade countries to disarm. At the Disarmament Conference of 1932–3 the Germans stated they would disarm if every nation disarmed. The French would not accept this.	• Hitler walked out of the conference and Germany left the League. • The failure of the League led to intensive rearmament programmes for Britain and France.

Study the information in the table. Make a list of the impacts for European peace based on the events that occurred.

Worked example

Why was the League of Nations seen as a failure by 1936? (6)

The League of Nations was intended to create stability and preserve peace in Europe. However, by 1935 the league seemed massively flawed due to a series of failures.

Through its failure to handle the Japanese invasion of Manchuria, the League appeared weak and lacking authority. Japan invaded Manchuria in 1931 and after an appeal to the League by Manchuria 40 nations voted that Japan should withdraw. Japan walked out of the League and the League was powerless to act, making it appear weak in the face of aggression by a great power.

In a similar vein, the League also failed to deal with the Abyssinian crisis of 1935. When Italy invaded Abyssinia in October 1935, Abyssinia appealed for help from the League. The League took action by imposing economic sanctions. The sanctions were ineffective though: Britain and France refused to support the action and the sanctions imposed failed to include essential commodities such as oil and coal so lacked real impact.

By failing to address either of these issues the League of Nations appeared to be weak and lacking credibility with countries when faced with a crisis.

Exam tip

For a 6-mark question, this is an excellent answer to use as a model: choose two good examples of the failure of the League and explain them fully. Adding a short summative sentence at the end, although not compulsory, shows a good understanding.

Key term

Lebensraum—the territory which a group, state, or nation believes is needed for its natural development - particularly relating to the post-First World War German concept of settler colonialism into eastern Europe.

How far was Hitler's foreign policy to blame for the outbreak of war in 1939?

Hitler had very clear aims for his foreign policy.

Hitler's foreign policy aims

1 Destroy the Treaty of Versailles

- The disarmament clause would be broken by introducing conscription and building up Germany's armed forces.
- The demilitarised Rhineland would be remilitarised, strengthening Germany's western frontier.
- Territory lost under the Treaty would be regained.
- Uniting with Austria was specifically banned by the Treaty but now formed part of Hitler's plans.

2 Create a Greater Germany

- All German-speaking peoples were to be brought into a German empire. This would include Austria and parts of Czechoslovakia and Poland.

3 Destroy communism (Bolshevism)

- Hitler was anti-communist. He believed that Bolsheviks were responsible for Germany's defeat in the First World War and that they wanted to take over Germany.

4 Acquire lebensraum (living space)

- Hitler wanted extra living space for Germans, believing this was their entitlement.
- This would be achieved by expansion eastwards into Poland and Soviet Russia.

5 Create a central European empire

- Having achieved his aims he would be at the head of the most powerful state in Europe and possibly the world.

▲ **Fig. 3.2** *Hitler's foreign policy aims*

What foreign policy actions were taken by Hitler from 1933–6?

1933	• Germany refused to pay any more reparations. • Hitler walked out of the Disarmament Conference and withdrew Germany from the League of Nations • The rearmament of Germany began in secret.
1934	• A non-aggression pact was agreed with Poland in January. This ensured that if Germany decided to attack Austria or Czechoslovakia, Poland would not intervene.
1935	• Hitler announced that conscription would be reintroduced. • A massive rearmament rally was held in Germany. Britain and France believed that a strong Germany was a buffer against communism. • Germany signed a naval agreement with Britain allowing Germany to have a navy up to 35 per cent of the size of the British navy. • A plebiscite was held in the Saar in accordance with the terms of the Treaty of Versailles. Over 90 per cent were in favour of a return to Germany.
1936	• Germany remilitarised the Rhineland. Britain and France made no effort to stop this. • Hitler and Italy signed the Rome–Berlin Axis. • The Anti-Comintern Pact committed Germany and Japan to hostility towards Soviet Russia. Neither Germany nor Japan would assist Soviet Russia if it attacked either country. • After the outbreak of the Spanish Civil War Italy and Germany supported Franco's nationalists in the Spanish Civil War. Britain and France decided not to become involved. Soviet Russia supported the Republicans.

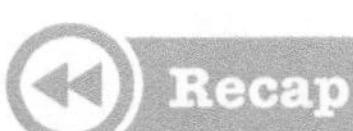

Recap

Germany had left the League of Nations, signed treaties with Italy, Poland, and Japan and also supported Franco in the Spanish Civil War. Although European conflict didn't seem imminent Hitler had taken steps to prepare for a future war.

Recap

By 1936 Germany had reintroduced conscription and rearmament and remilitarised the Rhineland, actions that all broke the Treaty of Versailles yet drew no major reaction from France and Britain.

The Spanish Civil War

- The Spanish Civil War gave Hitler an opportunity to test his new military equipment. His Luftwaffe was tested and committed a ruthless assault on Guernica.
- Hitler saw the Spanish Civil War as an opportunity to fight against communism.

  He succeeded in establishing Mussolini as an ally. They formed the Rome–Berlin Axis.

▲ **Fig. 3.3** *Guernica, Northern Spain, after a bombing raid, May 1937*

Worked example

Did Hitler's actions from 1933–6 reflect more an attempt to achieve equality with Britain and France than they were steps on the road to war? (10)

It can be argued that the actions taken by Hitler and Germany in the 1930s were an attempt to bring Germany more into line with Britain and France. This can be seen by the decisions in 1935 to introduce conscription and begin rearmament—it could be argued that Hitler was simply looking to restore Germany's status as a European power and exercise the same control over his country as other states.

However, the extent to which this is true can be questioned. In isolation these activities might be seen to be restoring Germany's power, but the other actions Hitler took in this period seemingly indicate he was preparing the country for an impending war. The support of Franco's nationalist forces in Spain show Hitler wanted to test his newly formed air force's capacity in conflict. The treaties with Italy, Poland, and the Soviet Union were an attempt either to form alliances or agree non-aggression pacts with potential rivals, ensuring that if the opportunity arose any attempt at seizing territory would be straightforward.

Exam tip

This is a tricky question, demanding that you offer a consideration of both arguments in the statement. You need to find evidence of the view that Hitler was looking to achieve equality with Britain and France and evaluate this; and then consider the opposing view, which is that Hitler always had war in mind.

What this answer does well is to develop the two sides of the argument and give specific actions that indicate the view. There isn't a conclusion though, and there should be in an answer of this length.

What happened from 1936–9?

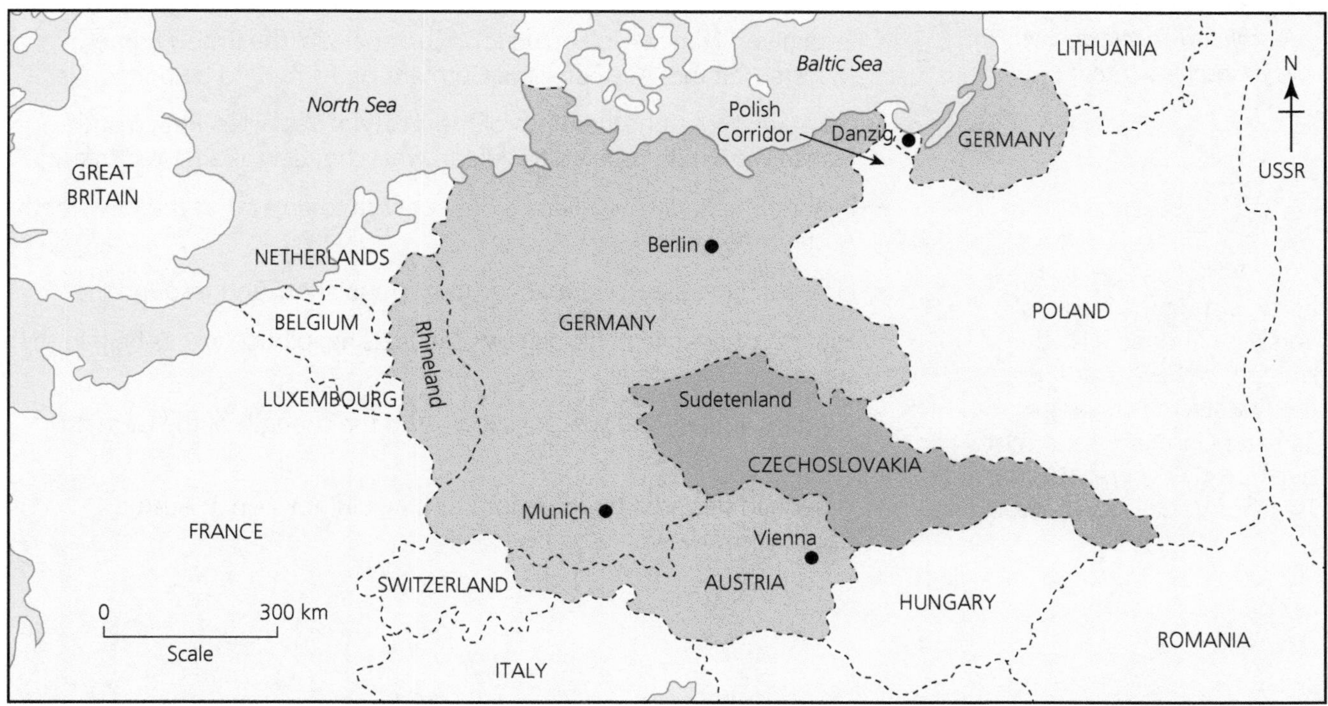

▲ **Fig. 3.4** *Map of central Europe after Austrian Anschluss (1938)*

Anschluss with Austria, 1938

Reasons for union with Austria

- Hitler was born in Austria and he had stated in *Mein Kampf* that he felt the two countries belonged together as one German nation.
- One of Hitler's aims was to form a "Greater Germany" that would include all German-speaking peoples. Austria had the largest number of German speakers outside Germany.
- Many in Austria supported the idea of union as their country was economically weak after it had been reduced in size by the Treaty of St Germain.
- Union with Austria was an opportunity to break the Treaty of Versailles further, as it had forbidden Anschluss.

Fig. 3.5 *Nazi poster for the Anschluss. The caption says: "The whole people say Yes!"*

Events

- In early 1938 Hitler encouraged the strong Nazi Party in Austria to provoke unrest. The Nazis staged demonstrations and started riots encouraging union with Germany.
- Hitler forcefully told the Austrian Chancellor Schuschnigg that political union was the only way to sort out the problems. Hitler persuaded Schuschnigg to agree but then Schuschnigg changed his mind, ordering a plebiscite to be held among the Austrian people.
- Hitler was furious, ordering Schuschnigg to withdraw the plebiscite and resign. At the same time Hitler ordered invasion plans to be drawn up.
- The new Austrian leader, Seyss-Inquart, asked Germany to send troops into Austria to restore law and order. On 12 March 1938 German troops invaded and two days later Austria was made a province of Germany.
- On 10 April, under the watchful eye of the Nazis, 99 per cent of the Austrian people voted for Anschluss.

Results

- Britain and France took no action. Chamberlain, the British Prime Minister, felt that Austrians and Germans had a right to be united.
- Germany broke another term of the Treaty of Versailles. Britain and France were not prepared to defend what they saw as a flawed treaty.
- In addition, Britain and France did not wish to go against the views of the Austrian people.
- Hitler had increased German territory, population, and resources.
- Hitler's confidence in his plans was increasing, particularly as he had the support of Mussolini.
- Austria's soldiers and weapons increased the strength of the German military.
- Hitler had declared his intentions and would not stop at Austria. Czechoslovakia would be next.

Recap

Hitler had managed to break a key term of the Treaty of Versailles and increase the strength of Germany. It was the first step to creating a "Greater Germany", and more significantly showed that the Treaty of Versailles was dead.

Worked example

What did Hitler achieve by the Anschluss? (4)

By joining together Germany and Austria in the Anschluss, Hitler had successfully broken the Treaty of Versailles and helped his development of a "Greater Germany". Through adding the country of his birth not only had Hitler increased the size of Germany, he had also increased the strength of Germany through the wealth of its industry and also by adding Austria's soldiers and weapons to its own army. The Anschluss showed that the Allies were not willing to go to war over the Treaty of Versailles, which encouraged Hitler to break it further.

Exam tip

To answer the question, you need to demonstrate thorough knowledge of the Anschluss. This example answer would be improved by focusing more heavily on what Hitler achieved rather than adding narrative detail. In your answer, remember to use the key wording from the question—in this case "achieve"—to show that you are focused on the question.

The Sudetenland, 1938

Reasons for the issue

- After the First World War Czechoslovakia had been created by the Treaty of St Germain.
- The Sudetenland formed the border area between Germany and Czechoslovakia.
- Three and a half million Germans lived in the Sudetenland area and many Sudeten Germans complained of discrimination by the Czech government.
- In 1938 Hitler demanded that Germany be given the Sudetenland. If this happened Czechoslovakia would be defenceless against a German attack.
- The British Prime Minister, Chamberlain, wanted to find a peaceful solution to the problem rather than allowing Hitler to use force.

Events

Meetings took place between Hitler and Chamberlain in an attempt to resolve the situation.

1. **Berchtesgaden, Bavaria, 15 September 1938**
   - It was agreed that areas of the Sudetenland where the majority of the population was German should be handed over to Germany. This was to be subject to the approval of the British, French, and Czech governments.
2. **Bad Godesberg, Rhineland, 22 September 1938**
   - Hitler went back on the agreement and stated that unless the whole of the Sudetenland was given to Germany by 1 October 1938 there would be war. Chamberlain was appalled by Hitler's new demand. Europe was on the brink of war.
3. **The Munich Conference, 29 September 1938**
   - This conference was attended by Chamberlain (Britain), Hitler (Germany), Mussolini (Italy), and Deladier (France). The Czechs and the Soviets were not invited.
   - Hitler gained what he had demanded at Bad Godesberg. The Czechs were forced to accept the agreement or face the full force of the German army on their own.
   - The following day, Chamberlain and Hitler signed a declaration promising that their countries would never go to war. Chamberlain returned to Britain saying "I believe it is peace in our time". He received a hero's welcome.

Results

- Britain and France had abandoned Czechoslovakia. On 1 October 1938, German troops marched into the Sudetenland.
- In March 1939 Hitler took over the rest of Czechoslovakia. There was no resistance from the Czechs. Britain and France did not help.
- Poland would be Hitler's next target. Britain promised Poland it would guarantee Poland's independence.

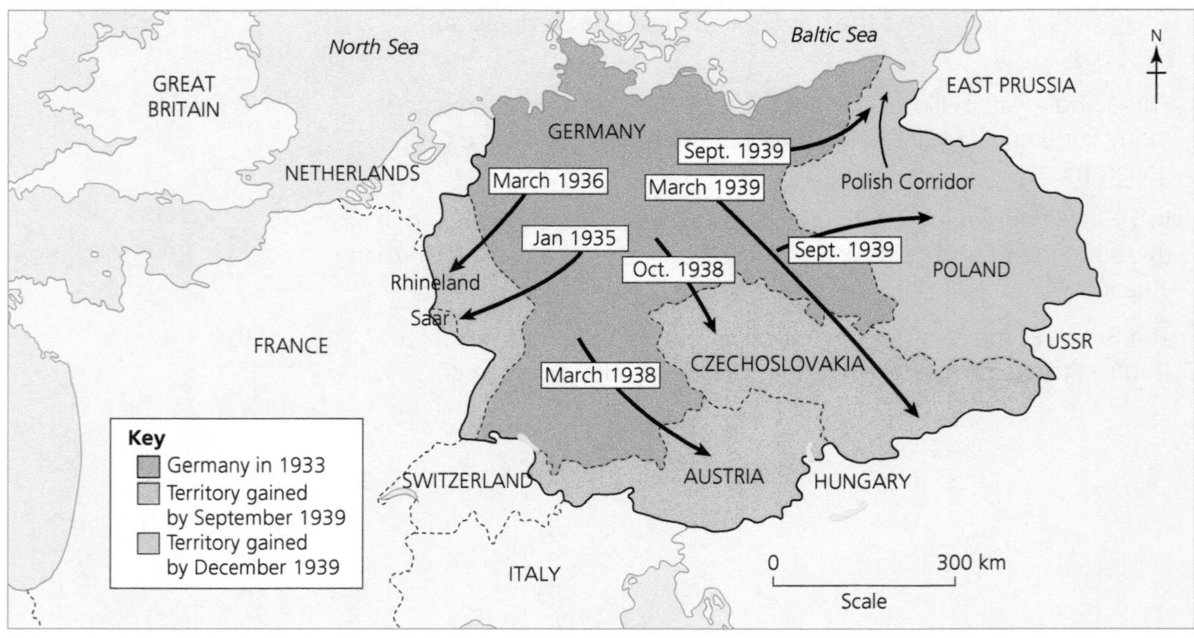

▲ **Fig. 3.6** *Map of Europe showing Hitler's territorial gains, 1935–9*

Source 1

"We have suffered a total and unmitigated defeat. . . You will find that in a period of time. . . Czechoslovakia will be engulfed in the Nazi regime. . . And do not suppose that this is the end. This is only the beginning of the reckoning."

▲ *From a speech made by Winston Churchill to the House of Commons in 1938. The speech was made soon after the Munich Agreement.*

Source 2

"It was thanks to Mr Chamberlain's courage that a senseless war was avoided. As I wrote to him then: 'Millions of mothers will be blessing your name tonight for having saved their sons from the horrors of war.' I also wrote at the time: 'The day may come when we may be forced to fight Germany. If we have to do so, I trust that the cause may be one in which the honour and vital interests of Britain are clearly at stake.' This was not the case in September 1938."

▲ *From Sir Neville Henderson's account, published in 1940, of his time as British Ambassador to Germany from 1937 to 1939.*

The Nazi-Soviet Pact

Reasons for the issue

- Ever since 1933, when Hitler came to power, Stalin had been concerned about the threat Germany posed. Hitler had openly stated his wish to crush communism and to gain land as lebensraum.
- Stalin signed a treaty with France in 1935. The treaty stated that France would help the Soviet Union if Germany invaded the Soviet Union. However, Stalin was not sure whether France would come to his aid if needed.
- Stalin's concerns were increased by the Munich Agreement in 1938. He had not been invited to the conference nor had he been consulted. He concluded that Britain and France would allow Hitler to take land in the east.
- Discussion with Britain and France over the spring and summer of 1939 came to nothing.

Events

- On 23 August 1939 the foreign ministers from each country signed a 10-year non-aggression pact.
- The clauses of the Nazi-Soviet Pact provided a written guarantee of non-aggression by each towards the other, and a declared commitment that neither government would ally itself to, or aid, an enemy of the other party.
- Secretly, Germany and Russia decided to split Poland between them. Stalin was interested in sections of eastern Poland and wanted the Baltic States that had once been part of Russia.

Apply

Study sources 1 and 2. How far do these sources provide convincing evidence that war in Europe was inevitable? Use the sources to explain your answer.

Exam tip

A general tip: when answering questions on sources, base your response closely on the content of the source as well as the context of what you know was happening at the time.

Results

- The two most ideologically opposed countries had signed a pact that made war seem inevitable.
- The pact gave Stalin time to build up his armed forces, which were weak following the purges, as he realised that eventually Hitler would break his promise and attack the Soviet Union.
- The pact gave Hitler the confidence to invade Poland, knowing he would not have to fight a war on two fronts.
- Hitler did not believe Britain and France would go to war over Poland and he assumed that Anglo-French opposition would not be any more serious than it had been over Czechoslovakia.

The invasion of Poland

Fig. 3.7

Reasons

- Under the terms of the Treaty of Versailles, the "Polish Corridor" was given to Poland in order to provide an outlet to the sea and Danzig was put under the control of the League of Nations. Hitler wanted to reclaim this land.
- The demand to return Danzig to Germany was not unreasonable as its people were mainly German-speaking.
- The destruction of Poland was an essential preliminary to the invasion of Russia, the destruction of communism and the acquisition of lebensraum.

Events

- On 31 March 1939 a British–French guarantee was given, promising that Poland would receive support and assistance if attacked.
- On 1 September 1939 Germany invaded Poland.
- Britain and France issued an ultimatum to Germany for the army to be withdrawn from Poland.
- On 3 September 1939, as Germany had not responded to the ultimatum, Britain and France declared war on Germany.

Apply

Create a timeline for 1933–9 of Hitler's actions in foreign policy. Mark on the line where you think France and Britain should have acted to stop Hitler. Would you have acted sooner than France and Britain did over Poland? Why?

Results

- It was clear that Germany was making a bid for European dominance and not just establishing the principle of self-determination for German-speaking peoples. Events in Czechoslovakia had shown Hitler's real aim of European dominance by force.
- Europe was at war.

Was the policy of appeasement justified?

Arguments for appeasement

- Many people agreed that the Treaty of Versailles was unfair and that Hitler should be allowed to recover what was rightfully Germany's.
- The Soviet Union under Stalin was seen as a much greater threat than Germany. The British hoped that a strong Germany would stop the spread of communism.
- Britain and France were militarily weak and still coping with the Great Depression's impact. Appeasement would give time for rearmament.
- It was hardly surprising that Britain and France wanted to avoid war. Memories of the horror of the First World War were still vivid.
- There was concern that Commonwealth countries might not give support. Some thought that support would not come from the United States. Would Britain and France be able to survive?

Arguments against appeasement

- It was morally wrong. Other leaders had allowed Hitler to go unchallenged and abandoned Czechoslovakia to its fate. Appeasement was another word for cowardice.
- The British and French assumed Hitler was a rational politician and they could negotiate on equal terms. His ruthlessness was misjudged.
- Hitler took any concession as a sign of weakness and demanded more.
- The opportunity to stop Hitler was missed. Had resistance been shown to Hitler in the Rhineland he may well have withdrawn. Although it gave Britain and France time to start rearmament it also gave Germany the opportunity to continue to grow more powerful.
- The policy alarmed the Soviet Union. Hitler made no secret of his wish to destroy communism and expand eastwards. Stalin was convinced that Britain and France would not stand in his way. As a result, the Nazi–Soviet Pact was signed.

Apply

Looking at the arguments surrounding appeasement, which of them would have appealed to:

- a senior member of the armed forces
- a mother who had lost her son in the First World War?

Review

1. In what ways did Hitler build up his armed forces before 1936? [4]
2. What measures had Hitler taken by 1938 to prepare Germany for war? [4]
3. What was Anschluss? [4]
4. What was the Nazi-Soviet Pact? [4]
5. What happened in the Saar in 1935? [4]
6. What actions had Hitler taken by 1936 to prepare for war? [4]
7. Describe events in 1938 relating to Czechoslovakia. [4]
8. Why did Britain and France not want to go to war with Germany? [6]
9. Why did some people argue that appeasement was the wrong policy? [6]
10. Why did Stalin agree to the Nazi-Soviet Pact? [6]
11. Why did Hitler become involved in the Spanish Civil War? [6]
12. Why was the Munich Agreement (1938) important? [6]
13. Why did Hitler's demands over Czechoslovakia not lead to war in 1938? [6]
14. Why did Britain and France end their policy of appeasement? [6]
15. "Hitler achieved his foreign policy aims." How far do you agree with this statement? Explain your answer [10]
16. "Hitler was an opportunist rather than a planner." How far do you agree with this statement? Explain your answer. [10]

For further information review this section in the Student Book.

1. What was the Munich Agreement? **[4]**

Analysis

- ✓ Answers to "what" questions require two good points about the topic in the question, which are then explained.
- ✓ A question like this needs a focused answer. Don't be tempted to include extra information just because you know it.
- ✓ The Munich Agreement was signed in September 1938 and relates to the agreement reached with Germany by France and Great over the future of Czechoslovakia.
- ✓ Hitler's claim was over the Sudetenland area of Czechoslovakia and the German speakers who lived there.
- ✓ The agreement was seen as a preserving peace in Europe at the time, and was greeted with great celebration in France and England.

Mark scheme

1 mark for each relevant point, additional mark for supporting detail, maximum 2 marks per point made.

Student answer

The Munich Agreement was a settlement reached by Germany, Britain, France, and Italy that allowed Germany to annex the Sudetenland, an industry-rich area of Czechoslovakia. In line with Hitler's aims of uniting German speakers within a "Greater Germany", he had laid claim to the area as there were some 3 million native Germans living there. The agreement was drawn up to avoid war—Hitler had made it clear he was prepared to take the area by force and France and Britain, despite the fact that France had an alliance with Czechoslovakia, wanted to avoid war.

Examiner feedback

The student makes two well-developed points—first, defining what the agreement was; second, explaining why the agreement was needed. 4 marks awarded.

2. Why did Britain and France allow Germany to remilitarise the Rhineland in 1936? **[6]**

Analysis

- ✓ The answer to this type of question needs to include two well-developed reasons for the event.
- ✓ There are various reasons why Germany had legitimate reasons to remilitarise in 1936. These included the idea that the Treaty of Versailles was out of date, and the fact that the Rhineland was part of Germany and so Germany should be allowed to do as it chose.
- ✓ The decision also formed a wider part of the policy of appeasement—Britain and France were looking to buy themselves time to rearm and at the same time avoid conflict.
- ✓ There is little doubt that the context is also important—in 1936 Hitler's demands didn't seem unreasonable, nor did any European country have an appetite for war so soon after the effects of the Great Depression.

Mark scheme

Level 1:	general answer lacking specific contextual knowledge (1 mark)
Level 2:	identifies AND/OR describes reasons (2–3 marks)
Level 3:	explains ONE reason (4–5 marks)
Level 4:	explains TWO reasons (6 marks)

Student answer

Britain and France allowed Germany to remilitarise the Rhineland as there was strong feeling that the Treaty of Versailles had been too harsh on Germany. There was a genuine feeling of empathy for the Germans and so when they moved into the Rhineland, rather than a massive public outcry, significant portions of the public and government accepted this as a fair action. Anthony Eden, the British Foreign Secretary at the time, remarked that it was just "Gerry going into his own backyard".

Examiner feedback

In this answer the reasoning is good, and certainly the Treaty of Versailles is a key reason why Britain and France reacted as they did, but for a 6-mark answer there needs to be another reason identified and explained. The quote at the end is correct—although it was actually said to Eden and he reported it in parliament—but an explanation of what it meant would improve the answer. 4 marks awarded.

3. "The Spanish Civil War was more important to Hitler than the remilitarisation of the Rhineland." How far do you agree with this statement? Explain your answer. **[10]**

Analysis

✓ The question is asking for a judgment about the importance of the Spanish Civil War to Hitler in relation to his attempts to militarise Germany and prepare for a future war.

✓ The war was important as it allowed Germany to test elements of its military, such as the air force, in an actual war zone.

✓ The importance of this war though needs to be balanced against the importance for Hitler of the remilitarisation of the Rhineland. This was the first territorial break of the Treaty of Versailles by Hitler, and it showed for the first time his aggressive intentions.

✓ It was also the first chance for France and Britain to respond to Hitler's actions.

Mark scheme

Level 1:	general answer lacking specific contextual knowledge (1 mark)
Level 2:	identifies AND/OR describes reasons (2–3 marks)
Level 3:	gives a one-sided explanation (4–5 marks) or one explanation of both sides (4–6 marks)
Level 4:	explains both sides (7–9 marks)
Level 5:	explains with evaluation (10 marks)

Student answer

The Spanish Civil War was certainly important to Hitler in the 1930s, as it allowed him the opportunity to test his new military equipment in a war zone for the first time. By offering support to Franco in his fight against his own people, Hitler was able to see how the newly developed Luftwaffe would fare in conflict as well as sending heavily armoured divisions as support.

Involvement in the Spanish Civil War also gave Hitler a chance to fight communism and paint communists as a natural enemy. This was something that would help later when fighting the Soviet Union.

However, it can be argued that by remilitarising the Rhineland, Hitler also greatly benefited.

Not only did the action win the support of the generals within Germany, it was a clear contravention of the Treaty of Versailles. It did not draw a significant reaction from Britain, France, or the League of Nations.

It was also part of Hitler's wider plan to regain military strength and territory, and would therefore have aided his popularity in his own country.

Examiner feedback

The candidate has attempted to explain both sides of the argument and does offer a balanced view. There is good material included, and some depth to knowledge. What is lacking though is evaluation, the student identifies and explains issues, but there is no sense of how important these issues are. Their importance could have been covered after the point about the Treaty of Versailles for example, explaining how this had an impact on the future. 7 marks awarded.

You need to know:

- why the United States–Soviet Union alliance began to break down in 1945
- how the United States reacted to Soviet expansion
- what the Berlin Blockade was and what its consequences were
- who was the most to blame for starting the Cold War: the United States or the Soviet Union

Background: tensions between the Soviet Union and the United States in 1945

By the end of 1944 it was becoming obvious that Germany was going to lose the war and that the Soviet Union was going to play a greater part in world affairs. By this time ideological differences and tensions between the United States and the Soviet Union were re-emerging.

The United States, the Soviet Union, and Britain set up two conferences in 1945 at Yalta and Potsdam. At the conferences it was evident that there were major differences over the future of Eastern Europe. The Soviet Union believed that the West wanted the recovery of Germany, which would make it a threat in the future, while the United States suspected the Soviet Union of trying to spread communism to as many countries as possible. The Soviet Union was now regarded by the West as the main threat to peace. The United States followed a policy of containment, introducing the Truman Doctrine and Marshall Plan in an attempt to prevent the expansion of the "iron curtain".

Why did the United States–Soviet Union alliance begin to break down in 1945?

- **Removal of the common enemy**—the threat from Germany was gone, and therefore there was no need for the Allied cooperation that had been extensive during the war.
- **Ideological differences**—the United States followed a democratic, capitalist approach opposed to the communist ideology of the Soviet Union. This made it more difficult to build up trust between the two.
- **History of distrust**—going back to 1918 and the intervention of the West in the Russian Civil War against the Bolsheviks, Stalin saw that the West frequently tried to limit Soviet interests and believed that the West had seen Hitler and the Nazis as the buffer against the spread of communism in the 1930s. In addition, Stalin was not invited to the Munich Conference.
- **The Soviet Union in world affairs**—by early 1945 it was obvious that the Soviet Union's "sphere of influence" was growing. Stalin was included with other European leaders in important conferences at Yalta (February 1945) and Potsdam (July 1945). Stalin made no secret of his desire to see communism spread to other countries, which worried the United States.

▲ **Fig. 4.1**

Issues to be addressed at the Yalta and Potsdam conferences

What the challenges were	What was decided at the Yalta Conference, February 1945	What was decided at the Potsdam Conference, July–August 1945
What to do with a defeated Germany	• Surrender was to be unconditional. • Germany and its capital Berlin were to be temporarily divided into four zones. • Germany's eastern border was to be moved westwards. • War criminals were to be punished. • Germany had to pay reparations.	• The Nazi Party was to be banned. • Germany was to be denazified and war crime trials held. • The decision to split Germany and Berlin into four zones was confirmed. • Each country was to take reparations from its own zone.
What to do with countries Germany formerly occupied	• Following liberation these countries were to be allowed to hold free elections for people to decide how they were to be governed.	
The future of Poland	• A provisional government would form, comprising pro-Soviet Lublin Poles and exiled London Poles who had fled in 1939. • Poland's border was to be moved westwards into German territory. • Free elections were to be held.	• The Polish–German border was to be the Oder–Neisse Line formed by two rivers. • No agreement was reached over the future government of Poland.
How war against Japan could be ended	• Stalin agreed to intervene in the war against Japan after Germany was defeated. • In return, Russia was to receive land in Manchuria and territory lost to Japan during the 1904–5 Russo-Japanese War.	• The Soviet Union wished to intervene in the war against Japan but this was refused by Truman.
How a lasting peace was to be maintained	• An organisation to be known as the United Nations was to be set up.	

Apply

Consider the issues discussed at the Yalta and Potsdam conferences. Draw a mind map of the issues you think are the most likely to cause tensions between the Soviet Union and the United States in the future.

Relations at the Yalta Conference had seemed good, and there had been plenty of agreement over the action needed, but the Potsdam Conference saw real tension and disagreement. What had changed?

In the United States: President Roosevelt died in April and was replaced by Harry S Truman. Truman was strongly anti-communist but inexperienced in international affairs. On the eve of the Potsdam Conference, Truman informed Stalin that the United States had successfully tested an atomic weapon.

In Britain: Churchill's Conservative Party was defeated in a general election. Churchill was replaced by Labour Party leader Clement Attlee.

In the Soviet Union: the Soviets had liberated Eastern Europe and were installing sympathetic governments. They failed to hold "free" elections.

The results of the Potsdam Conference–from wartime alliance to the Cold War

The United States and the Soviet Union emerged from the Second World War as superpowers and were prepared to face each other head on.

Former British Prime Minister, Churchill, referred to an "iron curtain", dividing Eastern Europe from Western Europe, democracy from communism.

Stalin accused Churchill of trying to provoke war against the Soviet Union. The Soviet Union had been invaded from the West twice in 30 years. Stalin was determined to set up a "buffer zone" of protective states to ensure that invasion never happened again. His reply to Churchill's speech was robust.

Apply

Read sources 1 and 2 (extracts from speeches by Churchill and Stalin). List the reasons why the two leaders' views differ so much.

Recap

The Yalta Conference put in place what would happen after the war. One key decision was to divide Germany into four zones.

The Potsdam Conference was the start of Cold War tensions and hostility. Little was agreed except to enlarge Poland and divide Berlin.

Recap

The change between the Yalta and Potsdam conferences was down to several factors—but all regarding trust issues between the United States and the Soviet Union. A new US President in Harry Truman, who was fiercely anti-communist, the emergence of the United States as a nuclear state, and also the Soviet Union's ambition in Eastern Europe meant that the Cold War was about to begin.

Worked example

What was agreed at the Potsdam Conference? (4)

There were several key agreements reached at the Potsdam Conference. The border between Poland and Germany was settled, as was the idea that Germany would be divided into four zones and each of these would be ruled according to the "4Ds"—denazification, demilitarisation, disarmament, and democratisation. It was also agreed that the Soviet Union would join the war against Japan, although due to the use of the atomic bomb by the United States this was never needed as the war ended shortly after.

Exam tip

To answer a question like this, focus on specifics. Address the question in the first few words—showing an understanding of what's being asked—then follow up with specific knowledge.

Source 1

"A shadow has fallen upon the scenes so lately lighted by the Allied victory. From Stettin on the Baltic to Trieste on the Adriatic, an iron curtain has descended. Behind that line lie all the states of central and Eastern Europe. The Communist parties have been raised to power far beyond their numbers and are seeking everywhere to obtain totalitarian control. This is certainly not the liberated Europe we fought to build. Nor is it one which allows permanent peace."

▲ *Adapted from a speech by Winston Churchill, March 1946.*

Source 2

"Mr Churchill now takes the stance of warmonger. The following circumstances should not be forgotten. The Germans made their invasion of the USSR through Finland, Poland and Romania. They were able to make their invasion through these countries because, at the time, governments hostile to the Soviet Union existed in these countries. What can there be surprising about the fact that the Soviet Union, anxious for its future safety, is trying to see that governments loyal in their attitude to the Soviet Union should exist in these countries?"

▲ *Stalin replying to Churchill's speech, 1946.*

Prepare a table showing what benefits the United States and the Soviet Union gained from the Yalta and Potsdam conferences.

How did the United States react to Soviet expansion?

The United States became committed to a policy of stopping the spread of communism. This was the policy of "containment". This was in response to the Soviet Union's actions in Eastern Europe.

How had the Soviet Union gained control of Eastern Europe by 1948?

- At the end of the war the Soviet Red Army remained in much of Eastern Europe.
- As agreed at the Yalta Conference, elections were held in Eastern European countries. By 1948 all these countries had communist governments, achieved through rigged elections and intimidation.
- The countries now under Soviet control became "satellite" states. COMINFORM, an alliance of communist countries, formed in 1947.
- Only one Eastern bloc country, Yugoslavia, rejected Stalin's leadership, although it remained communist.

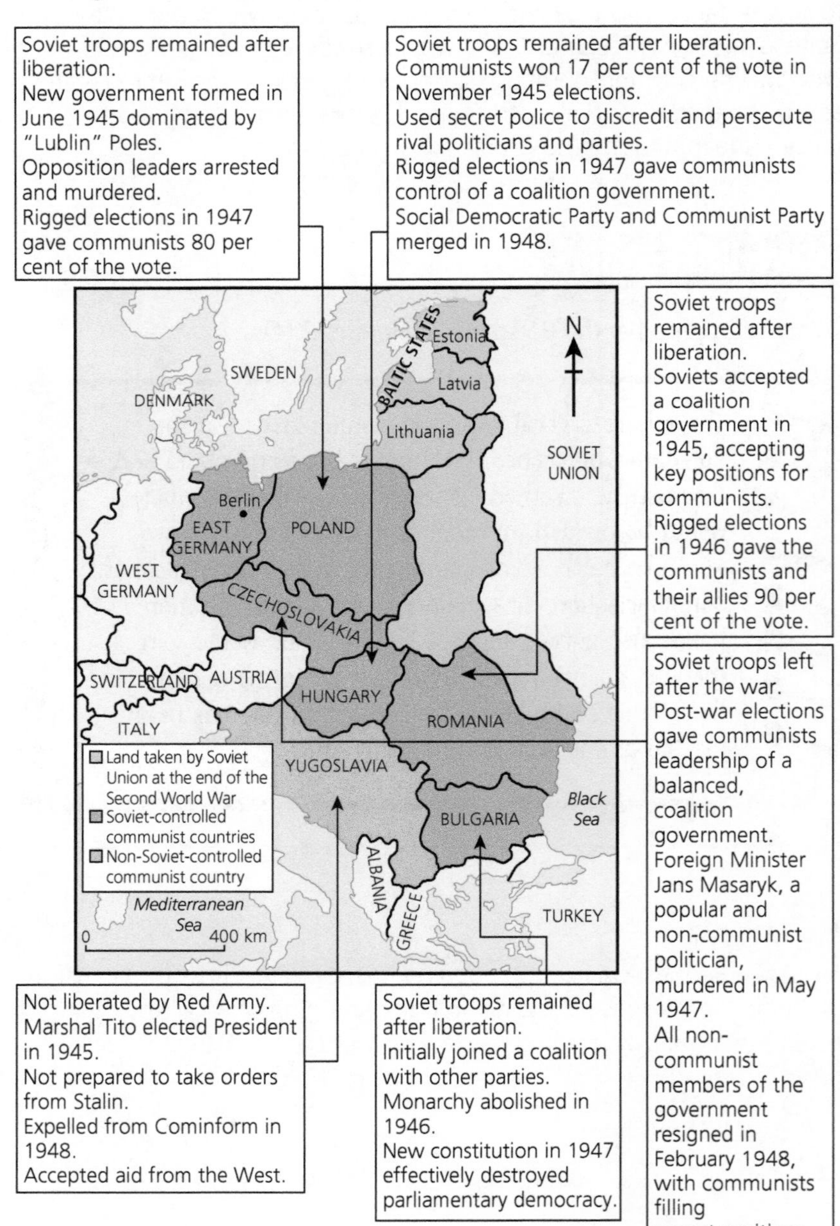

▲ **Fig. 4.2** *Map of Soviet expansion 1945–8*

The Truman Doctrine

Source 3

"I believe that it must be the policy of the United States to support all free people who are resisting attempted subjugation by armed minorities or by outside pressures. I believe that we must help free peoples to work out their own destiny in their own way."

▲ *President Harry Truman, March 1947.*

The United States feared that the Soviets were attempting to spread communism around the world. If they did nothing Greece and Turkey might be the next countries to fall to Stalin.

Truman persuaded the US Congress to provide aid in the form of arms and money for Greece and Turkey. In Greece, the communists were eventually defeated in 1949 following a civil war.

Marshall Aid

Source 4

"The United States should do whatever it is able to do to assist in the return of normal economic health to the world. Without this there can be no political stability and peace. Our policy is directed not against any country or idea but against poverty, hunger, desperation and chaos. Its purpose should be the rival of a working economy to permit the emergence of conditions in which free institutions can exist."

▲ *George Marshall, June 1947.*

Source 5

In June 1947 following a visit to Europe, the US Secretary of State George Marshall announced an economic recovery plan that provided aid to build up Europe's economy. This became known as the Marshall Plan.

To help war-torn Europe recover, the United States offered money, machinery, food, and technological equipment. In return, European countries would buy American goods and allow American investment in their industries. Sixteen Western European states accepted the offer. Between 1948 and 1952 the United States gave $13 billion of aid.

Recap

Stalin saw the United States' actions as an attempt to exert authority over Europe and he set up COMINFORM in return.

Why take this action?

- Truman believed that countries suffering from poverty were vulnerable to the spread of communism. Many countries in Europe were struggling to cope with the after-effects of the Second World War and were facing economic collapse.
- In addition, if Europe became prosperous again it could become a trading partner for the United States.

How did Stalin react?

Stalin refused Marshall Aid for the Soviet Union and banned Eastern European countries from receiving it. To counter the effects of the Marshall Plan, Stalin set up COMINFORM in 1947. This aimed to develop economic cooperation between communist countries.

The United States offered financial aid to European countries. As well as supporting these countries' recovery after the Second World War, the United States was also aware that this money would tie the countries most at risk to falling to communism more closely to the United States rather than establishing ties with Russia.

What was the Berlin Blockade?

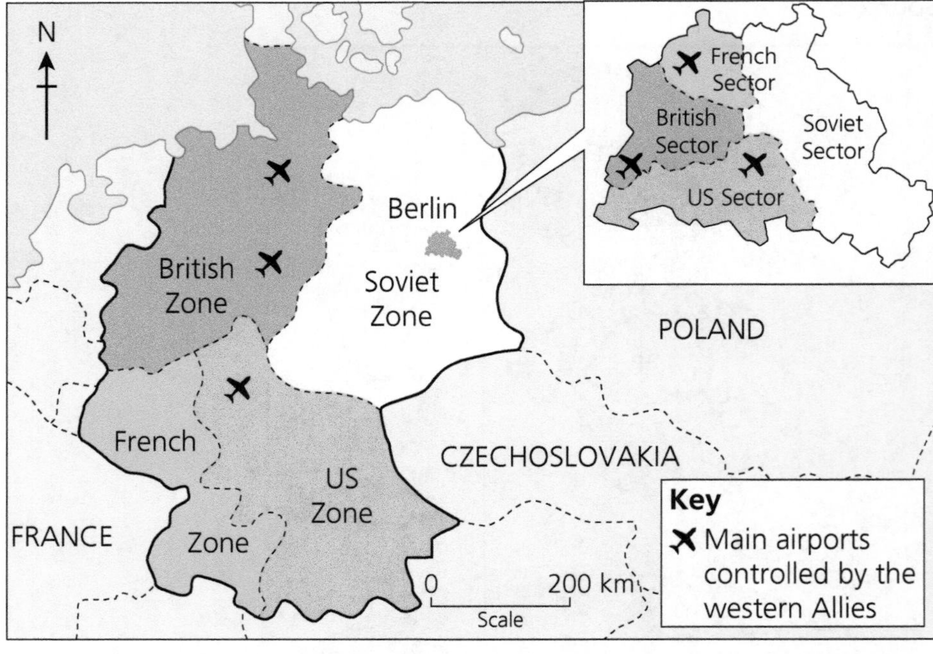

▲ **Fig. 4.3** *Germany in 1948*

Tensions over Germany

- Following the conferences at Yalta and Potsdam in 1945, the Allies had agreed to divide Berlin into four zones of occupation.
- Berlin, which was deep inside the Soviet zone, was also divided into four zones.
- The war had left Germany devastated and the Allies had different ideas about how to rebuild Germany.
- The United States and Britain wanted to help Germany recover quickly. The Soviet Union, however, wanted a weak Germany.
- Stalin was using German resources to rebuild the Soviet Union.

Causes of the blockade

Long-term causes of the blockade	Short-term causes of the blockade
• Within the Soviet zone, Soviet troops were able to control all access. • The Soviet Union believed the western Allies had no right to be in Berlin. The western Allies were seen as a threat as they had a base inside the Soviet zone. • The western Allies needed to be there to prevent the Soviet Union fully controlling Berlin. • The West could spy on Soviet activity behind the "iron curtain".	• In January 1947 Britain and the United States combined their zones to form "Bizonia". • France joined a year later. Stalin felt threatened by this, fearing he was being forced out. • Western Germany began to recover with the help of Marshall Aid. In East Germany there was poverty and hunger. • In 1948 the western Allies introduced a new currency into western Germany. Stalin refused to introduce it in the Soviet zone.

Stalin's motive

In June 1948 Stalin retaliated by blocking all road and rail links into West Berlin. Berlin was cut off from all supplies. Stalin increased the pressure by turning off all gas and electricity supplies. His aim was to force the other three powers to pull out of Berlin, making Berlin fully dependent on the Soviet Union.

The Berlin Airlift

- The airlift lasted for 11 months and involved nearly 300 000 flights.
- Cargo carried included coal, food, medicines, and petrol.
- Planes were landing in West Berlin at the rate of one every two minutes.
- Although they did not fire on incoming aircrafts, the Soviets used obstruction tactics, including jamming radios and shining search lights to temporarily blind pilots.

The Berlin Airlift was really the only solution available to the Allies. Other options, such as driving armed convoys through the blockade, would be highly provocative with a risk of war. However, pulling totally out of Berlin would render the Truman Doctrine an empty threat and mean countries would not trust the United States to stand up to communism in the future.

Stalin lifted the blockade on Berlin in May 1949 having failed to achieve his goal.

Exam tip

For a 6-mark question you need to ensure that you not only give reasons why something happened, but also fully explain them. You gain 1 mark for each point you correctly make, but full explanation of that point scores more highly. The example given is a good answer as it develops two points in relation to the question.

Worked example

Explain why the Soviet Union blockaded Berlin in 1948. (6)

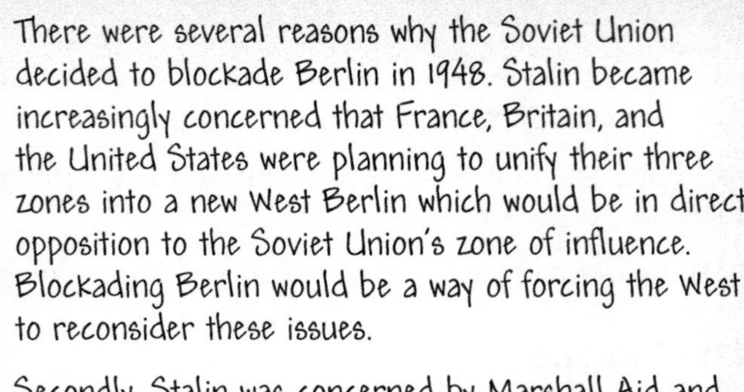

There were several reasons why the Soviet Union decided to blockade Berlin in 1948. Stalin became increasingly concerned that France, Britain, and the United States were planning to unify their three zones into a new West Berlin which would be in direct opposition to the Soviet Union's zone of influence. Blockading Berlin would be a way of forcing the West to reconsider these issues.

Secondly, Stalin was concerned by Marshall Aid and how Western influence was spreading into the Russian-controlled sector of Berlin. Berlin was deep within the communist zone of Germany and by blockading the city he was able to restrict travel to the Western zones and therefore limit influence. Marshall Aid also clashed with his idea for Germany—while the Allies wanted to rebuild the country in order to trade with it in the future, Stalin saw Germany as a source of raw materials to help rebuild his heavily damaged country.

Key term

The Warsaw Pact—a collective defence treaty signed between the Soviet Union and seven Soviet satellite states of central and eastern Europe in Warsaw, Poland in May 1955, during the Cold War. Its members were the Soviet Union, Albania, Poland, Romania, Hungary, East Germany, Czechoslovakia and Bulgaria.

The consequences of the blockade

October 1949
Stalin retaliated by turning the Soviet zone into the **German Democratic Republic.** This meant Germany was divided, with hostility between the two parts. East Berlin was part of East Germany. The division would last for 40 years.

May 1955
The **Warsaw Pact** was formed with eight communist countries unifying their armed forces under a central command. This was a direct response to the rearmament of West Germany and its incorporation into NATO.

May 1949
It was announced that the **Federal German Republic,** West Germany, had been formed by the merging of the zones of the Western Allies.

April 1949
The **North Atlantic Treaty Organisation (NATO)** was set up. Membership included the United States.

January 1949
COMECON was set up with the intention of establishing stronger links for Soviet bloc countries over economic issues

Key term

NATO—the North Atlantic Treaty Organization - a military alliance of countries founded on 4 April 1949 to strengthen international ties between member states, especially the United States and Europe, and to serve as a collective defence against an external attack. It remains in existence today.

Key term

COMECON—the Council for Mutual Economic Assistance - an economic organisation that comprised of the countries of the Eastern Bloc under the leadership of the Soviet Union between 1949 -91, along with a number of communist states elsewhere in the world.

Who was the most to blame for starting the Cold War: the United States or the Soviet Union?

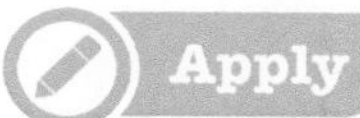

Write short fact files about:

- the Potsdam Conference
- the Truman Doctrine
- the Berlin Blockade.

For each event, how can it be argued that this was the start of the Cold War?

In what ways was the United States to blame?

Beliefs

The United States saw the threat of communism as a direct challenge to its own interests abroad. Therefore the actions taken by Truman looked to preserve American interests as well as protect the rights of citizens of other countries to access democracy. Its actions can be seen to reflect this—it can be argued that the true purpose of Marshall Aid was to provide a market for American goods and to ensure the preservation of a capitalist, free market system.

Actions

- The Marshall Plan promised aid to countries willing to stand up to the communist threat and therefore increased anti-communist sentiment.
- The creation of Bizonia and the introduction of a new currency into the western zones of Germany was a clear breach of the Potsdam Conference agreement and an attempt to impose a capitalist system.
- Truman was very aggressive in his dealings with officials from the Soviet Union and felt that as a powerful, atomic power the United States should be allowed to dictate terms at the Potsdam Conference.
- NATO was set up as a military alliance to defend its members against possible communist attack.

In what ways was the Soviet Union to blame?

Beliefs

The idea of communism was that it should be spread. It intended to impose its own system of government throughout the world. Stalin had a mistrust of the West. This led to concerns for Soviet security at the end of the war, which stemmed from historical fears about invasion from the west. These fears were caused by:

- the events of the Russian Civil War
- the belief that Britain and France encouraged Nazi Germany to expand eastwards during the late 1930s
- the belief that the western Allies deliberately delayed opening a second front in order to weaken the Soviet Union
- Britain refusing to share the German secret Enigma codes
- the secret development and testing by the United States of an atomic bomb.

Actions

- The creation of COMECON ensured that each Eastern European country followed the Soviet model of economic policy.
- The establishment of COMINFORM was a clear sign that Stalin intended to undermine capitalist society.

- Stalin did not abide by the agreements made at the Yalta Conference. He installed a communist government in Poland and went on to impose Soviet systems throughout Eastern Europe.
- Stalin's actions over Berlin in 1948 were drastic and destroyed any remaining trust between the two sides.

Review

1. What decisions, in relation to Germany, were agreed at Yalta and Potsdam? **[4]**
2. What was the Berlin Airlift? **[4]**
3. Explain the importance of NATO. **[4]**
4. Why was the Truman Doctrine significant? **[6]**
5. Why was the Potsdam Conference significant? **[6]**
6. "It was the Soviet expansion in Eastern Europe that caused the Cold War." How far do you agree with this statement? Explain your answer. **[10]**
7. To what extent was the failure of the Potsdam Conference the start of the Cold War? **[10]**

For further information review this section in the Student Book.

1. What was the "iron curtain"? **[4]**

Analysis

- ✓ The question is asking for two points focused on a key term relating to the Cold War.
- ✓ In addition to stating two points, the answer needs to explain in detail what they mean.
- ✓ The term was first used by Winston Churchill to describe the boundary that developed between the East and West.
- ✓ Churchill was referencing the division between East and West Europe that emerged at the Cold War developed.
- ✓ The term also symbolised the way in which the Soviet Union blocked its territories from open contact with the West.

Mark scheme

1 mark for each relevant point, additional mark for supporting detail, maximum 2 marks per point made.

Student answer

The "iron curtain" was the name for the division of Europe into two separate areas from the end of the Second World War. The name was used by Winston Churchill and made sense as a term because not only was there division between East and West and so a "curtain", it was also "iron" as Stalin and the Soviet Union restricted access to the West and attempted to control the actions of those countries through the Warsaw Pact.

Examiner feedback

The answer does well to identify that it was Churchill who established the term, and also offers a brief explanation of what the division did. The answer also offers some explanation of why it is an effective term, picking apart the meaning and placing it in context with the Warsaw Pact. 4 marks awarded.

2. Why was the Truman Doctrine introduced? **[6]**

Analysis

- ✓ As this is a "why" question, the answer needs to explain reasons why the United States introduced the Truman Doctrine.
- ✓ The answer shouldn't just list reasons why the United States acted, it needs to include two well-explained reasons in order to obtain a good mark.
- ✓ Truman wanted to support countries in Eastern Europe who were at risk of falling to communism in the uncertain and challenging post-war period.
- ✓ As well as political motives, there were also economic benefits for the United States—the Truman Doctrine led to the Marshall Plan which brought enhanced European trade for the United States.
- ✓ In the short term the Truman Doctrine was introduced due to the fear of Greece falling to communism, as other Eastern European countries had.

Mark scheme

Level 1:	general answer lacking specific contextual knowledge (1 mark)
Level 2:	identifies AND/OR describes reasons (2–3 marks)
Level 3:	explains ONE reason (4–5 marks)
Level 4:	explains TWO reasons (6 marks)

Student answer

President Truman was a fierce anti-communist who stated to Congress in March 1947 that he would try to counter the Soviet threat. Truman promised to send aid to Turkey and Greece because it was felt that without aid, both would inevitably fall to communism, with grave consequences throughout the region.

However, the Truman Doctrine was wider-ranging than just aiming at these two countries and implied American support for other nations allegedly threatened by Soviet communism. The Truman Doctrine became the foundation of American foreign policy, and led, in 1949, to the formation of NATO.

Examiner feedback

This is a good example of an answer from a student who clearly knows a lot about the Truman Doctrine, but hasn't answered the question asked. Although a lot of information about the Truman Doctrine is presented, the student doesn't tell us why this policy was introduced. The answer needs to be focused on the reasons the United States felt the need to react in this way. 2 marks awarded.

3. "The Soviet Union was to blame for the Cold War." How far do you agree with the statement? **[10]**

Analysis

- ✓ For the higher-mark questions remember that first you need to evaluate the factor specified in the question and then evaluate another side to the argument.
- ✓ The answer to this question should not be a simple list of reasons why the Soviet Union was to blame for the Cold War, with some detail added. Instead, try to give a full explanation of how the actions of the Soviets can be seen as a contributing factor to the cause of the war.
- ✓ The Soviet Union's attitude to Germany post-war undoubtedly led to tensions—their aim of using German resources to rebuild their country was certainly very different from that of the western Allies.
- ✓ As a communist state the Soviet Union wanted to spread Soviet beliefs and ideology across Europe. This caused concern among the western Allies, who feared their own interests would be compromised.
- ✓ To answer this question fully, you also need to consider issues other than the actions of the Soviet Union. For example, Winston Churchill's "iron curtain" speech was seen as very provocative, and it can be argued that the United States' use of aid through the Truman Doctrine also raised tensions.

Mark scheme

Level 1:	general answer lacking specific contextual knowledge (1 mark)
Level 2:	identifies AND/OR describes reasons (2–3 marks)
Level 3:	gives a one-sided explanation (4–5 marks) or one explanation of both sides (4–6 marks)
Level 4:	explains both sides (7–9 marks)
Level 5:	explains with evaluation (10 marks)

Student answer

It can be argued that the Soviet Union was to blame for the Cold War because of the beliefs and actions of Stalin in the period following the Second World War. The Soviet Union was a one-party communist state.

After the effects of the war the Soviets wanted to spread their control over Eastern Europe. By making other countries communist, suppressing free speech and establishing control through the creation of the COMINFORM

Stalin broke with what was agreed at Yalta and ignored the idea of free elections in Eastern Europe.

Stalin also increased tension in Europe through his behaviour in Germany. By blockading Berlin from the West, he forced the drastic action of the Berlin Airlift and this made tensions worse.

Examiner feedback

The student has presented a lot of information that is relevant to the question, but the mark scheme shows that the answer needs to be wider-ranging rather than just focusing on the Soviet Union.

There is no doubt that the actions of Stalin did lead to tensions between East and West, but this argument needs to be evaluated against the idea it was also the United States' fault that the Cold War broke out. The Truman Doctrine, the Marshall Plan, and the anti-communist stance of the United States meant that the Americans could also be seen as responsible for this war. 5 marks awarded.

You need to know:

- the role of the United States and events in Korea, 1950–3
- the role of the United States and events in Cuba, 1959–62
- how the United States was involved in Vietnam, examined using:
  - the events of the Cold War
  - case studies of:
    - American reactions to North Korea's invasion of South Korea, involvement of the UN, the course of the war to 1953
    - American reactions to the Cuban revolution, including the missile crisis and its aftermath
    - American involvement in the Vietnam War, including reasons for involvement, tactics, and strategy; reasons for withdrawal

Background: American concerns about communism

When the Second World War came to an end, the United States became increasingly concerned about the threat of communism, seeing it as a Russian attempt to dominate first Europe and then the world. This posed a challenge to American economic, political, and ideological interests.

Korea becoming communist in 1948 and China in 1949 led to concern that Asia would be engulfed by communism. To prevent this, the United States was willing to go to war. The spread of communism also threatened American interests in Cuba, while Vietnam presented a challenge to American influence.

Korea

Background to events in Korea

	1910	Korea had been controlled by the Japanese.
Division: the Japanese troops based in the north of Korea surrendered to the Soviet Union while those based in the south surrendered to the Americans. A temporary dividing line was drawn up between the north and south along the 38th parallel of latitude (38° north). Free elections were to be held for a united, democratic Korea.	**1945**	
	1948	Elections: separate elections were held. The south became the Republic of Korea, a capitalist dictatorship. In the north, now called the Democratic People's Republic of Korea, there was a communist dictatorship, supported by China and the Soviet Union.
25 June: North Korean soldiers, armed with Russian weapons, invaded South Korea.	**1950**	

▲ **Fig. 5.1** *Timeline summarising the background to events in Korea*

Exam tip

When answering a "why" question about the causes of a specific event, aim to explain two different reasons why the event occurred.

Worked example

Why did North Korea invade South Korea in June 1950? (6)

The ruler of North Korea, Kim Il-Sung, wanted a united Korea under communist rule. He felt that after the elections of 1948 the power the Communists had established in North Korea would be great enough to take control of the South too.

North Korea also felt that it had powerful allies and therefore would be successful in invading the South. North Korea had support from Stalin's Soviet Union as well as Mao's China. With this support North Korea's armed forces, using weapons supplied by the Soviet Union, were stronger than the armed forces of South Korea. In addition, China had developed its own atomic bomb, making the Chinese more powerful, and Kim il-Sung's view was that this made an American response unlikely, as Korea was not a major American priority.

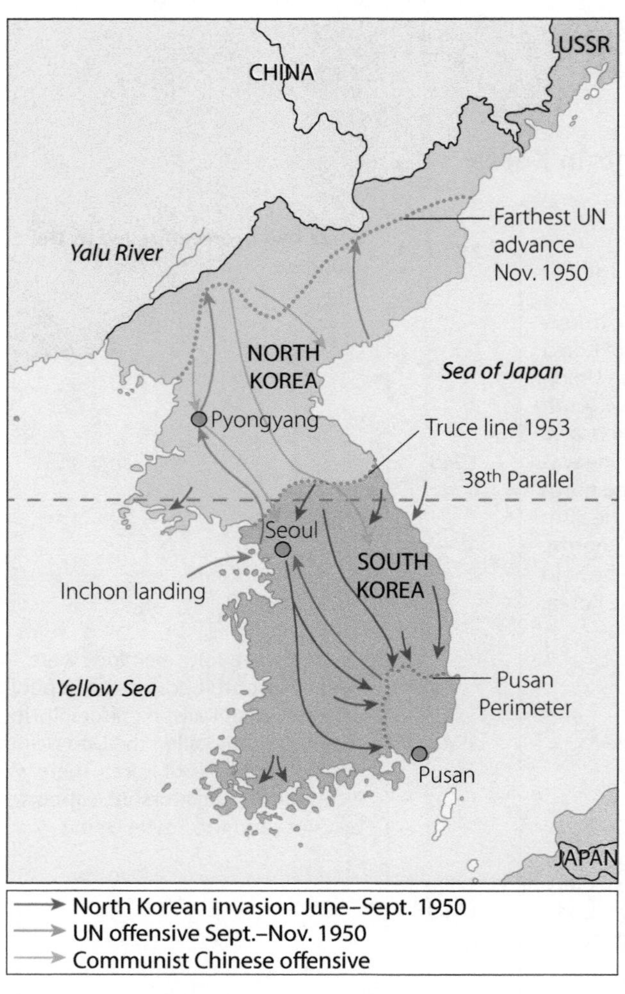

▲ **Fig. 5.2** *The Korean War, 1950–3*

How did the UN and the United States become involved?

President Truman sent the US Seventh Fleet to try to prevent a Chinese attack on Formosa (Taiwan). He ordered General MacArthur to go to Korea with military supplies.

The United Nations Security Council met on the day that North Korean troops crossed the border into South Korea. An American resolution was passed at the United Nations (UN) demanding the withdrawal of the North Koreans. Its passing was made possible by the absence of the Soviet representative on the Security Council. At that time the Soviets were not present, as a protest against the United State's treatment of communist China.

As North Korea had no intention of withdrawing, a second American resolution was put forward on the 27 June. A third resolution 10 days later made clear how military forces were to be deployed.

Troops from the United States and 15 other countries were sent to assist South Korea. The UN forces were to be commanded by the American General MacArthur, who took his orders directly from Truman rather than from UN officials. Half the ground forces were Americans, together with over 90 per cent of the air forces and over 85 per cent of the naval forces.

Key term

Containment—the United States' government policy under Truman, based on the principle that communist governments would eventually collapse provided they were prevented from expanding their influence.

Why did the United States become involved?

- The United States wanted to stop the spread of communism—it was determined to halt further communist expansion. The actions of North Korea were seen by the United States as part of Moscow's attempt to gain world domination.
- The Americans wanted to protect their interests. They feared that success in South Korea would encourage communist China to attack Formosa (the base of the non-communist Chinese). If South Korea and Formosa fell to the communists, Japan would come under threat. From the point of view of the United States, the fall of South Korea, Formosa, and Japan to the communists would represent a major shift in world power balance. The most effective way to prevent this was to oppose the North Korean invasion of South Korea.

Apply

Write a bullet list of the reasons why the Korean War developed.

The course of the war

In September 1950, UN troops landed at Inchon and forced the communists back into North Korea. UN troops invaded North Korea in an attempt to defeat the communists. In response, the Chinese leader Mao Zedong sent a large Chinese army to attack MacArthur's army.

In 1951 the UN army was forced to retreat to the south, followed by the communists. A UN counter-attack forced the Chinese and North Koreans back to the 38th parallel.

There were disagreements between Truman and MacArthur over the course of the war. President Truman did not want a lengthy or costly war in Asia but MacArthur wanted to carry on into China. He even suggested the use of the atomic bomb. Truman dismissed MacArthur in April 1951.

In 1953 a ceasefire was agreed that left Korea as two separate countries. Truman settled for communism being contained in North Korea.

Recap

The United States became involved because the Americans feared the spread of communism would threaten their own interests and make China more powerful.

Recap

American support meant that South Korea was able to resist North Korea's aggression. However, Korea would remain divided.

What were the results of the Korean War for the UN?

The UN had used military sanctions against an aggressor, showing that it was more purposeful than the League of Nations had ever been. The UN had failed in its objective of a "unified, independent and democratic government" for Korea. The massive involvement and influence of the United States made it look more like an American action than one by the UN.

UN support for the American motion had only been achieved by chance: when the Korean War began, Russia was boycotting the UN Security Council and so there were no Russian delegates to veto the UN decision.

What were the results of the Korean War for the United States?

- Forty thousand troops died.
- The American policy of containment had been successful as the spread of communism into South Korea had been prevented.
- Many American Republicans felt the United States had missed an opportunity to destroy communism in China. This feeling contributed towards the excesses of McCarthyism in the United States.
- American relations with China, as well as with the Soviet Union, were now strained, bringing a new dimension to the Cold War.

Exam tip

To answer a question like this it is important that you attempt a balanced answer—consider the question from both sides rather than arguing for one particular viewpoint.

Worked example

How great a threat was the Korean War to world peace? Explain your answer. (10)

It can be strongly argued that the Korean War did threaten world peace as it meant the Cold War had now spread to Asia and potentially could bring China, Russia, and other countries into full-scale conflict with the United States. At times war seemed very likely to spread beyond Korea: in November 1950, American troops reached the border between Korea and China, and the Chinese launched a large-scale counter offensive. If the war did move to mainland China, a growing power with a newly developed nuclear threat, then this would definitely threaten world peace.

The Korean War can also be seen to have threatened world peace as it increased mistrust between the Soviet Union and the United States. In the aftermath, the Soviet Union saw the United States as an expansionist country, and further deepened the growing Cold War tensions. On the United States' part, the fact that the Soviet Union gave arms to North Korea hardened the view that the Soviet Union was looking to undermine democracy in other countries and was a threat to the world interests of the United States.

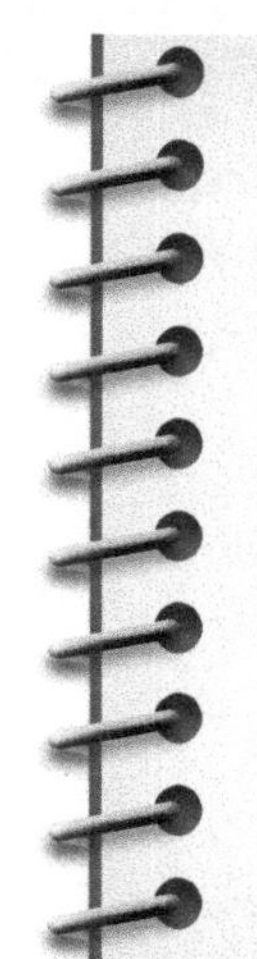

However, it also can be considered that the Korean War was not a threat to world peace. The UN stood up to an act of aggression by North Korea that had been supported by two major powers. The UN moved quickly to respond to the invasion of Korea and many member nations offered troops and military and medical equipment in assistance. Ultimately, the invasion was unsuccessful and in 1951 the United States, the Soviet Union, and China started negotiations to end the war. Neither side wanted to make the crisis any larger and when it looked as if it might spread to China, Truman immediately scaled back American involvement and replaced MacArthur as commander.

The United States and events in Cuba, 1959–62

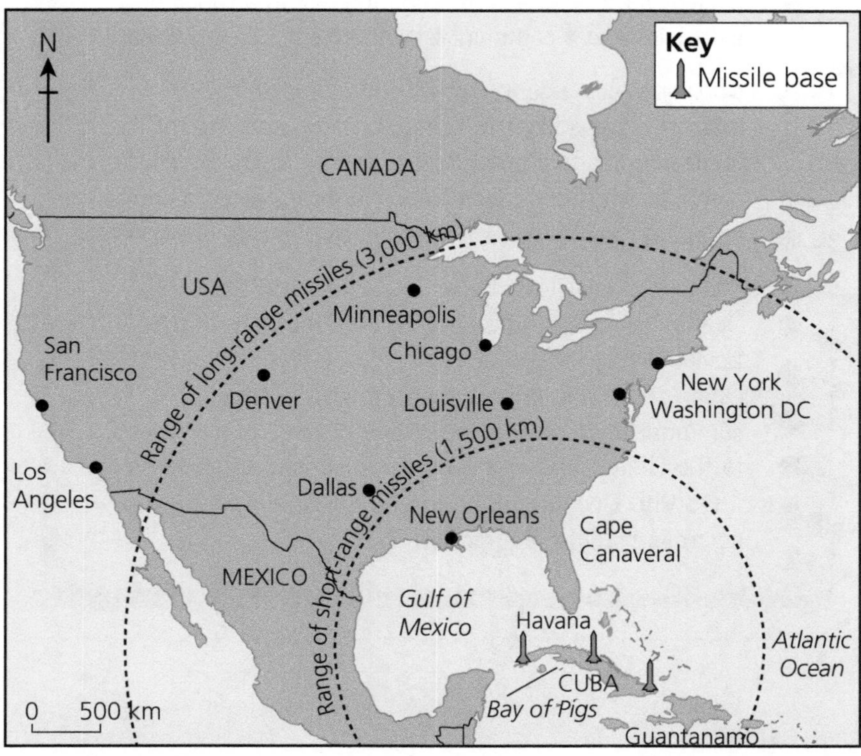

▲ **Fig. 5.3** *The threat to American cities posed by missiles in Cuba*

Background to events in Cuba

Cuba was important to the United States for a range of economic, military, and political reasons. The United States invested heavily in the Cuban economy, controlling the railways, telephone system and tobacco plantations. Cuba was also a significant importer of American goods, and Guantanamo Bay was an important US naval base. Cuba was also a holiday island for rich Americans, and the American mafia controlled much of the gambling, horse racing, and hotels in Cuba.

The United States was seen as corrupt by many in Cuba because of the interests it held there. This is an important reason why there was support for the new regime.

Recap

Cuba was very useful to the United States as a trading partner, a holiday destination, and also a naval base. The Americans did not want their influence in Cuba to be reduced.

Why did tensions develop between Cuba and the United States?

In 1959 there was a revolution in Cuba. The unpopular President Batista was overthrown by revolutionary Fidel Castro. Castro promised to end American influence and control. The United States was worried by this, as it had supported Batista. The Americans feared Castro would turn out to be a communist.

Castro negotiated trade agreements with the Soviet Union to export sugar and Khrushchev sent Castro advisers, military equipment, and economic aid.

Worked example

Why was the Cuban Revolution seen as a threat to the United States? Give two explained reasons. (6)

The Cuban Revolution was a threat to the United States as it threatened American interests within Cuba. The United States held a controlling interest in a range of industries and a communist takeover put these in danger.

Cuba was also a source of revenue for particular interest groups from the United States, such as the mafia who made a great deal of money from controlling gambling and hotels within the country. Any communist revolution would also threaten these American interests.

The Cuban Revolution also was a threat to the United States due to any links that were established with the Soviet Union. As the Cold War developed, the Soviet Union seemed intent on supporting the spread of communism to other countries and with Cuba so close to the United States, any communist state established there with strong links to the Soviet Union would be a potential route of aggression.

Exam tip

The key to answering the question is to consider the level of threat to American interests that the Cuban Revolution posed. Consider how profitable Cuba was to the United States and what things might change after the event.

How did tensions worsen between the two sides?

	January 1961	In response to Cuban trade links with the Soviet Union, the United States banned all trade with Cuba and cut off diplomatic relations.
President Kennedy made available weapons and transport for an attempt to overthrow Castro. In this invasion 1500 Cuban exiles landed at the Bay of Pigs to find themselves faced with 20 000 Cuban troops armed with weapons supplied by the Soviet Union. The anticipated support from the Cuban people did not materialise and the exiles were killed or taken prisoner. The invasion was a dismal failure.	**April 1961**	
	June 1961	Khrushchev met Kennedy in Vienna. The United States was concerned as Kennedy was thought to be weak and would not back the containment policy with force.
Castro nationalised all American industries.	**July 1961**	
	September 1961	Khrushchev publicly announced that he would provide arms to Cuba.

▲ **Fig. 5.4** *Timeline of events causing tensions to worsen*

Draw a spider diagram showing the reasons why Cuba was important to the United States.

The Bay of Pigs Invasion was a disaster for the United States. The details of the attack were leaked and Castro was prepared for the attack. The Cuban exiles were met by 20 000 Cuban troops. The invasion forces immediately came under heavy fire and although some escaped into the sea, most were killed or captured. The supporting air strikes missed many of their targets and few, if any, Cubans joined the invaders.

What was the Cuban Missile Crisis?

The Americans became increasingly alarmed about the Soviet military build-up in Cuba and were worried that a nuclear attack might be launched from Cuba by the Soviet Union. In September 1962 Khrushchev told Kennedy that he had no intention of placing nuclear missiles in Cuba. This was proved to be false, causing tension to heighten, when an American spy plane photographed the construction of nuclear missile sites in Cuba on 14 October 1962.

The Bay of Pigs invasion was a disaster for Kennedy, who was newly in post as President.

Why did the Soviet Union place missiles in Cuba?

Reason	Explanation
Placing missiles in Cuba would reduce the advantage held by the United States	The United States had missiles in Western Europe and had recently placed missiles in Turkey, which bordered the Soviet Union.
To act as a deterrent	Cuba was an ally of the Soviet Union. Missiles in Cuba would act as a deterrent against another attack. Cuba was the only communist country in the western hemisphere.
To send out a message of strength to the United States	Khrushchev was seen by some within the Soviet Union as not being strong enough in his dealings with the United States. Missiles close to the United States would give Khrushchev increased bargaining power.
The Soviet Union wanted a base close to the United States for its medium-range missiles	Cuba was only 90 miles away from the United States. Medium-range missiles would be able to reach the United States.
To "close the gap"	Khrushchev wanted to increase the number of Soviet warheads. Medium-range weapons were cheaper to produce and could threaten the United States from Cuba.

Thirteen days

Once the United States had confirmed that the missiles had been placed in Cuba, Kennedy and his advisers met for 13 days and nights to try and find a solution to the crisis.

Key fact

EX-COMM—the Executive Committee of the National Security Council—was a body of government officials that advised Kennedy during the Cuban Missile Crisis It was made up of members of the National Security Council, along with other advisers. The meetings were secretly recorded by Kennedy and the evidence from these tapes helps us understand this period of crisis.

Key fact

Robert Kennedy, JF Kennedy's brother, served as Attorney General and was a key adviser while JF Kennedy was US President.

Apply

Draw a spider diagram that shows the successes and failures in Kennedy's response to the Cuban Missile Crisis.

	Tue 16 October 1962	President Kennedy is informed of the missiles in Cuba. A group of advisers called EX-COMM meet in secret to discuss the United States' response.
EX-COMM continues to work on a response to the crisis.	**Wed 17 October 1962**	
	Thur 18 October 1962	Kennedy meets with the Soviet Foreign Minister. The minister denies the presence of missiles in Cuba. Kennedy does not reveal what he has discovered.
Kennedy decides to impose a blockade of Cuba. This decision is taken despite some members of EX-COMM favouring a show of force.	**Sun 21 October 1962**	
	Mon 22 October 1962	In a live broadcast on American television, Kennedy informs the American public of the missiles and that he is going to impose a blockade. He asks Khrushchev to withdraw the missiles from Cuba.
Khrushchev replies stating that there are no nuclear missiles in Cuba. He calls the blockade an act of piracy. Soviet ships sail towards the American blockade. If the blockade is ignored, the United States will fire on the ships. War seems certain to follow.	**Tue 23 October 1962**	
	Wed 24 October 1962	The Soviet ships reach the blockade. Kennedy stands his ground. One ship is allowed through, the others turn back. One crisis has been averted but the missiles still remain in Cuba.
Khrushchev admits to the existence of missiles in Cuba. Kennedy receives a letter from Khrushchev saying the Soviet Union will remove the missiles from Cuba if Kennedy agrees to lift the blockade and promises never to invade Cuba.	**Fri 26 October 1962**	
	Sat 27 October 1962	A second letter from Khrushchev revises his proposals of the first letter. His new condition for the removal of missiles from Cuba is the withdrawal of American missiles from Turkey. In another development an American spy plane is shot down over Cuba, killing the pilot. The advice to launch an immediate reprisal attack is ignored by Kennedy. Kennedy ignores the second letter but agrees to the demands made by Khrushchev in his first letter.
Khrushchev agrees to remove the missiles from Cuba. Conflict is avoided. Robert Kennedy informs the Soviet ambassador that the United States will not invade Cuba and that the missiles in Turkey will be removed within six months.	**Sun 28 October 1962**	

▲ **Fig. 5.5** *Timeline showing how the crisis unfolded, 16–28 October 1962*

Who won the Cuban Missile Crisis?

Countries	Positives	Negatives
The outcome for Cuba	Cuba remained communist, becoming a base for other communists in South America. Castro remained in power, keeping control of the American industries he had nationalised at the time of the revolution. Castro maintained the support and protection afforded to Cuba by the Soviet Union although he was disappointed with the deal Khrushchev agreed with the United States.	Unable to trade with the United States and dependent on the Soviet Union, Cuba remained a country poor and isolated in the western hemisphere.
The outcome for the Soviet Union and Khrushchev	Khrushchev was able to say that he had acted responsibly by agreeing to remove the missiles from Cuba. Cuba was maintained as a communist ally in the western hemisphere. This was a significant achievement in the face of American action. The United States had agreed to remove NATO missiles from Turkey. As this was a secret agreement, Khrushchev was unable to take the credit.	Many in the Soviet Union felt humiliated by the fact that Khrushchev had been forced to back down and remove the missiles from Cuba. Khrushchev's reputation was tarnished and he was replaced as Soviet leader within two years. His critics believed he had not been forceful enough.
The outcome for the United States and Kennedy	The possibility of nuclear war had been avoided. Kennedy's prestige in the world increased. He was seen by the West as a tough negotiator as he did not back down over his naval blockade. Some of Kennedy's military advisers, who were critics of containment, thought he should invade Cuba to turn back communism. He avoided this high-risk strategy by standing up to these hard-liners.	Cuba remained a communist state close to the United States. Restrictions on trade between Cuba and United States remained in force. The United States was criticised by some of its allies, including Britain. British newspaper articles were critical of the Americans' attitude that it was acceptable for them to have missiles in Turkey and other European bases but they complained about Cuba. The removal of missiles in Turkey had left some NATO members unhappy as technically the weapons were NATO missiles. The removal of the missiles was kept from the American public.

The aftermath of the crisis

Relations between the United States and the Soviet Union improved after the crisis. Both sides realised that brinkmanship had to be avoided in the future. The Cuban Missile Crisis was the nearest both sides came to conflict during the whole of the Cold War. They were now prepared to reduce the risk of nuclear conflict. A "hotline" telephone link was established between the Kremlin and the White House so that problems could be discussed. A Test Ban Treaty was signed in 1963.

American involvement in Vietnam

Background

Before the Second World War, Vietnam was ruled by France. In 1942 it was occupied by the Japanese. In 1945, following the defeat of Japan, the French returned, hoping to rule Vietnam. There was however strong opposition to French rule from the Vietnamese, who wanted to run Vietnam themselves.

In 1954 the Battle of Dien Bien Phu marked the end of French involvement in Vietnam. Under the Geneva Peace Accords of 1954, agreed by the Vietminh and the French, the following terms were set.

- Indo-China was split into three countries: Laos, Cambodia, and Vietnam.
- Vietnam was temporarily portioned into two parts (north and south) at the 17th parallel.
- Free elections were to be held in 1956.

These elections never took place because the United States feared the communists would win. The idea of the "domino theory" was introduced by the United States, where if one country became communist, others nearby would follow. Vietnam was therefore seen as a battleground against communism.

▲ **Fig. 5.6** *The domino effect*

In 1955 the Americans supported Ngo Dinh Diem to set up the Republic of South Vietnam. Diem was bitterly opposed to communism. The North meanwhile formed a Communist government under the Vietminh. Clashes began between the South and the Vietcong—communist members based in the South who used guerrilla warfare.

Why did the United States become involved in Vietnam?

- Diem's government was weak and needed support. By 1963 the communist Vietcong controlled 40 per cent of South Vietnam.
- American policy was based on the idea of "containment".
- President Eisenhower believed in the "domino theory"—if South Vietnam was allowed to become communist, then Laos, Cambodia, Burma, India, Thailand, and Pakistan would quickly follow.
- President Kennedy decided to increase American military presence because he saw Vietnam as crucial to the Cold War. He wanted to look strong after the failed Bay of Pigs Invasion and the Cuban Missile Crisis.

How did American involvement in Vietnam increase?

- Aid—after France had left, military and economic aid was offered to South Vietnam.

Key fact

Vietnam, along with Cambodia and Laos, was referred to as French Indo-China when ruled by the French. It was only when the French left that it officially became known as Vietnam.

Key term

Vietminh—a communist-dominated nationalist movement, formed in 1941, that fought for Vietnamese independence from French rule.

Key fact

The Vietcong, or National Liberation Front (NLF), was the guerrilla force that, with the support of the North Vietnamese Army, fought against South Vietnam and the United States. The Vietcong was based in the south of Vietnam.

Apply

Consider the effect of the Cuban Missile Crisis on the Soviet Union and on Cuba. Write a fact file focusing on how the crisis strengthened or weakened each country's position, and the reputation of its leader.

The United States' involvement in Vietnam was similar to that in Korea—the threat of communism and the belief in the domino theory forced the Americans to intervene.

Key term

Vietnamisation—support given by the United States to strengthen the South Vietnamese army to allow the gradual withdrawal of American combat troops from the Vietnam War.

- Advisers—President Kennedy sent military advisers to support the South Vietnamese army. In May 1961, 500 were sent. In 1963 the number of advisers totalled 16 000.
- "The Gulf of Tonkin incident"—in August 1964, two American warships were attacked by North Vietnamese gunboats while in international waters. This confrontation was known as the Gulf of Tonkin incident. In response, the US Senate granted Johnson permission to give armed support to South Vietnam.

The timeline below summarises the main events of the Vietnam War.

	February 1965	Operation Rolling Thunder—bombing of North Vietnam started, with targets that included the Ho Chi Minh Trail.
The first American combat troops were sent to Vietnam.	**March 1965**	
	January 1968	Start of the Tet Offensive—a large-scale communist attack on major towns and cities in South Vietnam. Targets included the American embassy in Saigon. Although the communists were defeated, the attacks were a major shock to Americans who had thought the war was almost won. The American media called it a defeat and public support for the war plummeted. Following the Tet Offensive peace talks started. A ceasefire was not achieved for a further five years.
A group of American soldiers was searching for Vietcong. The soldiers landed by helicopter close to the village of My Lai. They failed to find any Vietcong so rounded up the inhabitants of the village and massacred them all, including infants. When news of the massacre reached the American people there was shock and horror. Numerous anti-war demonstrations followed.	**March 1968**	
	October 1968	Operation Rolling Thunder finished. More bombs have been dropped on North Vietnam than were dropped by the United States on Germany and Japan during the Second World War. Also in this month the American policy of Vietnamisation was introduced by President Nixon.
President Nixon attacked Cambodia to prevent the Vietcong from using it as a base from which to attack American forces.	**1970**	
	1973	A ceasefire agreement was signed.

Recap

In November 1963 President Diem was overthrown by a military coup. Later the same month President Kennedy was assassinated. His successor President Lyndon B Johnson was more prepared to enter into full-scale conflict in Vietnam than Kennedy had been. (See the Student Book, pages 107–8.)

Fig. 5.7 *Timeline of the main events of the Vietnam War*

Were the military tactics of the United States or those of the communists the most effective?

Strategies used by the Vietcong during the Vietnam War

Strategy	Impact
Ho Chi Minh based the Vietcong guerrilla warfare strategies on the methods used by the communists to gain power in China. Features of Vietcong guerrilla warfare were as follows. • Guerrilla fighters did not have a base camp. • They did not wear a uniform, making it difficult to differentiate between villagers and Vietcong. • They used the element of surprise, carrying out attacks then quickly disappearing into the jungle, taking refuge in villages or their underground tunnels. • They ambushed American troops and set booby traps using trip wires and mines. • The closeness of fighting ("hanging on to American belts") negated the greater strength of American fire power.	• The morale of American troops, whose average age was only 19, was reduced. • The number of American casualties was increased. • Mistrust built between Vietnamese civilians and American soldiers who were unable to distinguish between friend and foe.

Strategies used by the United States during the Vietnam War

Strategy	Impact
Strategic bombing: during the war the United States bombed Vietcong strongholds, supply lines, and key cities. Operation Rolling Thunder started in 1965. Bombing continued after Operation Rolling Thunder stopped in 1968.	• Supply lines were disrupted but not stopped. The system of tunnels and underground passages was not affected by the bombing. • South Vietnamese targets were still attacked. Remember, this was the area the United States was supposed to be protecting. • Extensive bombing of Hanoi (the North Vietnam capital) encouraged the start of peace discussions. • The financial cost of this bombing was huge.
Use of chemical weapons	• The Americans developed "agent orange" and also used napalm. • Agent orange was used to carry out defoliation of the jungle in South Vietnam. The chemical was dropped from the air and removed the leaves from the trees in an attempt to prevent the Vietcong hiding in the jungle. The Vietcong underground supply lines were not affected. • Napalm was often dropped on villages to destroy them. Thousands of innocent Vietnamese civilians received terrible burns and many died. This shocked the American people, and meant that American troops lost any support from the villagers.

Strategy	Impact
Search and destroy: in response to the guerrilla tactics of the Vietcong the Americans carried out raids using helicopters. The helicopters would land near Vietnamese villages. The American forces would then kill hiding Vietcong fighters and set fire to the village.	• Although some Vietcong were killed, the impact was minimal. • The raids were often based on incorrect information resulting in villages being destroyed and large numbers of innocent villagers killed. • American troops became unpopular with the peasants who then gave their support to the Vietcong.
Imposing strategic hamlets: whole villages were moved to a new site enclosed by barbed wire.	• The Americans were able to control and check those who entered and left the village. • There was resentment from villagers who were forced to leave their homes to live somewhere else.

Key fact

The draft was the name given to the lottery system where men were conscripted into the US army. About one-third of those fighting in Vietnam were drafted, and once called they had to serve for two years.

Worked example

Describe the United States' tactics in Vietnam. (4)

The United States used a range of tactics in the war in Vietnam. In an attempt to combat the guerrilla warfare American troops faced, the United States used chemical weapons to try and limit the territory that the Vietcong could hide in. Agent orange and napalm were developed. Agent orange was used to bring about defoliation of the jungle in South Vietnam. The chemical removed the leaves from the trees in an attempt to prevent the Vietcong hiding in the jungle. However, underground supply lines were not affected. Both agent orange and napalm caused injury to thousands of innocent Vietnamese civilians.

The United States also used search and destroy tactics in an attempt to combat the Vietcong. Raids on villages would be based on information and would result in American forces killing or capturing Vietcong fighters and destroying the village. However, these raids were limited in effectiveness and often resulted in villages being destroyed and large numbers of innocent villagers killed.

Exam tip

In your answer focus on specific tactics of the American troops in Vietnam, using the relevant terms such as "search and destroy" and "strategic hamlets".

Why did the United States withdraw from Vietnam?

Reason	Explanation
Low morale	The use of guerrilla warfare affected the morale of the troops as they feared what might happen to them. Troops turned to drugs and thousands of soldiers deserted. The average age of American troops was 19. After 1967 they were "drafted" (conscripted) into the army. Many had recently left school and just wanted to return home safely. They were often from poorer homes or immigrant backgrounds.
The Tet Offensive	Up to 1967 the war had been going well for the Americans. During the New Year holiday in January 1967, communist troops attacked major Vietnamese towns and cities, including the American embassy in Saigon. The hoped-for revolution in South Vietnam did not materialise and the Vietcong were pushed back. The Tet Offensive was widely seen as a turning point for the United States as it was realised that without increasing the number of combat troops the war could not be won. Additionally, increased numbers of troops would bring even more casualties.
My Lai	In March 1968 an American troop patrol entered the village of My Lai. They were on a search-and-destroy mission, having been informed that members of the Vietcong were hiding there. No Vietcong were found, but nearly 400 civilians, many of whom were women and children, were massacred by the Americans. When details of the brutal massacre become known it shocked the American public, undermining support for the war. The horror of My Lai and the increasing view that the war was unwinnable led Johnson to decide not to run again for president.
Press and media	In the early years of the war, most American newspapers and news journalists were supportive of the war. The reports they produced were positive as they did not wish to undermine the American government's policy of containment. By 1967 reports from Vietnam were via television programmes that often showed scenes of shocking violence from search-and-destroy raids. At the same time television reporters were increasingly arguing that the war was unwinnable. One such reporter was CBS' Walter Cronkite. This changing attitude was not just influencing the American public but even President Johnson. American military leaders, including General Westmoreland, put forward the view that the media reduced support for the war effort in Vietnam.
Protests against the war	Public opinion was changing. As more and more bodies of young servicemen were brought home in body bags the public began asking if the United States could win the war. To show disapproval, "draft cards" were burnt and President Johnson was taunted by students. American student anti-war protests reached their height towards the end of the 1960s. Participating students held the view that the war was morally wrong and therefore did not wish to receive the draft. Often the protests involved the burning of the American flag and ended in violent clashes with the police. One such clash was at Kent State University where the US National Guard fired into a group of unarmed protestors. Four students were killed.
Human and economic cost	In 1967 *Life* magazine calculated that it was costing $400 000 for each Vietcong fighter killed. This meant cutbacks in the spending on social reforms in President Johnson's "Great Reform" programme. By 1968, 300 American soldiers were dying each week. Over 50 000 American troops eventually lost their lives.
Lack of support	There was declining support in South Vietnam. The winning of "hearts and minds" was seen as crucial to American success but the use of tactics that killed civilians lost the support of the Vietnamese people. At the same time, neighbouring countries of Vietnam showed sympathy to the Vietcong by allowing them to access arms and ammunition. The United States could not, for diplomatic reasons, enter these countries. Cambodia and Laos used the Ho Chi Minh trail to supply necessities to the Vietcong.

Exam tip

The key to answering this question successfully is to address the term "increasingly unpopular" by identifying the factors that changed public mood.

Worked example

Why did the Vietnam War become increasingly unpopular with the people in the United States? (6)

By 1968 the war was a stalemate. The United States could not defeat the Vietcong. The Tet Offensive showed that the Vietcong could not drive out the United States. However, the Tet Offensive and My Lai had horrified the American public as broadcasts showed wounded and dead soldiers, and innocent civilians massacred. The American public began to see the war as unwinnable.

The war was also huge drain on resources. The aim of President Johnson's "Great Reform" programme was huge social change, but with the vast sums spent on the war and the impact at home (such as through policing anti-war protests) the war lost popularity with ordinary Americans.

▲ **Fig. 5.8** *Nixon with advisors consulting on Vietnam*

The end of war in Vietnam

It was left to President Nixon to find a way to withdraw from the Vietnam War. This was a difficult task. From 1965 the American government had argued that the war was just and vital. Nixon introduced a policy of "Vietnamisation": the United States would train and equip the South Vietnamese so that American troops could withdraw. In February 1973 a ceasefire was agreed.

South Vietnam soon fell to the communists, as did Cambodia and Laos. During 1975 communist troops took South Vietnam including the capital, Saigon. In 1976 North and South Vietnam were reunited as a single communist country ruled by Ho Chi Minh. Relations between Vietnam and the United States remained hostile until 1993 when trade was resumed.

Review

1. Describe why conflict in Korea developed. **[4]**
2. Describe the Bay of Pigs invasion. **[4]**
3. Who were the Vietcong? **[4]**
4. Describe the My Lai incident. **[4]**
5. Why did the United States become involved in Vietnam? **[6]**
6. How successful was the United States in Vietnam in the period 1963–75? **[10]**
7. How successful was Kennedy's response to the Cuban Missile Crisis? **[10]**

For further information review this section in the Student Book.

1. What was the "domino theory?" **[4]**

Analysis

- ✓ The question introduces a key term so it is important that this is explained and the context of what it was referring to—in this case communism—is made clear.
- ✓ In the answer aim to make two good points that are well explained. The points should be what the theory was and how it applied to American foreign policy.
- ✓ The United States was concerned that as one country became communist, another would too.
- ✓ There is no need to explain why American politicians felt threatened by communism; instead, focus on the explanation of the theory.

Mark scheme

1 mark for each relevant point, additional mark for supporting detail, maximum 2 marks per point made.

Student answer

The domino theory was an explanation of how the United States feared communism would spread from country to country during the Cold War. The fear was that as a country turned communist, it would infiltrate neighbouring states, then momentum for communism would develop.

This belief was a defining factor in American military action in the period—intervention in Korea and Vietnam was an attempt to stop the spread of communism.

Examiner feedback

The candidate offers a good explanation of the theory, and also applies it to American foreign policy to show how it led to military action in Vietnam and Korea. 4 marks awarded.

2. Why did the United States become involved in Korea? **[6]**

Analysis

- ✓ The question references American involvement in the Korean War in the 1950s. For the answer aim for two well-developed reasons why the United States felt the need to become involved.
- ✓ The United States supported South Korea in the conflict against the North. The South was democratic while the North was communist.
- ✓ The US government viewed its involvement in the war as a way to prevent a communist takeover of the entire county.
- ✓ The United States' involvement was also prompted by the Soviet Union and China supporting North Korea.

Mark scheme

Level 1:	general answer lacking specific contextual knowledge (1 mark)
Level 2:	identifies AND/OR describes reasons (2–3 marks)
Level 3:	explains ONE reason (4–5 marks)
Level 4:	explains TWO reasons (6 marks)

Student answer

On 25 June 1950 the Korean War began when North Korea, supported by the Soviet Union and China, invaded South Korea, which was supported by the United States.

Korea had been separated at the end of the Second World War. North Korea became a communist regime under the leadership of Kim Il-sung. South Korea became a democratic state under Syngman Rhee. The Korean War therefore meant conflict between the communist and the democratic sides.

Examiner feedback

The answer gives detail about what the Korean War was, and does state that each side had foreign support. However, there is no focus on reasons for the United States' involvement—there needs to be more explanation of why the United States became involved. 1 mark awarded.

3. How far was American public opinion the most important reason for the United States' withdrawal from Vietnam? **[10]**

Analysis

- ✓ A "How far" question offers a chance to explore the factor in the question as well as considering other issues.
- ✓ In the answer you should explore the factor and relevant issues then come to a conclusion.
- ✓ Public opinion was definitely important, and this changed as the war went on.
- ✓ There is little doubt that by the late 1960s the reaction of the public to the war was becoming negative as protests rose.
- ✓ However, other issues need to be explored. The cost of war, the long duration of the conflict, and the fact that the war seemed unwinnable were all significant issues.

Mark scheme

Level 1:	general answer lacking specific contextual knowledge (1 mark)
Level 2:	identifies AND/OR describes reasons (2–3 marks)
Level 3:	gives a one-sided explanation (4–5 marks) or one explanation of both sides (4–6 marks)
Level 4:	explains both sides (7–9 marks)
Level 5:	explains with evaluation (10 marks)

Student answer

It can be argued that public opinion was the most important reason for the withdrawal of the United States from Vietnam. The major turning point for American public opinion was the Tet Offensive in 1968. In January the Vietcong attacked towns and bases of South Vietnamese troops all over Vietnam. Thousands of troops died during the attack and it came as a complete shock to Americans who thought that they had been close to winning the war. The US government and the public felt misled by the army leaders, from whom they had been receiving positive information about the war.

Events such as this along with many others, such as the My Lai incident, were all exposed by media coverage. This and the change in public opinion about the war were the most significant reasons for the withdrawal of troops from Vietnam. The Vietnam War was the first to have full media coverage and people were able to see exactly how awful the war really was.

A shift in public opinion was seen through people burning their draft papers and refusing to agree to conscription. There were also other significant protests. In May 1970 protests on campus became out of control at Kent State University. Four students died and a few were injured as a result of gunfire from the National Guardsmen.

However, it was also the high cost of the war that put pressure on the government to withdraw troops from Vietnam. By the end of the war over $100 billion had been spent. This was money that could have been directed to address inequalities in American society but instead was being spent on the war.

Examiner feedback

The answer is strong in terms of its explanation of the importance of, and reasons for, public opinion about the Vietnam War. The student also offers a balanced view by presenting in the final paragraph the additional factor of the cost of the war. To improve the answer there needs to be more of a counter argument and more evaluation in the points made. 7 marks awarded.

You need to know:

- why there was opposition to Soviet control in Hungary in 1956 and how the Soviet Union reacted
- why there was opposition to Soviet control in Czechoslovakia in 1968 and how the Soviet Union reacted
- similarities and differences between events in Hungary in 1956 and in Czechoslovakia in 1968
- why the Berlin Wall was built in 1961
- the significance of "Solidarity" in Poland for the decline of Soviet influence in Eastern Europe
- how far Gorbachev was personally responsible for the collapse of Soviet control over Eastern Europe

Background: Soviet control over Eastern Europe, 1945–53

The end of the Second World War had brought Soviet control over the countries of Eastern Europe. To some this generated hope based on the significant industrial growth achieved by the Soviet Union prior to the war. However, the reality of Soviet control was very different: the right to democratic government and free speech was lost; newspapers were censored; government critics were put in prison; travel to countries in the West was prohibited.

Eastern bloc factories produced the goods demanded by the Soviet Union rather than goods the ordinary people in Eastern European countries wanted. In Eastern Europe there were shortages of basics including coal, milk, and meat. Clothing was very expensive and consumer goods such as electric kettles and radios were unavailable. Wages were even lower than in the Soviet Union.

▲ **Fig. 6.1** *Eastern Europe*

When Stalin died in 1953 to be replaced by Khrushchev, Khrushchev talked of peaceful co-existence with the West and wanting to improve living standards for the people of Eastern Europe. He indicated to countries in Eastern Europe that they would be allowed greater independence to control their own affairs. Khrushchev even went as far as denouncing Stalin. A programme of de-Stalinisation was to follow. The people of Eastern Europe saw this changing attitude as a positive step towards greater freedom. How though would Khrushchev respond to any challenge?

Why was there opposition to Soviet control in Hungary in 1956?

Factor	Details
Politics	The country was run by the Hungarian Communist Party despite it only achieving 17 per cent of the vote. Political leaders were unpopular—the hard-line communist leader Rákosi lacked support and his replacement Gerö was just as unacceptable. The more acceptable Imre Nagy then took over to form a new government.

Key fact

Imre Nagy was a Hungarian politician who, although he was a communist leader with close ties to the Soviet Union, advocated greater liberalism and reform with more independence for the Hungarian people away from Soviet control. Following the Hungarian Revolution of 1956 Nagy was arrested, tried in secret, and executed.

Key fact

The Warsaw Pact was the name given to the treaty between Albania, Bulgaria, Czechoslovakia, East Germany, Hungary, Poland, Romania and the Soviet Union, which was signed in Poland in 1955. It called on the member states to come to the defence of any member attacked by an outside force and it set up a unified military command under Marshal Ivan S Konev of the Soviet Union.

Recap

Nagy believed that there was genuine chance of reforms being made and more freedoms granted to Hungary. By withdrawing from the Warsaw Pact he demonstrated that he wanted greater control for his own people over Hungary.

Factor	Details
Conditions	Following the war, Hungary was poor and needed rebuilding, yet much of its industrial production was sent to the Soviet Union. Food produced was often sent to the Soviet Union, causing shortages, and the standard of living to fall, in Hungary.
Soviet control	The Hungarians suffered from repression and strict control. Soviet control had brought censorship, secret police, and restrictions on education. Religion was banned for being subversive. The Hungarians resented the presence of thousands of Soviet troops and officials in their country, especially as they had to pay for the troops.

Actions planned by Nagy's government

When Nagy took over he introduced a plan to change life in Hungary.

- Free elections would be held.
- Law courts would become impartial.
- Farm land would be restored to private ownership.
- There would be a reduction in the Soviet influence on the daily way of life in Hungary, including the total withdrawal of the Soviet army. (Some troops had already withdrawn.)

Most dramatically, Nagy stated he intended to withdraw Hungary from the Warsaw Pact.

Why did the Hungarians think they would be successful?

- Khrushchev had stated that he was in favour of reduced control over the satellite countries following Stalin's death.
- When there had been a rising of workers in Poland in June 1956 Russia had given in to some of their demands.
- The Hungarians thought they would have support from the United Nations and also the new US President, Eisenhower, who had made supportive comments in speeches.

How did the Soviet Union react to this opposition?

At first Khrushchev appeared to be prepared to accept some reforms but he was not prepared to accept Hungary leaving the Warsaw Pact. On 28 October 1956 Khrushchev agreed to the demands of Nagy to remove Soviet troops from Hungary.

However, on 4 November thousands of Soviet troops and one thousand tanks moved into Budapest, the capital. Bitter street fighting followed as the Hungarians did not surrender. Approximately 3000 Hungarians died along with around 8000 Russians. Another 200 000 fled the country. Nagy was imprisoned and later executed.

Why was there opposition to Soviet control in Czechoslovakia in 1968?

There were two main reasons for opposition to Soviet control in Czechoslovakia.

- Communism was restrictive. Censorship, lack of freedom of speech, and the activities of the secret police were aspects of daily life hated by the people.

- During the 1960s the Czechoslovakian economy struggled and the standard of living fell.

The "Prague Spring"

Alexander Dubcek introduced the idea of the "Prague Spring" of 1968. This became known as "socialism with a human face". Dubcek's proposals for change included:

- the abolition of censorship, allowing the press to print what they wanted
- freedom of speech, allowing criticism of the government in industry, the creation of workers' councils and increased rights for trade unions
- freedom of movement for all people.

Wary of what had happened in Hungary, Dubcek made a clear statement that Czechoslovakia did not wish to leave the Warsaw Pact or end its alliance with the Soviet Union.

Dubcek, however, planned to cooperate with Romania and Yugoslavia, two countries with less close ties to the Soviet Union. This increased Soviet concerns.

Alexander Dubcek was a politician who served as the leader of Czechoslovakia from January 1968 to April 1969. He attempted to reform the Communist government during the Prague Spring but was forced to resign following the Warsaw Pact invasion in August 1968.

How did the Soviet Union react to this opposition?

Reaction to Dubcek

In 1968 Brezhnev had taken over as leader of the Soviet Union. He was just as determined as his predecessors to maintain Soviet control of Eastern Europe.

Czechoslovakia was an important country within the Warsaw Pact because of the strength of its industry. Brezhnev knew that if Czechoslovakia gained more freedom other Eastern European countries would want the same. He took action to stop reform in Czechoslovakia.

- Brezhnev instructed Dubcek to stop his reforms.
- Pressure was put on Brezhnev by the East German Leader, Ulbricht.
- Troops from countries within the Warsaw Pact carried out training exercises on the Czech border.

On 20 August 1968, Soviet tanks moved into Czechoslovakia. While some fighting occurred, there was nothing comparable to what had happened in Hungary. Generally the Czechs refused to cooperate. Dubcek was removed from power and taken to Moscow.

Czechoslovakia's attempt at reform was less revolutionary than in Hungary, and was met with a softer response from the Soviets. However, they refused to allow reforms and Dubcek was unsuccessful.

The Brezhnev Doctrine

This was introduced in order to stop such events happening again in other countries. It stated that all Warsaw Pact countries should work together to prevent any attempt by a country to leave the treaty. Military force could be used by the Soviet Union if any attempt to leave the Warsaw Pact was made by a member country.

Events in Hungary in 1956 and in Czechoslovakia in 1968–similarities and differences

	How were events similar?	How were events different?
Causes	Both countries had a long-term resentment of Soviet rule.	Hungary was affected by issues in other countries: the rebellion in Poland inspired the Hungarians to act. Czechoslovakia was affected by issues at home: economic depression and a desire for political change.
Aims of the rebels	Both sets of rebels wanted to give their people more rights and lessen the control of the communist state.	In Hungary the political changes included withdrawing from the Warsaw Pact and Soviet influence. Czechoslovakia did not want to go that far.
Actions of the people	Both rebellions involved groups of people protesting.	In Czechoslovakia, the people's actions were largely started by the role of their leader. It was his changes that encouraged them to protest. In Hungary, it was the people who acted first.
Why the Soviet Union intervened	The Soviet Union was very suspicious and fearful that any form of rebellion or change would spread and lead to a split in its control in other countries.	The political nature of Czechoslovakia was particularly dangerous for the Soviets; they had faced people-led rebellions before, like that in Hungary, but the "Prague Spring" was started by people who were meant to be under Soviet control.
How each state responded to Soviet intervention	Both leaders were removed from office. In both states there was mass emigration.	In Hungary the people armed themselves and fought when the Soviets attacked. In Czechoslovakia, following orders from the government, the people did not fight back. In Czechoslovakia there were several protests after the Russian invasion, including suicides.
Reaction of the wider world	Reactions to both were wholly negative to Soviet use of force. The situation in Hungary was discussed at the United Nations; with Czechoslovakia the Soviet actions were condemned by different countries, including the United States.	With the Czechoslovakian invasion some members of the communist Warsaw Pact expressed shock at Soviet actions. The Romanian leader complained about Russian intervention.

There are significant differences between the rebellions in Czechoslovakia and Hungary. However, this might be due to the timing. The harsh response to the events in Hungary might explain not only why the Czech rebellion was less radical in its demands but also why the Soviets reacted differently.

Worked example

"There were more similarities than differences between the revolts in Hungary and Czechoslovakia." To what extent do you agree with this statement? Explain your answer. (10)

It can be argued that there were clear similarities between the two uprisings. Both had a similar cause in that both in Hungary and Czechoslovakia there had been a long-standing resentment of Soviet rule since the Second World War. People had grown tired of the repressive nature of the Soviet-backed governments that had been put in place. In addition, both wanted to lessen Soviet influence in their countries as well as giving the people personal freedoms and a greater sense of democracy.

Another similarity is the way that both revolts were dealt with. Russian troops were moved into Hungary and Czechoslovakia to take back control and the countries' leaders were forcibly removed.

However, there were clear differences between the two revolts. When the Russians arrived in Hungary the people armed themselves and attempted to fight back but in Czechoslovakia, following orders from the government, the people did not retaliate. While some protested in different ways, including through suicide, there were no clashes with troops. The revolts were also different regarding what the protesters wanted. The Hungarians wanted to be free of Soviet influence. The Czechs did not share this aim, and made that clear.

Exam tip

In the answer avoid simply agreeing with the question and only providing similarities between the two revolts. It is important to offer a balanced answer—so make sure you also consider the differences between the revolts.

Why was the Berlin Wall built in 1961?

What was the Berlin Wall?

At the end of the Second World War, the city of Berlin was split into four zones. A wall was constructed to seal East Berlin from the West. The wall was constructed on 13 August 1961. Originally the wall was constructed of barbed wire but over time it became a permanent concrete structure. All crossing points were sealed except one, which became known as Checkpoint Charlie.

Berlin was now divided by a wall 87 miles long. The wall was to prevent the movement of people from East to West. Already nearly 2.6 million had left East Germany for the West. Anyone trying to defect to the West was shot.

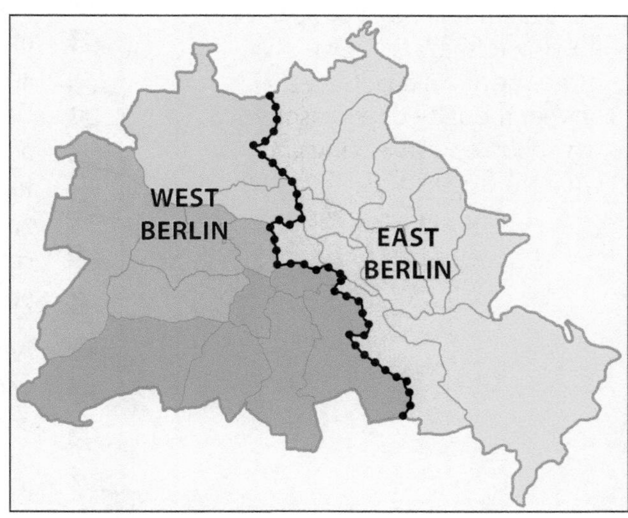

▲ **Fig. 6.2** *Map of the Berlin Wall*

6 How secure was the Soviet Union's control over Eastern Europe?

Recap

- Berlin had been divided into four zones after the war.
- The wall was put up to stop people leaving—they could only cross from East to West and vice versa via the tightly controlled checkpoints.
- As the quality of life was better in the West, people were leaving the East in vast numbers.

Apply

Draw a spider diagram showing the factors that led to the building of the Berlin Wall.

Why were people leaving East Berlin?

- The quality of life was much better in the West. West Germany had been able to use Marshall Aid to rebuild following the devastation of war.
- In West Berlin shops were full of a variety of goods and freedom was greater, as was wealth. The attraction of capitalism was significant compared to the harsh regime of East Germany under hard-line communist leader Ulbricht.

What was the impact of this movement on East Germany?

The communists feared a "brain drain" as skilled workers, including engineers, physicians, teachers, and lawyers were all leaving in high numbers.

Negative propaganda was created. In the context of the Cold War the number of people who were leaving a communist country created a feeling of unpopularity for communism. It became good propaganda for the West—the West was attractive while the East had to erect a wall to keep people in.

What were the immediate consequences of the building of the Berlin Wall?

There were two immediate consequences.

- The flow of people from East to West stopped.
- Berlin became a focus of the Cold War.

The West's reaction to the Berlin Wall was to be publicly horrified and demand that free transport to and around West Berlin continued. However, US President Kennedy stated that there would be no military action to remove the wall or any barriers between East and West Berlin.

Exam tip

The Berlin Wall was built by the Soviet Union to address the large numbers of people moving to the West. Give more specific detail in the answer though—offer reasons why people were leaving and what the impact was.

Worked example

Describe why the Berlin Wall was built. (6)

The Wall was built in 1961 due to an increasing number of people migrating from the East to the West. The crushing of the Hungarian revolt in 1956 showed Eastern Europeans that it was impossible to rebel against a communist rule. It appeared that the only way to escape from communist rule was to leave their roots and move to the West. But the hatred of communist rule was not the only reason people moved: the pro-communists left due to poor living conditions.

Among the thousands of people fleeing to the West were many of the Soviet Union's most skilled workers and highly qualified managers. The Soviet government couldn't afford their loss. Khrushchev thought that thousands of people fleeing a communist rule for a better life under capitalism undermined communism in East Germany and in general.

What was the significance of "Solidarity" in Poland for the decline of Soviet influence in Eastern Europe?

The rise of Solidarity

From the end of the Second World War, Soviet control of Poland increased in unpopularity. Over the years there had been numerous protests about wages and food prices in an attempt to improve the standard of living but nothing challenging the rule of the Soviet Union.

	1979	The Polish economy reaches crisis point. Food prices are rising and wages remain low.
The government was forced into increasing the price of goods, including food, further while at the same time blocking any pay increases. People were facing poverty and responded by going on strike. The strikes spread quickly across the country.	**July 1980**	
	14 August 1980	The workers at the Lenin Shipyard in Gdansk (Danzig) went on strike. Dismayed with the conditions they were facing, they produced a list of 21 demands as well as demanding the right to form a trade union. The strike was led by Lech Walesa.
The right to form a union free from government control was accepted and by mid-September "Solidarity" was formed.	**End of August 1980**	

▲ **Fig. 6.3** *Timeline of events leading to the rise of Solidarity*

Why did the communist Polish government agree to meet the demands of Solidarity?

- Fear of a general strike: the government was afraid because a general strike would devastate Poland's economy. The government thought there might be a general strike as originally the Solidarity membership came mainly from important areas of shipbuilding and heavy industry.
- Methods: Walesa was careful not to provoke the Soviet Union, working to reinforce the view that Solidarity was not an alternative to the Communist Party. Violence was avoided. The strikers used methods such as distributing newspapers to spread their message of the need for reform.
- Popularity: the movement was thought of as trustworthy and represented around 80 per cent of workers from across Polish life. Walesa was seen as a folk hero by many.
- Support of the Catholic Church: in Poland the government was unable to crush the church because of the strong faith of the people.

6 How secure was the Soviet Union's control over Eastern Europe?

Key fact

Foreign support for Solidarity: the movement had gained support in the West through positive media coverage and the charisma of Walesa. Attempting to crush the movement would reflect badly on the Soviet Union.

Key fact

Pope John Paul II's influence in the Solidarity movement should not be forgotten. Pope John Paul II was Polish, and spoke several times in the late 1970s and 1980s in support of the Polish people. He was seen to be a public face that gave the Polish people hope of change.

Key fact

Mikhail Gorbachev was the eighth and last leader of the Soviet Union. He believed that the Soviet Union was in urgent need of modernisation, and that the people of Eastern Europe should be allowed self-determination.

Exam tip

One of the key reasons the Solidarity movement was able to succeed was timing. In the answer point out that the context of what was happening in the Soviet Union gave Solidarity a far greater chance of success than the movement would otherwise have had.

Why was action taken against Solidarity in December 1981?

General Jaruzelski became Prime Minister of Poland in February 1981. He and Walesa tried to work together but their relationship was tense. It finally failed in December. Jaruzelski claimed he had evidence that the Solidarity leaders were planning a coup, imposed martial law and Solidarity was outlawed. Walesa and most of the Solidarity leaders were put in prison.

How important was Solidarity?

In 1985 Gorbachev became leader of the Soviet Union. His reforms included the release of political prisoners connected with Solidarity. However, his reforms did not improve Poland's economic situation.

Although Jaruzelski was technically still in power, Solidarity held the real power. It was only a matter of time before communism collapsed in Poland. By 1988 strikes had swept through Poland as food costs rose by 40 per cent. Walesa negotiated with the Polish government to find a solution.

In April 1989 Solidarity was again legalised, fielding candidates in the upcoming elections. Solidarity won every seat it contested and the first non-communist government of the post-war era was formed, with Walesa as President. Solidarity had demonstrated to the rest of the Eastern bloc that communist control could be resisted.

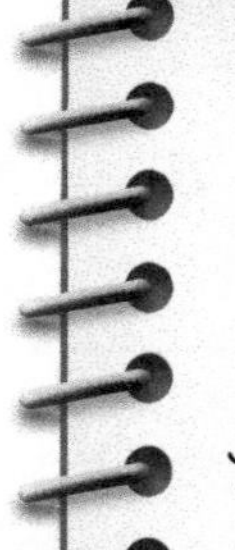

Worked example

Why did the Solidarity movement succeed while other similar movements failed? (6)

The Solidarity movement was able to succeed because its followers were well organised and it attracted mass support. The timing of the revolt was also a factor.

In 1980 and 1981, 10 million people from across Polish society, including students, workers, and intellectuals, joined Solidarity. This represented over 80 per cent of Poland's workforce. No other popular movement had gained such support, and this can be seen as a reason for its success. Solidarity also succeeded in appealing to a wide range of people by championing national, not local issues—securing the support of many people and affecting the major industries.

Solidarity supporters were also well organised. The trade union's newspaper, *Solidarnosc*, was printed on the shipyard printing press. It enabled members to spread their message. The committee and spokesmen also ensured that a consistent message was clearly heard.

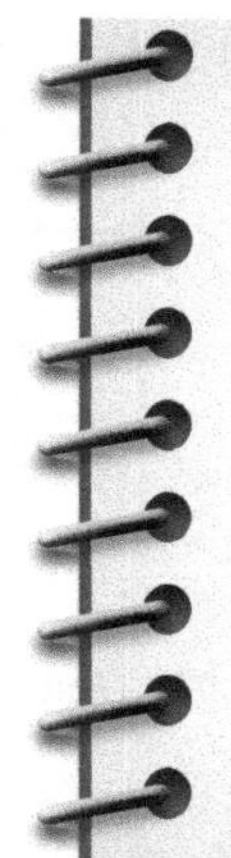

Finally, Solidarity succeeded because of timing. The initial Solidarity uprising in 1980 didn't succeed in the long term. While it did achieve some success and widespread support, it wasn't until 1989 that it was able to establish control over Poland and bring about all of the change it wanted. This came at the right time as by 1989 Gorbachev had allowed Eastern Europe a greater freedom, meaning there was more freedom and opportunity for movements such as Solidarity. Before then, as events in Prague and Hungary had shown, the Soviet Union was too repressive.

How far was Gorbachev personally responsible for the collapse of Soviet control over Eastern Europe?

What was the state of the Soviet Union in 1985 when Gorbachev became leader?

- The controlling of other countries was outdated. The Soviet Union could no longer afford the cost of maintaining a military presence in European satellite states.
- The economy was very weak as too much money was being spent on the arms race and an unwinnable war in Afghanistan. The economy was still run as it was at the time of Stalin. Factories produced cheap, poor-quality goods. Food was in short supply.
- The standard of living was low compared to that in the West.
- There was much corruption in government.
- Soviet rule was unpopular across Eastern Europe—as dissatisfaction grew it became harder to keep control.

The role of Gorbachev

Gorbachev introduced two key policies.

One was **"glasnost"** (openness)—the freedom of expression with more freedom for the media, allowing news of government corruption and the criticism of government officials. Citizens became aware of some of Russia's past, with details about some of Stalin's brutal excesses being revealed.

The other was **"perestroika"** (restructuring). This aimed to make the Soviet economy more modern and efficient. It included:

- encouraging private ownership of Soviet industry and agriculture
- reducing state control over imports and exports
- allowing trade with non-Eastern bloc countries
- allowing foreign investments in Russian businesses
- an increase in the production of and trade in consumer goods.

Crucially, Gorbachev realised that Eastern Europe must be allowed to choose its own destiny. He made it clear he would not stand in the way of attempts at democracy in Warsaw Pact countries, and unlike in the past, troops would not be used to keep countries tied to the Soviet Union. He abandoned the

Apply

Write a fact file that gives the main reasons why Solidarity was important.

Recap

Compared to other Soviet leaders, such as Brezhnev, Gorbachev held a reformist attitude. The two policies of glasnost and perestroika were central to this.

Apply

List the main things Gorbachev did that changed Eastern Europe. Explain the results of each action.

Brezhnev Doctrine, making moves to establish a more friendly relationship with the West. Arms reduction treaties were signed with the United States.

The table below summarises the role of other factors.

Factor	Explanation
The war in Afghanistan	The war badly overstretched the Soviet economy and demoralised the military. Soviet actions were condemned by other countries who applied pressure for the Soviets to withdraw. The cost was significant, as was the loss of 10 000 Soviet soldiers. Even more important was the impact of the war on the Muslim world.
The role of the United States	US President Reagan sought to end the Cold War. The Soviet Union found it could not compete with the United States in the "arms race" and so had to use diplomacy to secure peace. Additionally, its outdated industry was causing environmental problems, such as the explosion at the Chernobyl nuclear power plant in 1986. Reagan and Gorbachev signed treaties to limit nuclear weapons.
The role of other countries	Between the spring of 1989 and the spring of 1991 every communist or former communist Eastern European country held democratic parliamentary elections. Many people in Eastern Europe were suffering from poverty. They were affected by food shortages, crime, and alcoholism. Gorbachev was unable to shield the public from the fact that Eastern bloc countries were much poorer than the majority of people in the capitalist West.

Review

1. Describe the Hungarian revolution of 1956. **[4]**
2. Why did Berlin remain a focus of Cold War tensions during 1960–2? **[6]**
3. Why was Solidarity a threat to Soviet control? **[6]**
4. Why did the Polish government agree to Solidarity's demands in 1980? **[6]**
5. How significant was the part played by Solidarity in the loss of Soviet control in Eastern Europe? **[10]**
6. How similar were events in Hungary in 1956 and in Czechoslovakia in 1968? **[10]**
7. How did Gorbachev change Eastern Europe? **[10]**
8. Why was there opposition to Soviet control in Hungary in 1956 and Czechoslovakia in 1968, and how did the Soviet Union react to this opposition? **[10]**

For further information review this section in the Student Book.

1. What was the "Prague Spring"? **[4]**

Analysis

- ✓ The answer should include two explained points that refer to the question.
- ✓ Contextual knowledge is important—add details to explain a little about the uprising.
- ✓ The "Prague Spring" took place in 1968 in Czechoslovakia and the answer should place the uprising in this context.
- ✓ Alexander Dubcek introduced the idea of the "Prague Spring" in an attempt to push for "socialism with a human face".
- ✓ It is important to note that the uprising wasn't against the Czech government, it was in response to the control imposed over the country by the Soviet Union.

Mark scheme

1 mark for each relevant point, additional mark for supporting detail, maximum 2 marks per point made.

Student answer

The "Prague Spring" was an attempt by the people to gain some control over their own lives and reform the communist system. That meant keeping the socialist model of government but creating a fairer system to ensure greater freedoms for the people and fewer restrictions imposed by Soviet control. This lasted for four months until it was crushed by the Soviet Red Army.

Examiner feedback

This is a good answer that defines what the protestors wanted to achieve, as well as providing some detail over the ultimate outcome. There is a lack of detail though—the student should state when the revolt took place, in which country or who led it. 2 marks awarded.

2. Why were the Soviets worried about events in Czechoslovakia in 1968? **[6]**

Analysis

- ✓ In the answer aim to explain two reasons why the Soviets were worried, giving enough supporting detail for a full explanation.
- ✓ The Soviet Union was very suspicious and fearful that any uprising would spread and lead to a split in its control in other countries.
- ✓ The support that the attempted reforms had was widespread and potentially difficult to stop.
- ✓ Events in Hungary, where the Soviet Union had suppressed another uprising, had made the Soviets look oppressive and they were keen to avoid another similar issue.

Mark scheme

Level 1:	general answer lacking specific contextual knowledge (1 mark)
Level 2:	identifies AND/OR describes reasons (2–3 marks)
Level 3:	explains ONE reason (4–5 marks)
Level 4:	explains TWO reasons (6 marks)

Student answer

Soviet leaders were worried about events in Czechoslovakia in 1968 as they seemed similar to the uprising in Hungary, which had resulted in the need for Soviet action and the deaths of thousands of anti-communist protestors. Any similar event would mean more loss of life and would add to the view that the Soviet Union was very oppressive.

Leaders in Moscow were also worried that if Czechoslovakia pushed for reform, other Eastern European countries would do the same. There might be widespread rebellion against Moscow's leadership of the Eastern Bloc, weakening Moscow's power and influence over these states.

Examiner feedback

This is a good example of how it is possible to obtain full marks without writing a long answer. The student makes two well-developed points, focused on the fear of the spread of reformist ideas and also the need to avoid a similar event to that which occurred during the "Prague Spring". 6 marks awarded.

3. Was Gorbachev personally responsible for the collapse of Soviet control over Eastern Europe? **[10]**

Analysis

- ✓ In the answer explain the role of Gorbachev and his actions in bringing change in Eastern Europe. As well as this, compare Gorbachev's involvement to other factors that led to reform in Eastern Europe.
- ✓ Gorbachev's rule in the Soviet Union led to dramatic change and saw the end of Soviet influence across many countries in Europe.
- ✓ His openness to reform, and key policies such as glasnost and perestroika, meant that the tight restrictions of communism were lifted and the economy took on more capitalist elements.
- ✓ Crucially, Gorbachev believed that Eastern Europe should be allowed to choose its own destiny, and had no wish to keep countries that were dissatisfied as part of the Soviet Union.
- ✓ However, other factors are important. US President Reagan was also key in pushing for an end to the Cold War, and external events such as the war in Afghanistan further strained the Soviet Union's resources and ability to keep control in Eastern Europe.

Mark scheme

Level 1:	general answer lacking specific contextual knowledge (1 mark)
Level 2:	identifies AND/OR describes reasons (2–3 marks)
Level 3:	gives a one-sided explanation (4–5 marks) or one explanation of both sides (4–6 marks)
Level 4:	explains of both sides (7–9 marks)
Level 5:	explains with evaluation (10 marks)

Student answer

Gorbachev was responsible for the collapse of the Soviet empire to some extent. In 1985 when he came to power, he realised that the Soviet economy was devastated and facing many problems, with communism making the situation much worse. Gorbachev realised that reforms were needed to stabilise the economy. He also realised that the controlling of other countries was outdated. The Soviet Union could no longer afford the cost of maintaining a military presence in other states, particularly those who wanted reform.

Gorbachev introduced two key policies—glasnost and perestroika. Glasnost meant that freedom of expression was allowed with more freedom for the media, allowing reports of government corruption and the criticism of government officials. Perestroika reformed the economy, encouraging private ownership of Soviet industry and agriculture, reducing state control over imports and exports and leading to an increase in the production of and trade in consumer goods. Gorbachev was also responsible because he implemented an end to the Brezhnev Doctrine in the satellite states and in Russia. This broke the bond of unison and ended the enforcement of communism.

Examiner feedback

The student clearly understands the role of Gorbachev in the collapse of Soviet control and makes good points about glasnost, perestroika and the end of the Brezhnev Doctrine. However, the answer is too one-sided. It needs to explore the wider issues that didn't involve Gorbachev. The role of the United States, the war in Afghanistan and populist movements such as Solidarity are all factors. 5 marks awarded.

You need to know:

- why Saddam Hussein was able to come to power in Iraq
- the nature of Saddam's rule in Iraq
- why there was a revolution in Iran in 1979
- the causes and consequences of the Iran–Iraq War, 1980–8
- why the First Gulf War took place

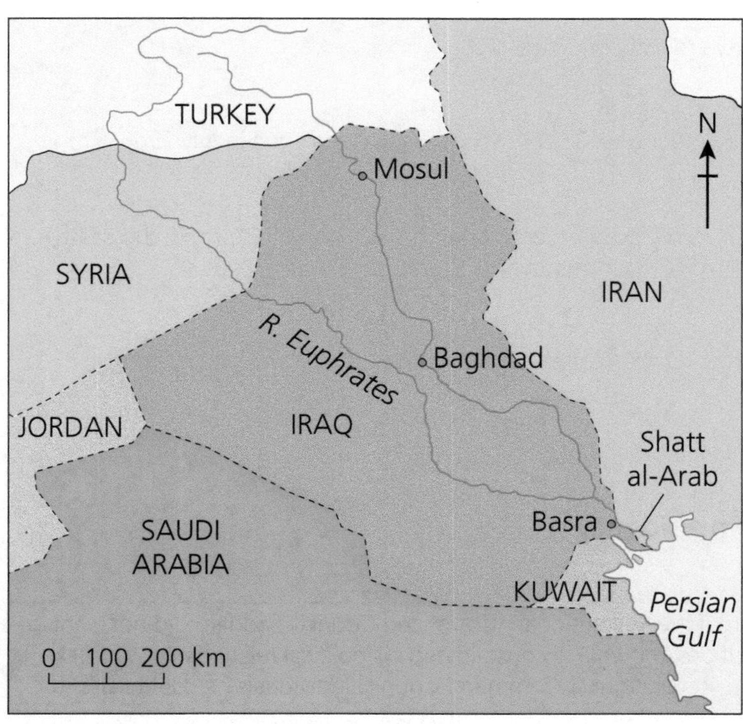

▲ **Fig. 7.1** *Iraq and its neighbouring countries*

Background: the importance of events in the Gulf

By the final third of the 20th century, oil was a vital commodity for the industrialised nations of the world. The states located around the Persian Gulf (Iran, Iraq, Kuwait, Saudi Arabia, Bahrain, Qatar, United Arab Emirates, and Oman) collectively housed around half of the world's known oil reserves. It was vital that countries followed diplomatic and foreign policies that promoted peace and stability in this part of the world. Events in the Gulf were of prime importance to the rest of the world to ensure steady supplies of oil at stable prices. Yet throughout this period the Gulf region was one of instability and volatility.

Why was Saddam Hussein able to come to power in Iraq?

Early life

Saddam Hussein:

- was inspired by Arab nationalism, and joined the Baath party in 1957
- was involved in violent anti-government activities
- was selected by the Baath party to participate in an attempted assassination of General Qassem, the ruler of the newly established republic of Iraq in October 1959; the attempt failed and Saddam had to go into exile in Egypt
- achieved a minor position in a new government formed when Qassem was overthrown in 1963.

Saddam's rise to power

Saddam held a minor position in the new government under Bakr

↓

He was promoted to the Regional Command: the Baath Party's decision-making body

↓

He was placed in charge of the Party's military organisation

↓

He was involved in a coup against President Arif; spent two years in jail; escaped in July 1966

↓

He worked with senior army officers in key government positions who sympathised with the Baath cause. After a successful coup in July 1968 Bakr became President

↓

Saddam became Deputy Chairman of the Revolutionary Command Council: the second most important government position.

▲ **Fig. 7.2** *Saddam's rise to power*

The road to presidency

Factor	Explanation
Political support	As Deputy Chairman of the Revolutionary Command Council, Saddam did not want his presidential ambitions known. He consolidated his political relationship with Bakr and appointed to the Revolutionary Command Council individuals he could trust.
Foreign interests	Saddam ensured that Iraq had a superpower ally by negotiating a Treaty of Friendship and Cooperation with Soviet Russia.
Improving lives	Using money from the nationalised oil industry he improved ordinary people's lives by building schools and hospitals, and improving transport.

In 1979 an aging, ailing President Bakr was "encouraged" to resign. At the age of 42, Saddam Hussein became leader of Iraq.

Worked example

Describe Saddam Hussein's rise to power in Iraq. (4)

Saddam Hussein held a powerful position as Deputy Chairman of the Revolutionary Command Council and formed positive relationships with important people. Using money from the nationalised oil industry he gained the support of ordinary people by building schools and hospitals.

Exam tip

The focus of the answer needs to be on Saddam's rise to power, such as how he built his power base through the positions he took within Iraqi government.

What was the nature of Saddam Hussein's rule in Iraq?

Saddam Hussein ruled as a dictator. As President he was Commander-in-Chief of the armed forces. His political hero was Stalin, the leader of Soviet Russia. Saddam closely followed many aspects of Stalin's method of governing.

Purges and terror	Hundreds of party members and military officers were removed from their positions, with many being executed. False accusations, arrests, torture, and trials became a regular feature of Saddam's rule by terror. In most instances the accused received lengthy prison sentences or were executed. An example was Mashhadi, the Secretary General of the Revolutionary Command Council, who questioned the validity of Saddam's appointment. He was dismissed and brought before the senior Baath Party members. He gave a fabricated confession of crimes against the state and named 66 alleged co-conspirators. At a special court, 55 were found guilty and either sentenced to death or imprisoned.
Waging war on his own people	The make-up of the Iraqi people was varied: 20 per cent of the population were Kurds, who wanted independence, and 60 per cent were Shiites. The Shiites were hostile to the Sunni-dominated regime. In 1987, 1988 and again in 1991 Saddam tried to suppress the Kurds. He destroyed half of Kurdistan's villages and towns, killed thousands of Kurds using mustard gas and cyanide, and displaced more than a million people, who fled to Iran or Turkey or were housed in concentration camps in the Iraqi desert. In 1991 the Republican Guard carried out arrests and summary executions of Shiites. Civilians were used as human shields, fastened to the front of tanks. Women and children were shot on sight. In the south-east of Iraq Saddam wanted to destroy the marshes to enable a new waterway to be constructed. The Marsh Arabs were victims of chemical weapon attacks or were starved to death.
Personality cult	Saddam set out to cultivate an image of a father-style leader. This was achieved by: • establishing a permanent exhibition about himself in Baghdad • glorifying himself though articles in newspapers and on television • hanging portraits on street corners and in party and government offices • renaming roads after himself; commissioning statues, murals, and paintings. Schools and Baath organisations brainwashed the young to believe in a glorious leader. Censorship ensured that critical views of Saddam were never heard or read. It was a capital offence to criticise government. The law courts were under Saddam's influence, and all economic production was geared to the needs of the state. Membership of the Baath Party was essential if a career in public office was to be followed.
Modernisation	From Iraq's massive oil revenues Saddam carried out an extensive modernisation programme. Wages rose, taxes were cut and basic foodstuffs were subsidised. Other benefits were: • supplying electricity to even remote villages and building a countrywide network of oil pipelines • developing heavy industry including, steel, petrochemicals, and coal • establishing a new radio and television network to enable the spreading of propaganda • major building programmes for schools, houses, and hospitals • introducing a major campaign to end adult illiteracy • making hospital treatment free.
Military expansion	Iraq became a major military power, with Soviet Russia providing most supplies. Saddam purchased tanks, planes, helicopters, surface-to-air missiles, and electronic equipment. By the middle of 1979 Saddam had constructed his first chemical warfare plant and was soon producing chemical weapons, including agents such as anthrax.

Apply

Write a fact file of the effects of Saddam's actions on these groups of Iraqis: those employed in the military, other workers, families, and children.

Why was there a revolution in Iran in 1979?

The Shah of Iran left the country in January 1979, never to return. He had upset almost every sector of society and the last year of his rule was one of demonstrations, violent deaths, and widespread strikes. The pressures for the Shah to go had been building for over 25 years.

Why was the Shah unpopular?

Social issues

- **His reforms were unsuccessful.** In the 1960s the Shah introduced the "White Revolution". The reforms were seen as inadequate—land reform didn't work, education reforms failed to address high levels of adult illiteracy and while health reforms increased the number of doctors, nurses, and hospital beds they failed to reduce infant mortality rates.
- **Society was becoming more divided.** By the end of the 1970s the rich were living in palaces while the poor were condemned to shanty towns lacking proper roads and other essential facilities.
- **Money was badly spent.** The vast sums of money from oil were used to build up military capability while the majority of the population saw little improvement in their living standards.

Political issues

- **The Shah was seen to favour foreign countries.** In 1953 the Shah, supported by the CIA and MI6, overthrew the popular Prime Minister Mohammed Mussadeq. The main interest for the United States and Britain was the safeguarding of oil supplies to the West.
- **The Shah's autocratic government was resented.** In March 1975 the Shah established a one-party state. The new Resurgence Party immediately made enemies by waging an anti-profiteering campaign in the bazaars, attacking the clerical establishment and introducing a new calendar.
- **Repressive measures were used.** The secret police (SAVAK) rooted out opposition to the Shah's rule. SAVAK became known for its brutal tactics, including torture, forced confessions, and summary executions.

Exam tip

To answer this "Why" question choose two reasons that explain the cause of the revolution. The answer may focus on the failings of the Shah, or the appeal of the other side.

Worked example

Why was there a revolution in Iran in 1979? (6)

The key to the cause of the revolution in Iran was the unpopularity of the Shah. His policies meant that he lost support from the people as the ideas he promoted seemed to have failed. His attempt at a "White Revolution", bringing reforms to education, health, and land were seen as failures. By the end of the 1970s the rich were living in palaces while the poor could only live in shanty towns without proper roads and other essential facilities. The Shah was also seen to be in the control of foreign powers—both the United States and Britain worked closely with him to overthrow the popular Prime Minister Mohammed Mussadeq. This was deeply unpopular—people saw that foreign interests were maintained in Iran not for the good of the Iranian people but to safeguard oil supplies to the West.

The leadership of Ayatollah Khomeini

In contrast to the Shah was Ayatollah Khomeini. He had been forced into exile in 1964 for undermining the Shah. His developed his support while abroad and made it clear he opposed the Shah's readiness to agree to foreign influences and in supporting Israel against the Muslim world. He made it clear that he would not return until the Shah had left the country. He returned on 1 February 1979 to be met by over 3 million people. Thousands of civilians celebrated the popular revolution on the streets.

▲ **Fig. 7.3** *Ayatollah Khomeini returns to Iran from exile, 1 February 1979*

What were the causes and consequences of the Iran–Iraq War, 1980–8?

In September 1980 Iraq's land and air invasion marked the beginning of war that destabilised the region. The causes were both long-term and also more immediate.

Territorial disputes

- Iraq and Iran shared a land border of 1400 kilometres so it is hardly surprising that there was friction related to territorial issues.
- A key argument was the Shatt al-Arab waterway. This waterway was important because it provided a link to the Persian Gulf. It was Iraq's only outlet to the sea. Iraq had a historic agreement that gave the country control over the waterway, but in 1969 the Shah of Iran rejected this treaty and refused to pay any further shipping tolls.
- The leaders of the two countries had encouraged rebels in the opposing country. Saddam encouraged the Arabs who lived in the oil-rich Iranian province of Khuzestan to revolt against the Shah's rule. Iran had begun encouraging Kurds in the north of Iraq to take up arms against Saddam's regime. The Shah provided training bases and military equipment.
- The Algiers Agreement between the two countries in 1975 ended these disputes. Iran ended its support for the Kurds and Iraq dropped its claims to Khuzestan. It was also agreed that the border along the Shatt al-Arab waterway was to be more equitable. Saddam renounced this agreement shortly before invading Iran in September 1980.

Domination of the Gulf

Iraq and Iran were the only serious contenders to be the dominant country in the Gulf as they alone had the necessary financial and military resources. Saddam believed that with Khuzestan and the Shatt al-Arab waterway, his oil reserves would expand at the expense of his main rival. Gaining power was seen by Saddam as an aid to being made leader of the Arab world, following Egypt's expulsion as a result of its peace accords with Israel.

The opportunity provided by the Islamic Revolution

The overthrow of the Shah brought to an end the alliance between the United States and Iran, depriving the Iranian army of much-needed spare parts for its military weapons. The revolution also brought a major purge of senior officers in the Iranian army, which reduced its effectiveness. Saddam saw Iran as being politically unstable, in diplomatic isolation and with its military disintegrating.

Recap

- Territorial disputes centred on the Shatt al-Arab waterway.
- Both countries supported rebels in the other country.
- The underlying factor was the desire of both leaders to be the dominant power in the Arab world.

Ayatollah Khomeini's opposition to Saddam Hussein

Khomeini had been expelled from Iraq in 1977. Iran was a Shiite Muslim state governed in accordance with Muslim law and Khomeini looked upon Saddam's rule as inferior. From June 1979 Khomeini encouraged the Iraqi Shiites to overthrow the Baath regime and establish another Islamic republic. Anti-Baath riots broke out and Saddam became convinced that Khomeini was deliberately trying to undermine his government.

Exam tip

There were many reasons for the war between Iran and Iraq 1980–8. To answer the question include two specific issues, such as the territorial issues, the battle for dominance in the region, or support for rebels.

Worked example

Why did Iraqi troops invade Iran in September 1980? (6)

The tensions between the two sides had been building for a while. Both were competing to be the dominant country in the region. Saddam saw that by establishing dominance over Iran and gaining control of the Shatt al-Arab waterway his oil reserves would increase. He would be seen as the leader of the Arab world, following Egypt's expulsion as a result of its peace accords with Israel.

There were also tensions between Iran and Iraq over specific issues. The leaders of the two countries had encouraged rebels in the opposing country, particularly in Khuzestan where Saddam encouraged the Arabs who lived in the oil-rich Iranian province to rebel against the Shah's rule. At the same time, Iran was encouraging Kurds in the north of Iraq to take up arms against Saddam's regime, and supported this by providing training bases and military equipment.

The course of the war

Iraq invaded Iran on 22 September 1980, triggering a bitter eight-year war that destabilised the region and devastated both countries.

↓

By 1982 Iranian forces had regained the territory they had lost but Khomeini rejected an offer of a ceasefire.

↓

The conflict turned into a war of attrition with each side disregarding the human cost: thousands of young Iranians were sent to their death in "human wave attacks"; chemical weapons were used against the Iranians by Saddam and against the Kurds of Halabja—his own people; the civilian population of both sides was constantly bombarded from the air.

↓

Both sides attacked opposition oil tankers in the Gulf in an attempt to prevent trade. The "tanker war" changed the war into an international one: both the United States and Soviet Union became involved in response to Kuwait's appeal for protection.

↓

Faced with this opposition, Iran became exhausted and isolated.

↓

A ceasefire was accepted by Khomeini in July 1988.

▲ **Fig. 7.4** *Stages in the Iran–Iraq War, 1980–8*

Other countries' involvement in the war

The United States was concerned that the oil trade would be disrupted and the economy affected. The Americans sent billions of dollars of aid, provided military training, and sold arms. The United States became more involved from May 1984, sending warships to the Gulf to help guarantee oil supplies as each side was attacking the other's tankers and merchant shipping.

Britain, France, and West Germany also feared a disrupted oil trade and also that an Iranian victory would threaten their interests by the installation of Islamic revolutionary governments in the Gulf states. They supplied military equipment.

China and North Korea sold arms to the Iranians, but the weapons were not at the same level of sophistication, and did not match the quantity, of the arms Iraq was purchasing.

The consequences of the war

The aftermath of war

- Economic damage was considerable with both countries' annual oil revenues halved. Both faced bankruptcy and had incurred substantial foreign debt.
- There was no winner.
- For the people of both countries, living standards plummeted and social projects in Iraq stopped.
- Neither side achieved its war aims.
- Saddam and Khomeini both remained in power.
- Both sides suffered substantial casualties of at least half a million. In addition many suffered from serious wounds or psychological damage.
- The economic plight of Iraq was one of the factors why Saddam invaded Kuwait in 1990.

▲ **Fig. 7.5** *The aftermath of war*

Apply

Complete a two-column table of information about the Iran–Iraq War, 1980–8. In one column list key issues leading to the war. In the other column, for each key issue, note how the war changed the situation.

Recap

The war was expensive and lengthy for both sides. Despite foreign involvement supporting both countries, neither could force a breakthrough.

Why did the First Gulf War take place?

Why did Iraq invade Kuwait?

Economic reasons	• Iraq was economically weak following the Iran–Iraq War and needed to increase the wealth of the country. Kuwait had valuable oil wells that could be taken over. • In 1990 world oil prices dropped steeply. Saddam blamed Kuwait and the United Arab Emirates for deliberately overproducing to undermine the Iraqi economy.
Historical relationship with Kuwait	• Saddam claimed that Kuwait was historically part of Iraq although Kuwait had existed as a separate territory for much longer than Iraq. In the early 1960s the British recognised the full independence of Kuwait. At first Iraq did not and border tensions existed. • Saddam was angry that Kuwait was demanding the repayment of a $14 billion loan made during the war with Iran. Many Iraqis thought the Kuwaitis ungrateful after being protected from the threat of Iranian expansion.
Standing in the world	• Saddam had failed to gain regional leadership from the war—this had been another opportunity to become the most powerful Arab leader in the Middle East. • Iraq was militarily the strongest country in the area and Saddam did not believe the United States or Europe would take any action. The United States had supplied Saddam with arms during the Iranian war and had taken no action when he had crushed the Kurds and suppressed the Shiites.
Problems within Iraq	• After the war with Iran, the Iraqi economy was in tatters and factions had started to emerge within society. Several attempts to overthrow Saddam had been made between 1988 and 1990. • A successful war against Kuwait would take the focus away from these issues.

Exam tip

Remember that for a "Why" question about a particular event you should aim to explain two key reasons for the event (in this case, specifically why this war broke out).

Worked example

Why did the First Gulf War take place? (6)

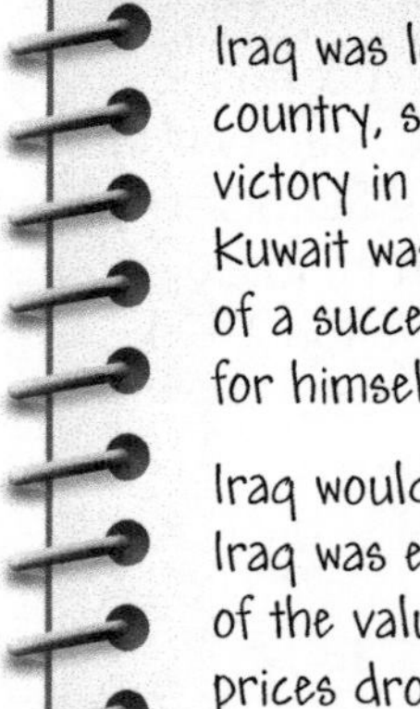

Iraq was looking to establish itself as a powerful country, something it had failed to do without a decisive victory in the Iran–Iraq War. Saddam claimed that Kuwait was historically part of Iraq and saw the chance of a successful invasion as a way of boosting popularity for himself with the Iraqi people.

Iraq would also benefit financially from the invasion. Iraq was economically weak and wanted to take control of the valuable oil wells of Kuwait. In 1990 world oil prices dropped steeply, and Iraq saw the overproduction by Kuwait as a cause of this—if Iraq could control oil production it could further increase its own revenue.

The wider-world reaction to the invasion of Kuwait

As in the case of Iran, Saddam had miscalculated. If he had foreseen his invasion creating such a storm he would have taken diplomatic means to achieve his aim. The UN took the following actions.

- Trade sanctions were placed on Iraq—no country was to trade with Iraq, effectively preventing the country's oil exports.
- Saddam was ordered to remove his troops from Kuwait by 15 January. If he did not, the UN would use "all necessary means" to remove them.
- Saudi Arabia, Syria, and Egypt all supported the UN action.
- British Prime Minister Margaret Thatcher and US President Bush decided that Saddam's power should be curbed.

The interests of the West were at risk as Saddam was threatening the West's oil supplies.

The course of the war

- Saddam's Iraqi troops invaded and occupied Kuwait in August 1990.
- An international force of over 600 000 troops assembled in Saudi Arabia.
- A coalition of 34 nations contributed troops, armaments, and cash. The involvement of troops from Arab countries such as Egypt and Syria, as well as from Muslim countries such as Pakistan and Bangladesh, meant Saddam could not claim that this was the West against Arabs and Islam.
- Operation Desert Storm, the liberation of Kuwait, began on 17 January 1991.

Air war

- Bombing attacks were carried out on Baghdad (the Iraqi capital), causing many civilian casualties.
- Military targets, bridges, and roads were also attacked.
- Iraq launched SCUD missile attacks on Israel, hoping to provoke a split between the West and their Arab allies. This did not happen.

Ground war

- Kuwaiti oil wells were set on fire and blown up by Iraq. Millions of gallons of crude oil poured into the Persian Gulf.
- Iraq carried out a brief invasion of Khafji in Saudi Arabia but was driven out by coalition forces.
- Within four days the Iraqis had been routed and driven out of Kuwait. Estimates put the number of Iraqis killed at 90 000, compared to fewer than 400 of the coalition. Around 10 000 were killed on the "Highway of Death", the six-lane motorway from Kuwait to Basra.
- The retreating Iraqis were at the mercy of the coalition but Bush called a ceasefire as he feared the Allies would lose the Arab nations' support.

What were the consequences of the First Gulf War?

After the ceasefire, peace terms imposed on Iraq by the UN were:

- recognition of Kuwait's sovereignty and payment of reparations
- Iraqi cooperation with the UN to uncover and destroy all biological, chemical, or nuclear "weapons of mass destruction" (WMD)
- trade sanctions that virtually cut off Iraq from the rest of the world
- "no-fly" zones that were to be established and policed by American planes flying out of Saudi Arabia as it was feared that Saddam would carry out further atrocities against his own people in the south and north.

Exam tip

The war was a disaster for Iraq. The answer should focus on the high casualties, mass damage, and the range of impacts on the civilian population that were the direct consequences of the war.

Worked example

Describe the consequences of the First Gulf War for Iraq. (4)

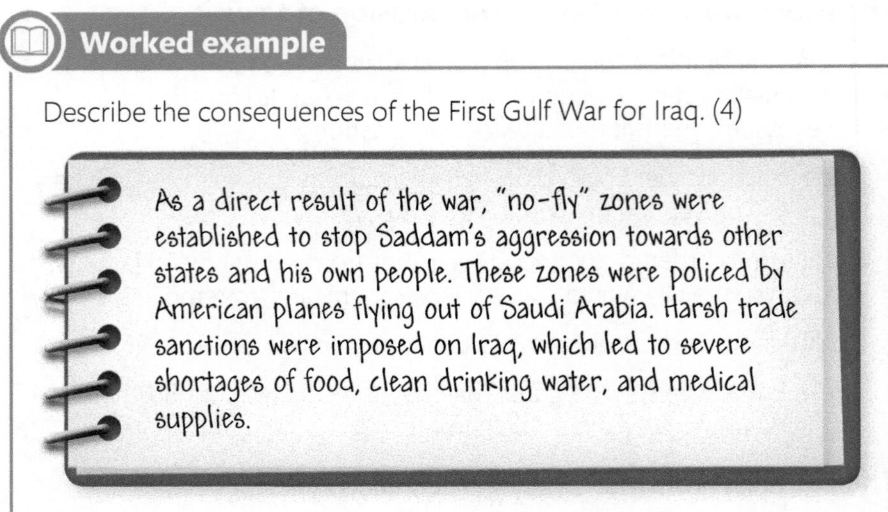

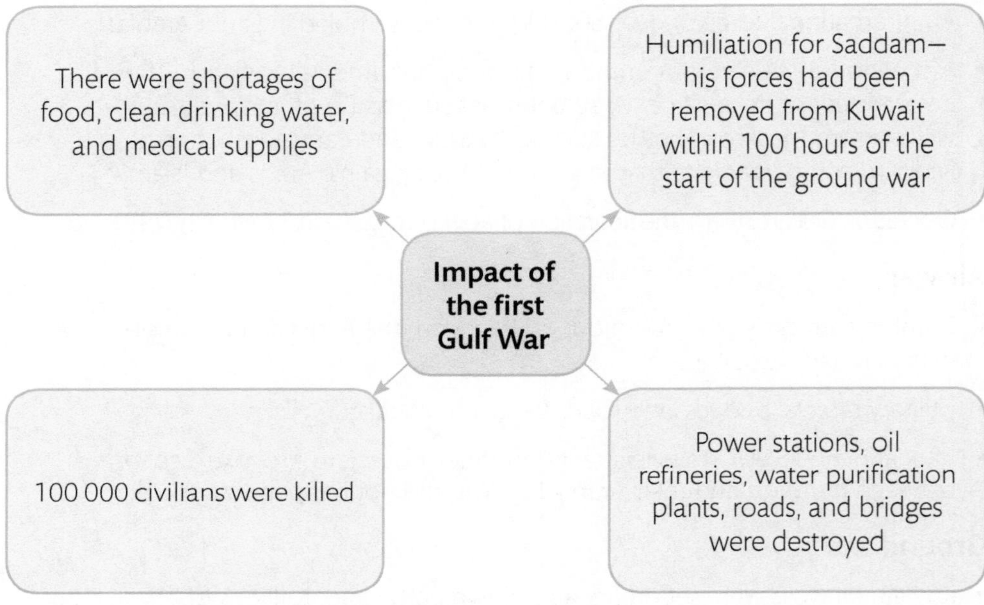

▲ **Fig. 7.6** *The impact of the Gulf War, 1990–91*

Review

1. Describe the involvement of the western powers in the Iran–Iraq War, 1980–8. **[4]**
2. Describe the Iranian Revolution of 1979. **[4]**
3. Why was there opposition within Iran to the Shah's rule? **[6]**
4. Why was Saddam Hussein able to come to power in Iraq? **[6]**
5. "Iraq suffered more than Iran as a result of the war between the two countries." How far do you agree with this statement? Explain your answer. **[10]**
6. "The most serious aspect of the Iran–Iraq War of 1980–8 was the threat to the stability of the Arab World." How far do you agree with this statement? Explain your answer. **[10]**
7. How significant were the roles of Thatcher and Bush in the First Gulf War? **[10]**

For further information review this section in the Student Book.

1. What were the causes of the Iran–Iraq War, 1980–8? **[4]**

Analysis

- ✓ To answer this 4-mark question you need to provide two reasons for the outbreak of the war. Make sure you explain the reasons rather than simply identifying them.
- ✓ Both countries had the ambition of becoming the dominant country in the Gulf.
- ✓ Clashes between the two countries were over territory such as the Shatt al-Arab waterway.
- ✓ The two leaders were encouraging rebels in each other's countries.
- ✓ Clashes such as that over the Algiers Agreement only added to tensions between the two sides.

Mark scheme

1 mark for each relevant point, additional mark for supporting detail, maximum 2 marks per point made.

Student answer

The main cause of the war between Iran and Iraq was a dispute over land. Iraq and Iran shared a land border and clashed over a series of issues, including the Shatt al-Arab waterway. This water was Iraq's only outlet to the sea. Despite a treaty giving Iraq control over the water, the Shah of Iran refused to pay any further shipping tolls, leading to tensions. The waterway had also led to tensions over the border that it formed—both countries claimed the land and Iraq's refusal to accept the Iranian border was one of the causes of the war.

Examiner feedback

The student has done well to provide detail regarding one of the key causes of the war, and offers two well-developed points on the issue of land as a factor. 4 marks awarded.

2. Why did the Iranian revolution take place in 1979? **[6]**

Analysis

- ✓ In the answer aim to make two well-developed points that address the question.
- ✓ The unpopularity of the Shah came from failed reforms within Iranian society and poor political decisions.
- ✓ His "White Revolution" failed and money was inappropriately used on the military while society remained divided.
- ✓ Politically, Iran faced issues under the Shah—close links to foreign nations proved unpopular, as did repressive measures and an autocratic style of government.
- ✓ In contrast, the Ayatollah Khomeini offered a more open and liberal reform programme that favoured the people.

Mark scheme

Level 1:	general answer lacking specific contextual knowledge (1 mark)
Level 2:	identifies AND/OR describes reasons (2–3 marks)
Level 3:	explains ONE reason (4–5 marks)
Level 4:	explains TWO reasons (6 marks)

Student answer

It can be argued that the Iranian revolution occurred because the Shah was so unpopular. His actions had been badly received and had failed to have a positive impact on his people. His attempt to introduce the "White Revolution" failed, as big ideas such as land and education reforms failed to address the serious issues in Iranian society, for example poverty and high levels of adult illiteracy. The "White Revolution" had been an attempt to address the issue of a divided society but it failed—and the gap between rich and poor grew wider.

At the same time the Shah failed to address political issues facing Iranians. He was seen to favour foreign countries, and this was only made worse when he overthrew the popular Prime Minister Mohammed Mussadeq with support from the United States and Britain. All this meant that the Iranian people wanted significant change.

Examiner feedback

The answer explains two key reasons why the revolution took place, both focusing on the unpopularity of the Shah. 6 marks awarded.

3. "It was the pursuit of power by Saddam Hussein that caused the First Gulf War." How far do you agree with this statement? Explain your answer. **[10]**

Analysis

- ✓ The argument that Saddam wanted more power for Iraq needs careful explanation and should be balanced against the view that there are other factors that caused the conflict.
- ✓ Iraq was economically weak following the Iran–Iraq War and needed to increase its wealth. Kuwait had valuable oil wells that could be taken over.
- ✓ Saddam claimed that Kuwait was historically part of Iraq.
- ✓ Saddam was keen to add to the power he held in the region and saw oil-rich Kuwait as a way to do this.
- ✓ A successful war for Iraq would boost Saddam's failing popularity among his own people.

Mark scheme

Level 1:	general answer lacking specific contextual knowledge (1 mark)
Level 2:	identifies AND/OR describes reasons (2–3 marks)
Level 3:	gives a one-sided explanation (4–5 marks) or one explanation of both sides (4–6 marks)
Level 4:	explains both sides (7–9 marks)
Level 5:	explains with evaluation (10 marks)

Student answer

Saddam Hussein certainly saw the invasion of Kuwait as a way to increase Iraq's power in the world. It was clear that if he could add oil-rich Kuwait to his own country, the wealth of Iraq would significantly increase. This was another opportunity for Saddam to become the most powerful Arab leader in the Middle East. The war with Iran had failed to establish Iraq as the dominant power in the region, but if Kuwait could be conquered Iraq would gain this dominance.

Saddam was also hoping to increase power within Iraq and re-establish his popularity. The lengthy war with Iran had left the Iraqi economy in tatters and factions had started to emerge within society. A successful seizure of territory would help Saddam regain popularity among his own people.

Examiner feedback

This is a good answer focusing on the factor specified in the question. However, there needs to be greater balance and the inclusion of another cause of the war is needed. The example used could be economic reasons for the conflict, or Iraq's worsening relations with Kuwait. 5 marks awarded.

You need to know:

- why the war was not over by December 1914
- how successful the British Expeditionary Force (BEF) was
- why there was stalemate on the Western Front
- the importance of new developments such as tanks, machine guns, aircraft, and gas
- the significance of the Battles of Verdun and the Somme
- the importance of other fronts
- why the Gallipoli campaign of 1915 failed
- why Russia left the war in 1918
- the impact of war on civilian populations
- why the German offensive in 1918 was unsuccessful
- why Germany asked for an armistice in 1918
- why the armistice was signed

Background: events immediately before the First World War

On 28 July 1914 Austria declared war on Serbia. Two days later, despite warnings from Germany, Russia began the mobilisation of its armed forces. On 1 August Germany declared war on Russia and then, on 3 August, on France. The following day the Schlieffen Plan was put into operation with Germany invading Belgium. This action brought Britain into conflict with Germany.

The First World War had started.

Why was the war not over by December 1914?

How was the Schlieffen Plan intended to work?

The Schlieffen Plan was originally designed to prevent Germany having to fight a prolonged war on two fronts. By dealing with the French threat in the west within six weeks, Germany would then be able to turn east to fight Russia; the German General Staff believed it would take Russia 10 weeks to mobilise its forces. Moving the army through neutral Belgium, Germany planned to avoid the heavily defended Franco-German frontier and did not expect to encounter much resistance from the Belgians.

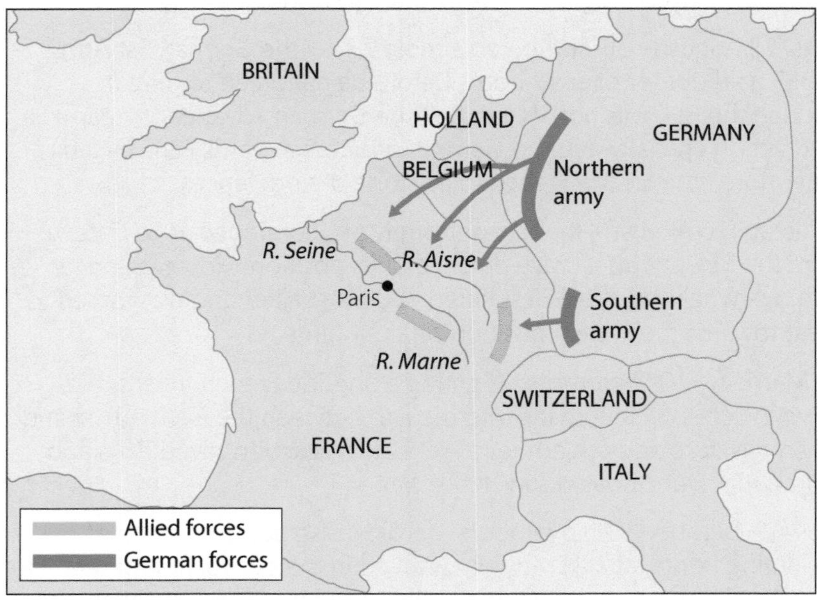

▲ **Fig. 8.1** *The Schlieffen Plan*

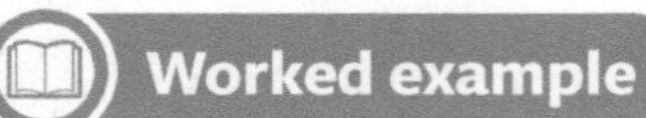

What did Germany hope to achieve through its use of the Schlieffen Plan? (4)

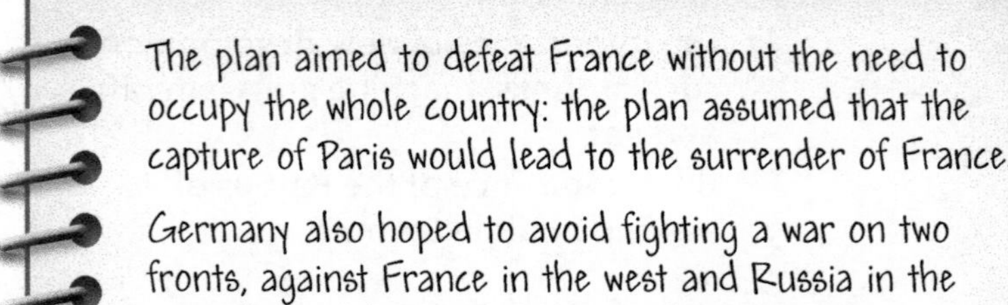

The plan aimed to defeat France without the need to occupy the whole country: the plan assumed that the capture of Paris would lead to the surrender of France.

Germany also hoped to avoid fighting a war on two fronts, against France in the west and Russia in the east. This was because France and Russia were part of a rival alliance against Germany when the plan was written in 1905. The plan enabled Germany to defeat France first before turning east to fight Russia who, it was believed, would take a lot longer to mobilise troops.

Exam tip

To answer this question you need to give two examples of what Germany hoped to achieve, supported by relevant factual detail.

Recap

The success of the Schlieffen Plan depended upon several important assumptions proving to be correct.

Apply

List the important assumptions that were made about the successful operation of the Schlieffen Plan, but did not come true.

In practice, the plan did not proceed as von Schlieffen had envisaged.

- In 1906 von Schlieffen's successor as Chief of Staff, von Moltke, revised the plan to avoid going through Holland.
- Von Moltke also weakened the German right flank to strengthen Germany's border with France.
- The many assumptions von Schlieffen had made about the operation of the plan did not come true.

Key term

The British Expeditionary Force (BEF)—the British Army sent to fight in the Low Countries alongside France against Germany prior to the First Battle of Ypres on 22 November 1914. Unlike the conscripted forces of Germany and France, the BEF consisted of volunteer troops, who were renowned for their shooting skills.

How successful was the British Expeditionary Force (BEF)?

Dismissed by Kaiser Wilhelm II as "General French's contemptible little army", the BEF played a vital role in holding up the German advance in 1914. The BEF played a significant role in the following battles.

- Mons (23 August)—outnumbered almost 2:1 by the German 1st Army, the BEF held out for over six hours before being forced to retreat. Although the BEF was not able to halt the German advance, its rear-guard action crucially delayed German progress towards Paris by a day, giving more time for the French to organise their defences.
- Le Cateau (26 August)—the retreat from Mons continued at Le Cateau where the BEF put up a brave defence of its position. However, once again overwhelmed, the BEF suffered 7000 casualties and was forced to retreat towards the French position on the Marne.
- The Marne (6–10 September)—fighting alongside French troops, the BEF was successful in moving into the gap between the German 1st and 2nd armies, forcing both armies to retreat. This action saved Paris and ensured that France could stay in the war.
- Ypres (19 October–30 November)—heroic resistance in the face of unrelenting frontal attacks virtually resulted in the destruction of the BEF, but this resistance saved the town and ensured that the Germans were not able to make the breakthrough on the northern wing of the Western Front.

Worked example

Why was the role of the BEF important in contributing to the Schlieffen Plan's failure? (6)

The most important way that the BEF contributed to the failure of the Schlieffen Plan was in its role at Mons. The Schlieffen Plan assumed that Britain would remain neutral, but the delay to the advance of German troops through Belgium was compounded by the intervention of the British. The quality of the BEF's shooting inflicted heavy casualties on the Germans and delayed their advance by at least a day.

The BEF also contributed to the plan's failure through its fighting alongside the French at the Marne in early September. The German advance had started to slow by the time its troops reached the Marne, and the French and British action at the Marne brought an end to the Schlieffen Plan and forced the Germans to retreat.

Exam tip

To answer this causal question you need to provide two fully explained reasons. Remember to provide precise examples to support the points you make.

Key term

"Race to the sea"—the attempt by both sides to capture the Channel ports and outflank each other from the middle of September until the middle of October 1914.

Why did both sides introduce trenches?

By the middle of September 1914 both sides had started to dig shallow trenches as defensive positions. By the end of the year, a complex network of trenches had emerged, stretching from the Belgian coast to the Swiss frontier. The inability of either side to achieve a breakthrough or outflank the enemy meant that both armies were forced to dig trenches to protect their soldiers from enemy machine gun and artillery fire.

Worked example

"The failure of the Schlieffen Plan was the main reason why both sides introduced trenches on the Western Front." How far do you agree with this statement? Explain your answer. (10)

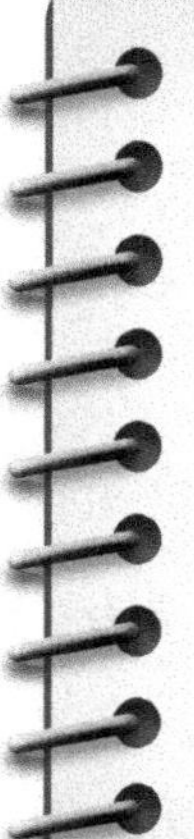

On the one hand, this statement is correct. After the battle of the Marne, von Falkenhayn ordered his troops to dig trenches in order to provide protection from enemy artillery but also to ensure that his forces did not lose the land that they had gained in France and Belgium since the start of the war. He had assumed that the war would be a war of movement, and that the Schlieffen Plan would be successful; however, Belgian defence along with British involvement alongside the French brought the German advance to a standstill by the end of September 1914.

Exam tip

The answer should provide a balanced response, ideally providing two arguments for each side and a conclusion evaluating how far you agree with the statement.

The failure of the Schlieffen Plan was also a significant reason for the introduction of trenches as its failure meant that the war was now unlikely to be a short one, and both sides needed to prepare strong enough defensive positions to resist an attack from their enemy and from which to launch attacks themselves.

The failure of either side to outflank the other in the "race to the sea" after the Schlieffen Plan had failed was also important in the introduction of trenches. The British defence of Ypres in November 1914 prevented the Germans gaining access to the French channel ports, but meant that they were faced by the Germans on three sides at Ypres. Digging trenches therefore provided some protection from the enemy. Both sides were now facing each other from the Belgian coast down to the Swiss frontier without the opportunity to achieve a breakthrough in the winter of 1914.

However, both sides also introduced trenches because of developments in weapon technology. The development of machine gun technology, so a typical machine gun could fire 11 rounds per second, meant that soldiers needed to dig trenches in order to protect themselves after an attack had broken down.

Overall, the failure of the Schlieffen plan was the most important reason why both sides introduced trenches because if the plan had succeeded then France would likely have fallen and the war would have been a short one.

Fig. 8.2 *Soldiers in a First World War trench*

Key term

"Morning hate"—all sides in the First World War would attempt to prevent a surprise dawn raid by firing rifles and throwing grenades in the direction of the enemy; this was frequently repeated at dusk.

Why was there stalemate on the Western Front?

What was living and fighting in the trenches like?

The nature of a soldier's routine would depend upon which part of the Western Front he found himself on and the level of fighting at any given time. Typically, he would follow a cycle of time on the front line, followed by time in close support trenches, then in reserve, followed by a short break.

The daily routine would invariably begin with the "stand to" when soldiers were woken by an officer, quickly followed by the "morning hate". After breakfast, there would be kit inspections and daily chores, with time for sleep and personal duties, such as writing letters home, allowed once the chores were done. As dusk approached, the trench systems teemed with activity with trench repairs, patrols into "no man's land", supply missions to the rear, and relief of front line units taking place at night.

Soldiers faced many hazards in the trenches.

- Artillery: shelling and mortar fire became increasingly important as methods for smashing enemy trenches after the end of the war of movement. Artillery fire caused most of the casualties, and it has been estimated that approximately 10 million tons of shells were fired during the course of the war.
- Snipers: raising one's head above the parapet for even a second could mean death, such was the quality of snipers on both sides. Many snipers kept tallies of how many men they had killed, particularly how many officers.
- Raids: trench raids were tactics intended to gain intelligence on enemy position, and to capture or kill enemy prisoners.
- Rats: apart from the enemy, rats were the biggest source of fear for soldiers in the trenches. Feeding off remains of food and even human corpses, they could be as big as cats, and carried infectious diseases.
- Lice: these bred rapidly and were often found in the seams of soldiers' clothing. Even when soldiers washed, lice were very hard to shift.
- Trench fever: this was an especially unpleasant and contagious disease. The main symptoms were high fever, headaches, aching muscles and sores. Treatment often involved 12 weeks away from the trenches. By 1918 it was established that having body lice was the main cause of trench fever.
- Trench foot: a fungal infection that could lead to gangrene, this was caused by cold and wet conditions. Severe cases could result in amputation.

How important were new developments such as tanks, machine guns, aircraft, and gas?

Machine guns: by 1914 machine-gun technology allowed gunners to fire around 500 rounds per minute and up to 2700 metres in range which, coupled with the use of enfilade tactics, allowed defenders to create virtually impenetrable "force-fields" of fire. Specialist gunners contributed to attacks across no man's land by concentrating fire over their own men's heads.

Gas: the first gas attack was launched on the Eastern Front in January 1915. Within four months both sides were using this new method of warfare on the Western Front. Different types of gas were used, the first being an early form of tear gas, followed by chlorine, phosgene, and mustard gas.

Aircraft: aircraft played several important roles during the conflict, evolving from a reconnaissance function in the early stages to operating as fighter and bomber aircraft as the war developed.

Tanks: first used by the British at Flers in September 1916, tanks were initially slow, mechanically unpredictable and unsuited to trench warfare. When allied to better tactics they could be highly effective weapons, but they still did not prove to be the war-winning weapon Britain and France had hoped for.

Key term

Enfilade fire—First World War tactic of firing across the longest line of soldiers to create a "beaten zone" of fire which would entrap enemy troops as they attempted to progress forward.

Key term

Mustard gas—chemical weapon used by the Germans for the first time at Ypres in 1917, its sulphuric compound created blisters, burning the eyes, skin, and lungs.

Exam tip

You should not attempt to include a long list of problems in the answer to this short, descriptive question. Instead, focus on two main problems and include relevant supporting details.

Worked example

What problems did many soldiers face when living in trenches on the Western Front? (4)

Serious injury or death were constant threats on the front line. Snipers, shelling, and mortars, as well as the dangers posed by enemy raiding parties, all contributed to the risks faced by soldiers in trenches.

Living conditions were also poor and created further problems for soldiers. The numerous rats, which could eat rations as well as spread disease, along with the risk of trench foot caused by prolonged exposure to damp conditions, and the risk of catching trench fever from lice, made life a misery for men in the trenches.

What was the significance of the Battles of Verdun and the Somme?

Recap

The failure of the Verdun campaign was attributable to several factors, not least the determination of the French despite huge casualties.

By early 1916 German and British commanders were keen to achieve a breakthrough that would bring the war to a swift end.

Verdun (February–December 1916)

At the end of 1915 German Chief of General Staff Erich von Falkenhayn proposed a new strategy for ending the war: eliminate France from the war, which would lead Britain to seek peace, deprived of its ally on the Western Front. He therefore settled on a prolonged attritional attack on the historic town of Verdun, which he believed France would attempt to defend at all costs. In the process, France would be required to sustain unbearable losses, leading to its withdrawal from the war.

The Verdun offensive lasted from February to December 1916 and was the longest offensive of the entire war. Each side suffered approximately 350 000 casualties during the battle, which ultimately failed to remove France from the war.

The Somme (July–November 1916)

The Allies were also developing their own plans to win the war at the end of 1915. Britain agreed to take greater responsibility for the fighting on the Western Front, and Field Marshal Haig agreed a plan with the French to launch a joint offensive on the Somme in the summer of 1916. Haig's plan was to batter the German lines across a 20-mile front with a week-long artillery barrage, creating holes in the lines. His infantry and cavalry could rush through the damaged lines then they could fan out into open country.

Haig's plan appeared, in the short term, to have failed spectacularly: 20 000 British soldiers died on the first day, 1 July, with nearly 70 000 dying during the entire offensive. Although some troops made gains on the first day, by mid-November the front line had only shifted 10 kilometres.

Some historians, however, view the Somme offensive in a different light and suggest that it was vital in helping relieve the pressure on Verdun. They point out that the Germans suffered such heavy casualties on the Somme that they realised they would not be able to win the war on the Western Front. They therefore decided to retreat to a shorter, easier-to-defend line (the Hindenburg Line) in February 1917, and switched their offensive strategy away from the Western Front and towards a campaign of unrestricted submarine warfare.

Worked example

Why did the Somme Offensive fail to achieve its objectives? (6)

The main reason why the Somme Offensive failed to achieve its objectives was that the preparations for the attack were not good enough. Although there was a week-long bombardment immediately prior to the men going over the top, a quarter of the shells did not explode. Those that did explode failed to destroy the German barbed wire, as they had been expected to. This meant that the German defences were not as badly damaged as Haig had hoped they would be.

The week-long bombardment gave the enemy advance notice that an attack was imminent, and as soon as it stopped the German soldiers were able to get to their machine guns before the British and French started to move. This contributed to another key reason why the attack failed: the sheer loss of men throughout the campaign. On the first day Britain suffered nearly 20 000 fatalities, and lost nearly 70 000 men in total during the Somme offensive.

Exam tip

It might be tempting to respond to this question by disputing the assumption behind it—that the Somme Offensive was a failure—but that would be a mistake. Remember to focus on what the question is asking, and give two explained reasons why the Somme Offensive failed.

How important were other fronts?

Who won the war at sea?

In the years 1914–16 the primary naval objective of Britain and Germany was to gain control of the North Sea. This culminated in the Battle of Jutland 31 May–1 June 1916. The extent to which Jutland proved to be a British victory is a hotly debated topic.

The case for a British victory	The case for a British defeat
The German High Seas Fleet never risked a major naval battle again.	More British ships (14) than German ships (11) were sunk.
Britain kept control of the North Sea.	There were more British casualties (6784) than German casualties (3058).
Britain was able to maintain its blockade of the German coast.	

Key term

Unrestricted submarine warfare—a German naval strategy in the First World War which declared the waters around Great Britain to be a war zone; all shipping in that zone could be targeted, without warning.

Arguably the main naval contribution to the Allied victory was through the British blockade of the German coast. This had a devastating effect on imports, creating unsustainable pressure on Germany's ability to feed its population or provide sufficient raw materials to service its war needs.

Germany attempted to carry out its own blockade of the British coast through the use of submarines; in particular, with its campaigns of unrestricted submarine warfare in 1915 and 1917. To cope with the significant threat this posed to its own ability to feed its population, Britain used a variety of tactics to tackle the U-boat threat.

- Q ships: heavily armed, converted merchant ships were deployed.
- Convoy system: battleships escorted packs of merchant ships across the Atlantic, providing protection and the ability to sink U-boats.
- Mines: thousands of anti-submarine mines were placed across the North Sea.
- Sonar: sound waves helped to detect submarines under the water.

Apply

Write a list of bullet points to answer this question: To what extent was the Battle of Jutland a success for Germany?

Why did the Gallipoli campaign of 1915 fail?

With stalemate established on the Western Front, First Lord of the Admiralty Winston Churchill devised an ambitious plan to win the war by defeating Turkey and coming to the aid of Britain's ally, Russia. The campaign resulted in over 140 000 Allied casualties and a humiliating withdrawal from the Turkish peninsula. Several explanations for the campaign's failure have been put forward.

- The plan was flawed from the start: Churchill, Kitchener, and Hamilton have all been criticised for their roles in devising a beach-landing plan, and having poor understanding of the terrain or of Turkish defences.
- Conditions at Gallipoli: with most of the Turkish defences on hills overlooking Allied positions, the chances of progress were slim. In addition, extreme heat, flies, and dysentery hindered the campaign.
- The trench system: with little progress moving off the beaches and towards the Turkish lines, a complicated network of trenches quickly emerged, providing the Allied forces with the type of stalemate they were trying to break out of on the Western Front.
- Turkish defences: at the start of the war, Liman von Sanders helped construct Turkish defences. After the failure of the British naval assault in March 1915 he reinforced the defences along the Gallipoli coast, using natural defences along with existing fortifications.

Why did Russia leave the war in 1918?

On the Eastern Front, Russia's war started better than expected, with a rapid mobilisation and advance into eastern Germany. However, following defeats at Tannenberg and Masurian Lakes in the first two months of the war, the Russians were steadily pushed back, and continued to suffer defeats against the German army throughout 1915.

Although the Russians experienced some successes against the Austrians, for example in the Brusilov Offensive in summer 1916, the devastating impact of war contributed to the downfall of Tsar Nicholas II in February 1917, and ultimately to the rise to power of the Bolsheviks in October 1917. In March 1918 Russia negotiated the Treaty of Brest-Litovsk with Germany, which resulted in Russia withdrawing from the war.

These are the main reasons why Russia had to withdraw from the war.

- Russian forces were not strong enough to defeat the German military. They were badly led by the Tsar and his senior officers.
- Ordinary Russian soldiers lacked motivation. They were fighting in a war as a result of treaty obligations. This unwillingness led to several mutinies and mass desertions.
- Political events in Russia resulted in a new government led by the Bolsheviks who had no intention of continuing the war against Germany.
- Russian forces lacked essential supplies, including food and weapons.

Key fact

The Bolshevik Party consisted of communists led by Lenin. After the fall of the Tsar, Lenin returned from exile and committed the Bolsheviks to opposing continued participation in the war and opposition to the ruling Provisional Government.

Worked example

How important was the role of Nicholas II in contributing to Russia's defeat in the First World War? (40)

Arguments that Nicholas II was important in contributing to Russia's defeat in the First World War include:

- the poor commanders he had appointed to lead the Russian army when the war started
- his move to Commander-Chief in August 1915
- his rejection of support from the Duma.

Arguments that other reasons were more important in contributing to Russia's defeat in this war include:

- lack of equipment in 1914–5, especially rifles, shells
- deteriorating support for the war from the Russian people
- the Bolshevik seizure of power.

Exam tip

This is an example of a paper 4 question: in one hour you are expected to answer one question from the Depth Studies. To score highly you must provide a focused, balanced, and well-argued response.

This worked example suggests arguments that could be used to answer this question—but note that, in addition, a conclusion is required. The conclusion needs to make a clear judgment, evaluating the relative importance of the main reasons given.

Key fact

"Ersatz goods" were introduced by Germany to help to deal with food shortages caused by the Royal Navy blockade. Ersatz goods were substitute goods; for example, acorns and beechnuts were used as a coffee substitute.

What was the impact of war on civilian populations?

Civil liberties: the outbreak of war brought many restrictions to the lives of civilians. The British government introduced the Defence of the Realm Act (DORA). The United States also passed major legislation to ensure that the war effort was not threatened. Measures passed included making it illegal to release classified information or to interfere with the recruitment of troops.

Conscription: each of the major combatants introduced conscription, although Britain relied on a volunteer army until 1916. Some men refused to be conscripted and were known as conscientious objectors.

Food shortages: most combatant nations suffered from food shortages. Common causes were a loss of farm workers to the military, and blockades. Britain was vulnerable to blockade, with the German campaign of unrestricted submarine warfare having a devastating effect on the import of essential food. Germany's civilians suffered similarly as a result of the Royal Navy blockade. Food shortages in Russia were mainly caused by the poor quality of the railway network and the backward agricultural system.

France was less affected by food shortages as it was able to feed its population from agricultural land unaffected by the war. The United States was also self-sufficient and able to provide essential supplies for its allies.

Rationing of food was introduced in both Britain and Germany.

Employment of women: Britain created the Women's Land Army in 1915. Another area where opportunities for women increased was within the industrial workforce, often in munitions factories. In Britain women accounted for 37 per cent of the workforce by 1918.

Civilian deaths: it is thought around 940 000 civilians lost their lives as a result of military action. Almost 6 million died from disease, malnutrition, and accidents.

Recap

In Britain rationing was introduced gradually.

- Voluntary rationing was introduced in February 1917.
- Compulsory rationing was introduced in stages between December 1917 and February 1918.
- Ration books were introduced in July 1918 for butter, margarine, lard, meat, and sugar.

Worked example

How important was the role of women in assisting the war effort in Britain during the First World War? (40)

Arguments that the role of women was important in assisting the war effort in Britain are as follows.

- The Suffrage movement, including the WSPU, abandoned the campaign for the vote and devoted themselves to winning the war.
- The Women's Land Army was essential in helping with food production.
- Women played a role in the recruitment campaign.

Arguments that the role of women was not that important in assisting the war effort in Britain include the following.

- Rationing (voluntary and compulsory) was the important factor in ensuring that demands for food were met.
- The increase of the role of women was simply part of a wider sense of patriotism that was present.

Exam tip

This is another paper 4 question. As with the previous example, a range of possible arguments that could be used to answer the question are provided.

Why did Germany ask for an armistice in 1918?

What was the importance of the United States' entry into the war?

The United States entered the war in April 1917 as a result of Germany resuming its campaign of unrestricted submarine warfare and because of the publication of a telegram, intercepted by the British. This telegram was sent by the German Foreign Minister to the German ambassador to Mexico and offered United States territory to Mexico in return for joining the war on Germany's side.

Initially, the United States was not prepared for war and American troops were slow to arrive. When they did arrive, the first ones were short of uniforms and equipment.

Destroyers and merchant ships were sent to increase anti-submarine capabilities. Additional support aided the destruction of mines in the North Sea.

American forces reached France in small numbers. By March 1918 there were 300 000 American soldiers in France; by July a further 800 000 were in position. These soldiers provided valuable support in combating the German offensives of June and July.

The arrival of the Americans provided a tremendous morale boost following the disasters of 1917 when the effects of the German unrestricted submarine campaign, the Battle of Passchendaele, and Russia's withdrawal from the war, threatened victory.

What was the Zimmerman Telegram? (4)

The Zimmerman Telegram was a message the German Foreign Minister sent to the German ambassador in Washington instructing him to offer Mexico the states of Arizona, New Mexico, and Texas if the Mexicans agreed to enter the war against the United States.

The message was intercepted by the British in January 1917, who presented and decoded it for the Americans. When it was published in newspapers, and the German minister admitted sending it, the American public was horrified. Already furious at the resumption of unrestricted submarine warfare, Americans increased calls for the United States to enter the war against Germany, which it did in April 1917.

Exam tip

One mark will be awarded for each relevant point, with additional marks for supporting details. To achieve 4 marks you need to make two relevant points and explain each of them.

Why was the German offensive of 1918 unsuccessful?

In January 1918 German war prospects were not good. German troops were still fighting on the Eastern Front, the submarine campaign had failed to achieve its target, and recruits for the army were drying up. Furthermore, the United States was expected to send large numbers of fighting men to the Western Front.

On 21 March 1918 Germany launched Operation Michael, conceived by General Ludendorff. The offensive was initially a success: German forces, including many transferred from the Eastern Front, broke through the Allied lines and advanced 56 kilometres in the first 3 weeks. The German army was now 8 kilometres from Paris.

This German push was stopped by an Allied counter-offensive, but at great cost. Britain suffered 178 000 casualties and France 77 000. German casualties numbered over 1 million during the offensives of 1918.

German troops of 1918 were not as good as those of 1914. Their discipline was poor and they were badly fed and supplied. Crucially, they did not have reserves to call upon. The numerical advantage of the well-equipped Allies was beginning to make an impact and between May and August the Germans made no further progress.

The failure of Ludendorff's plan can be firmly placed within the reasons for its initial success. By breaking out from the heavily fortified Hindenburg Line, the Germans changed the war from one of attrition into one of movement.

Key term

Operation Michael—a German offensive launched in 1918 to push troops into France; also referred to as the Ludendorff Offensive or Spring Offensive.

Fig. 8.3 *Soldiers in a First World War trench*

This transformation played into the hands of the Allies who had more tanks, men, and aircraft than Germany. On 8 August the Allies launched a counter-attack along the Western Front and by late September, they had reached the Hindenburg Line. September saw the Germans in full retreat.

A serious influenza epidemic within the German army left only 2 of its 13 divisions fit for action, and by the end of September it had become a question of when, rather than if, Germany would surrender.

Write a short fact file stating when and where the Hindenburg Line was created, and what its purpose was.

Why did revolution break out in Germany in October 1918?

The war effort	Generals Hindenburg and Ludendorff began to interfere in domestic affairs under the pretext of directing the country's war effort. At the same time, the Reichstag started to question the war effort. The long-term cause of the German revolution was war weariness and by July 1917 the Reichstag was demanding peace.
New government	The first stage of the revolution in October 1918 occurred following the formation of a new government under the newly appointed Chancellor von Baden. He asked US President Wilson for an armistice. This was refused until Germany agreed to allow "true representatives of the German people" to negotiate. On 26 November the Kaiser introduced the October reforms that transferred power to the Reichstag.
Mutiny	The second stage was triggered by the mutiny of sailors at the naval bases of Kiel and Wilhelmshaven.
Riots	Riots broke out across Germany and the Kaiser abdicated, fleeing to the Netherlands. Friedrich Ebert was appointed as the new Chancellor.

Why was the armistice signed?

- To avoid a Russian-style revolution: revolutions were threatened across Germany and Ebert feared a Bolshevik (communist) revolution.
- Conditions in Germany: the blockade had brought terrible shortages of food, causing ill health.
- To take advantage of Wilson's 14 points.
- Fear of invasion: on 28 September, Ludendorff and Hindenburg agreed that Germany had no choice but to surrender. Failure to do so would result in the destruction of the army and the invasion of Germany.
- Morale: by early November the morale of German forces was extremely low and the troops were in a state of permanent retreat.
- The Central Powers were defeated: Bulgaria called for an armistice following defeat at Monastir-Doiron. Turkey agreed a peace deal on 30 October and four days later Austria did the same.

Exam tip

The key to success with this type of question is to provide two fully explained reasons. Remember to answer what is being asked of you: do not think that this is a question about the defeat of Germany in the war.

Worked example

Why did revolution break out in Germany in October and November 1918? (6)

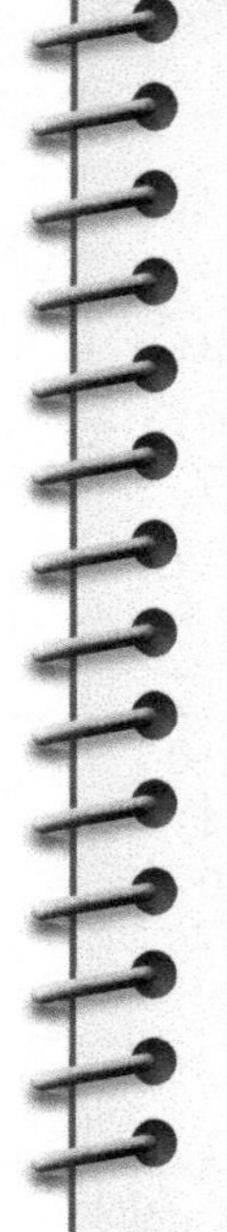

The German revolution in October and November 1918 was caused firstly by war weariness. In July 1917 the Reichstag had passed a peace resolution calling for a peaceful end to the war, which was ignored by both the German government and the Allies. However, at the end of October 1918, sailors at Wilhemshaven and Kiel mutinied in protest at plans to take the German fleet out to sea again. These protests spread across Germany as sailors' councils, or soviets, were set up.

The hardship caused by the war was also a key long-term cause of the revolution. The food shortages worsened by the Allied naval blockade resulted in average daily rations of 1000 calories in early 1917, while ersatz goods replaced many staples. For example in the winter of 1917, the turnip replaced the potato as a staple in the German diet. In addition, the onset of influenza in 1918 caused over 400 000 fatalities among Germans who lacked the diet to survive the onslaught of the disease.

Review

1. Describe the role played by Belgium in the failure of the Schlieffen Plan. [4]
2. What new methods of technology were used to break the stalemate on the Western Front? [4]
3. What did Germany hope to achieve through the 1918 Spring Offensive? [4]
4. Describe the main features of the Treaty of Brest-Litovsk. [4]
5. Describe the main features of the 1914 Defence of the Realm Act. [4]
6. Why did the United States enter the war in 1917? [6]
7. Why did Russia withdraw from the war in 1918? [6]
8. Why was conscription introduced in Britain in 1916? [6]
9. Why did Britain introduce rationing in 1918? [6]
10. "The failure of the Gallipoli campaign was mostly due to poor leadership." How far do you agree with this statement? Explain your answer. [10]
11. "The weakness of Germany's allies was the decisive factor contribution in its decision to seek an armistice in 1918." How far do you agree with this statement? Explain your answer. [10]
12. How important was the entry of the United States into the war in 1917 in the defeat of the Central Powers? [40]

For further information review this section in the Student Book.

> **1.** Describe the main features of unrestricted submarine warfare. **[4]**

Analysis

- ✓ The answer to this question should include two main features of unrestricted submarine warfare and relevant supporting details, such as when and where the strategy was carried out.
- ✓ Unrestricted submarine warfare was a German navel strategy.
- ✓ The Germans' aim was to carry out a blockade of the British coast using submarines.
- ✓ The strategy was used in 1915 and 1917.
- ✓ The Germans declared that the waters around Britain were a war zone and that shipping there would be targeted without warning. One ship attacked, causing American fatalities, was the Lusitania.

Mark scheme

1 mark for each relevant point, additional mark for supporting detail, maximum 2 marks per point made.

Student answer

Unrestricted submarine warfare was a German strategy for defeating Britain by cutting off all supplies to the country. U-boats sank any ship that sailed to and from Britain, including foreign ships.

Examiner feedback

The answer to question 1 shows a broad understanding of unrestricted submarine warfare, but this response lacks sufficient precise detail and explanation. It would have been useful to see the candidate demonstrate knowledge of how this campaign took place, and to offer a more specific description of its features, for example the fact it was operated in 1915 and then in 1917, and who the target was. The student should have provided two relevant features with supporting detail. 2 marks awarded.

> **2.** Why did the Schlieffen Plan fail to achieve its objectives? **[6]**

Analysis

- ✓ The answer to a 6-mark causation question needs to include two well-supported reasons.
- ✓ There are several reasons why the Schlieffen Plan failed, but the answer could focus on two general areas of German mistakes in implementing the Plan, such as weakening its right wing, and opposition actions that contributed to its defeat, such as the intervention of the BEF at Mons.

Mark scheme

Level 1:	general answer lacking specific contextual knowledge (1 mark)
Level 2:	identifies AND/OR describes reasons (2–3 marks)
Level 3:	explains ONE reason (4–5 marks)
Level 4:	explains TWO reasons (6 marks)

Student answer

The Schlieffen plan failed to achieve its objectives for three main reasons.

First, Britain intervened in the war, which Germany did not expect.

Second, the French held the Germans up at the Marne, slowing the German timetable for success in the West.

Third, the Russians mobilised much quicker than German war planners had believed possible when the Schlieffen Plan was drawn up in 1905.

Examiner feedback

Three relevant reasons are provided in this answer. To develop the response, the student should instead offer two reasons that are much better developed and explained. 4 marks awarded.

3. Why was the Gallipoli Offensive launched in 1915? **[6]**

Analysis

✓ To score highly on the question two well-explained reasons for the launch of the offensive should be included.

✓ These could include that it was important to seek an alternative to the stalemate on the Western Front and there was a desire to support Russia.

Mark scheme

Level 1:	general answer lacking specific contextual knowledge (1 mark)
Level 2:	identifies AND/OR describes reasons (2–3 marks)
Level 3:	explains ONE reason (4–5 marks)
Level 4:	explains TWO reasons (6 marks)

Student answer

The Gallipoli Offensive was launched because fighting on the Western Front had ground to a halt by the end of 1914 and the British government, especially Winston Churchill, believed that an assault on Turkey would be successful and therefore remove an important ally of Germany's from the war.

Another reason was that Russia requested that its allies Britain and France open up a front against Turkey, as a way of distracting Turkey from its campaign against Russia in the Caucasus.

Examiner feedback

This response is closely focused on the question, and attempts to provide two explained reasons. To develop the answer, the student could have provided more detail for each reason. For example, the student could have mentioned that Turkey was bombarding Russian ports and had sealed off the Dardanelles Straits, which Russia hoped to capture in order to access the eastern Mediterranean. 4 marks awarded.

4. "The Verdun campaign of 1916 failed because of the start of the Somme offensive." How far do you agree with this statement? Explain your answer. **[10]**

Analysis

- ✓ This question needs a balanced response, so you should first explain how the start of the Somme offensive contributed to the failure of the Verdun campaign, then explore other factors.
- ✓ The Germans had to divert men and artillery away from Verdun in July.
- ✓ Other factors were the French troops' strong defence of Verdun and the diversion of German troops to the Eastern front to support Austria.

Mark scheme

Level 1:	general answer lacking specific contextual knowledge (1 mark)
Level 2:	identifies AND/OR describes reasons (2–3 marks)
Level 3:	gives a one-sided explanation or one explanation of both sides (4–6 marks)
Level 4:	explains both sides (7–9 marks)
Level 5:	explains with evaluation (10 marks)

Student answer

The Verdun campaign failed because the British started their offensive on the Somme on 1 July, which meant that the Germans had to divert forces away from Verdun and up to the Somme.

It also failed because the French were determined that Verdun would not fall, and sent the large part of their forces to defend the town.

German troops also had to be diverted to the Eastern Front to support Austria, which was in retreat as a result of the Brusilov offensive.

The most important reason the Verdun campaign failed was because of the Somme Offensive.

Examiner feedback

Although the student does engage with the reason given in the question and provides two other reasons, this response requires more development of each point. It also requires a better conclusion, where there is evidence of evaluation of the question: the student has to state why this reason is more important than the others in the answer. 5 marks awarded.

> **5.** "Haig deserves his reputation as butcher of the Somme." How far do you agree with this statement? Explain your answer. **[10]**

Analysis

- ✓ This question needs a balanced response: first, a range of arguments to support the statement, then a counter argument.
- ✓ Arguments to support the statement could include the number of casualties suffered during the Somme Offensive, Haig's tactics, and the length of the campaign.
- ✓ The counter argument could defend Haig's reputation and challenge the statement with points such as the Somme was ultimately a British victory, and Haig was anxious to protect his untested new army.
- ✓ Remember to finish with a conclusion that gives a final judgment on the statement.

Mark scheme

Level 1:	general answer lacking specific contextual knowledge (1 mark)
Level 2:	identifies AND/OR describes reasons (2–3 marks)
Level 3:	gives a one-sided explanation or one explanation of both sides (4–6 marks)
Level 4:	explains both sides (7–9 marks)
Level 5:	explains with evaluation (10 marks)

Student answer

General Haig was a very controversial officer in the First World War, and has been described as the butcher of the Somme because of the large number of soldiers who died in France between 1 July and mid-November. The Somme Offensive was intended to smash a hole in the French lines, leading to a cavalry and infantry charge through the German rear. It was also intended to relieve pressure on Verdun, which had been besieged by Germany since February.

The offensive was a complete failure, with Allied forces only managing to capture approximately 10 kilometres of land. It is estimated that 70 000 British soldiers lost their lives during the campaign, meaning that Haig does deserve his reputation as butcher of the Somme.

Examiner feedback

This question requires a candidate to analyse and evaluate, not to describe events. Unfortunately, this response is largely descriptive and does not attempt any meaningful analysis. Instead, it should have presented an argument that Haig does deserve this reputation, perhaps referring to the number of casualties sustained in the face of continuing lack of success but looking at the other side of the argument as well, pointing to the achievements of the Somme campaign. Finally, some kind of evaluative judgment is required. 3 marks awarded.

6. How important was the role of technology in the defeat of Germany by 1918? **[40]**

Analysis

- ✓ As this is a 40-mark question taken for a Depth Study, you are expected to display depth and range of knowledge, and avoid producing something superficial and limited in scope.
- ✓ The best responses will provide a range of well-supported arguments, leading to a sustained conclusion.
- ✓ This question requires you to focus on the role of technology in the defeat of Germany, so you would have to relate the role of technology to wider factors that contributed to Germany's defeat, for example the role of tanks in the combined approach used on the Western Front in the summer of 1918, or the development of sonar or Q ships to enable Allied shipping to survive and defeat the U-boat campaigns.
- ✓ You should also provide a counter argument that technology did not contribute much to the defeat of Germany, perhaps explaining the limitations of technology: the issues with tanks 1916–18 would be one good example to use.
- ✓ Other factors in the defeat of Germany should then be provided, with a final conclusion where you weigh up the relative importance of technology in Germany's defeat.

Mark scheme

Level 1 (1–8 marks)	• Demonstrates little relevant contextual knowledge. • Demonstrates limited ability to select and organise information. • Describes a few key features, reasons, results, and changes of societies, events, people, and situations relevant to the question. • Answer shows little understanding of the question.
Level 2 (9–16 marks)	• Demonstrates some, but limited, contextual knowledge. • Selects and organises some relevant information. This is only deployed relevantly on a few occasions. • Identifies and describes key features, reasons, results, and changes of the societies, events, people, and situations relevant to the question, but with little awareness of the broad context. • Attempts conclusions but these are asserted, undeveloped, and unsupported. • Presents a recognisable essay structure, but the question is only partially addressed.
Level 3 (17–24 marks)	• Demonstrates and selects relevant contextual knowledge and deploys it appropriately to support parts of the answer. • Selects and organises mostly relevant information, much of it deployed appropriately with a structured approach, either chronological or thematic.

	• Demonstrates some understanding of the key features, reasons, results, and changes of the societies, events, people, and situations relevant to the question with some awareness of the broad context. • Produces structured descriptions and explanations. • Points support conclusions although they are not always well substantiated.
Level 4 (25–32 marks)	• Deploys mostly relevant and accurate contextual knowledge to support parts of the answer. • Selects a range of relevant information which is generally well organised and deployed appropriately. • Demonstrates a reasonable understanding of the significance of the key features, reasons, results, and changes of societies, events, people, and situations relevant to the question with awareness of the broad context. Has some understanding of the interrelationships of the issues in the question. • Can produce developed, reasoned, and supported conclusions.
Level 5 (33–40 marks)	• Selects and deploys a range of relevant and accurate contextual knowledge to effectively support the answer. • Selects, organises, and deploys effectively and relevantly a wide range of information to support conclusions. • Demonstrates a good understanding of the key features, reasons, results, and changes of societies, events, people, and situations relevant to the question. Demonstrates an awareness of the importance of the broad context and of the interrelationships of the issues of the question. • Produces well-developed, well-reasoned, and well-supported conclusions.

Student answer

Technology did not play an important role in the defeat of Germany. Instead, the fact Germany had to fight a two-front war after the failure of the Schlieffen Plan was the most important reason why Germany lost the war. Fighting on two fronts meant that Germany always had to divide its forces between the west and the east, while also having to send troops onto the southern part of the Eastern Front to prop up Austria in the conflict with Russia. This was especially important in 1916 when von Falkenhayn was attempting to destroy the French at Verdun but was forced to send troops not only to defend the Somme once the Allied campaign had begun there, but also to Galicia to prevent Austria completely collapsing as a result of the Brusilov Offensive.

Another factor that contributed to the defeat of Germany was the British naval blockade, which had had caused severe suffering in Germany by the end of 1918. One effect was that money became virtually worthless and Germans had to resort to bartering. As a result, the government found it difficult to pay suppliers for the war effort, and many ordinary Germans found it difficult to buy essential items. Working-class Germans felt that wealthier Germans were able to survive because of the black market, and food riots took place from 1916. The shortages caused by the blockade were blamed on the government and became a major cause of the revolution in October 1918, which led to the agreement to the armistice.

Technology did play a part, but only in an indirect fashion. For example, the development of Q ships and sonar helped defeat the U-boat threat in 1917, ensuring that Britain could continue in the war. Tanks were not effective until allied with appropriate tactics in 1918 when they were used with infantry to blaze a trail through enemy lines.

In conclusion, German defeat became virtually inevitable after the failure of the Schlieffen Plan in autumn 1914 as the war would now be fought on two fronts and the side with the greatest capacity of men and materials would be most likely to win.

Examiner feedback

This example of a paper 4 question would require a lengthy response (the paper requires one question to be answered in an hour), featuring a strong analytical approach: each paragraph should explicitly answer the question, providing a clear reason for the defeat of Germany. The student should have started by explaining the role of technology, before introducing alternative explanations for Germany's defeat in 1918, so as to produce a balanced answer. Reasons should be fully explained and illustrated by relevant supporting details, with the answer culminating in a substantiated judgment and conclusion.

You need to know:

- to what extent the Weimar Republic was doomed from the start
- the impact of the Treaty of Versailles on the Weimar Republic
- to what extent the Republic recovered after 1923 under Stresemann
- why Hitler was able to dominate Germany by 1934
- why Hitler was able to become Chancellor by 1933
- how Hitler consolidated his power in 1933–4
- how effectively the Nazis controlled Germany, 1933–45
- what it was like to live in Nazi Germany

The Weimar Republic and Ebert: Germany was declared a republic on the day the Kaiser abdicated. Ebert, leader of the Social Democrat Party (SDP), became the first President. His first tasks were to restore law and order but he faced a number of challenges.

Background: the formation of the Weimar Republic

The First World War was brought to an end by the signing of the armistice on 11 November 1918. Shortly before the signing, Kaiser Wilhelm II of Germany abdicated and a democratic government, the Weimar Republic, was set up. By removing the Kaiser, Germany hoped for a more lenient peace settlement. This didn't happen and the Weimar Republic was to last 14 years before Hitler's accession to power and the establishment of the Nazi dictatorship until 1945.

Was the Weimar Republic doomed from the start?

How did Germany emerge from defeat at the end of the First World War?

Ebert's priority when he became President in 1918 was to tackle the challenges faced by the new government. These included the following.

Anger at the Treaty of Versailles	The new government became immediately unpopular by signing the Treaty of Versailles in 1919. The government's members became known as the "November Criminals". Most Germans were furious that the government had accepted the terms of the Treaty of Versailles. They thought their treatment was too harsh, especially as most did not believe that Germany had lost the war.
The threat from the extreme left	The communists in Germany, known as Spartacists, wanted a revolution similar to the one that occurred in Russia in 1917. In January 1919, the left-wing activists led by Rosa Luxemburg and Karl Liebknecht seized power in Berlin. They were crushed by the Freikorps, who were ex-soldiers and bitter enemies of the communists.
The threat from the extreme right	In March 1920 Wolfgang Kapp, an extreme nationalist, together with some Freikorps units, seized power in Berlin. This was known as the Kapp Putsch. The nationalists wanted a strong government. The army refused to intervene. Kapp was not supported by the Berlin workers, who went on strike, refusing to cooperate. After four days Kapp and his supporters fled Berlin. In 1923 another right-wing attempt to seize power was led by Adolf Hitler and his growing NSDAP party. The Munich Putsch attempted to seize power and install a right-wing government. It was unsuccessful and put down by loyal troops. Hitler was arrested and imprisoned for two years.

A new constitution

As a Republic, Germany needed a new constitution and its new governments were to be more democratically elected than ever before.

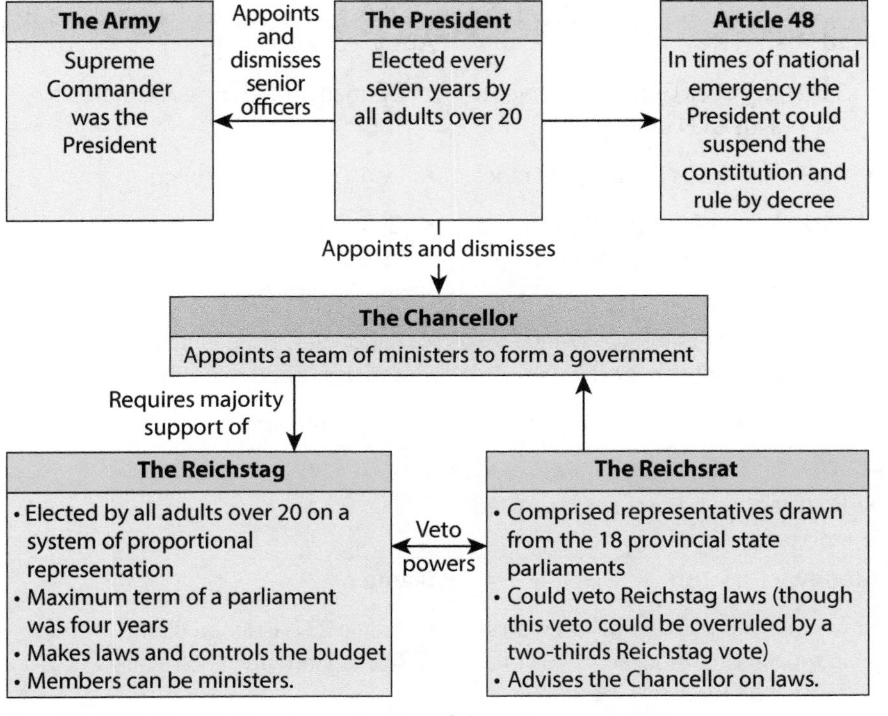

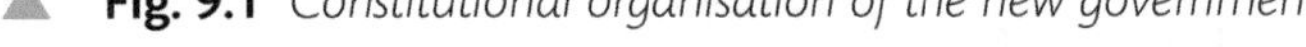
▲ **Fig. 9.1** *Constitutional organisation of the new government*

The new system created a few issues for the Weimar Republic.

- Through proportional representation some extremist parties were represented in the Reichstag, giving them a voice and publicity.
- Proportional representation prevented overall control by one party—coalition governments were made up from several political parties.
- Article 48 gave the President so much power that he had the opportunity to act undemocratically.

Recap

- Germany had expected a lenient settlement after it had changed the leadership of the country and tried to become more democratic.
- Germany would face serious difficulty in rebuilding economically. Not only did the Treaty of Versailles restrict Germany's ability to raise revenue through the loss of territory, but also reparations were set so high that a significant amount of money would be spent repaying the debt to the Allies.
- The psychological impact was also significant—the army and the people felt that they had been let down by those who had signed the treaty.

Apply

Draw a timeline from 1918 to 1923 that shows the events that were Ebert's main challenges as President.

Key term

Coalition government—a government formed by multiple political parties promising to cooperate for the common good, reducing the dominance of an absolute party within that coalition. The usual reason for this arrangement is that no single party can achieve a majority in the parliament.

What was the impact of the Treaty of Versailles on the Weimar Republic?

The table below summarises the terms of the treaty.

Land	Army
• Surrender of all German colonies to the League of Nations • Return of Alsace-Lorraine to France • Poland given a "corridor" to the sea, cutting East Prussia off from the rest of Germany • Other territories lost to Poland, Denmark, and Lithuania • Germany forbidden to unite with Austria • Rhineland to be occupied by Allied troops for 15 years	• German armed forces restricted to 100 000 • Conscription prohibited • German naval forces limited to 15 000 men, 6 battleships, 6 cruisers and 12 destroyers • Poison gas, armed aircraft, tanks, and armoured cars prohibited • Rhineland demilitarised
Money	**Blame**
• Germany to pay 226 billion marks in reparations; reduced in 1921 to 134 billion marks • France awarded the coal-producing region the Saar until a plebiscite in 1934	• Article 231 assigned blame for the war to Germany and its allies

Exam tip

The answer needs to include two well-explained points about why the Republic seemed at risk. You could choose issues relating to the Treaty of Versailles or to the constitution.

Worked example

Why was the Weimar Republic in danger of collapse in 1919–23? (6)

A range of challenges in 1919–23 severely tested the new Republic. The German people bitterly resented the Treaty of Versailles' terms of reparations, war guilt, and loss of territory. There were challenges from right-wing groups, such as the Kapp Putsch (1920) and the Munich Putsch (1923)—both were serious attempts to remove the government.

The treaty also caused major economic issues. Germany had lost territory, and struggled to pay reparations fixed at 226 billion marks. This led to the Ruhr crisis of 1923: French troops occupied the German region to take raw materials when Germany defaulted on payments. There was hyper-inflation in Germany, and great economic instability, endangering the new Republic.

The Germans had believed the Treaty of Versailles was to be based on Wilson's Fourteen Points. They were furious at its harsh terms and it was regarded as a "diktat"—a dictated peace. The Germans were not allowed to attend the Conference to discuss the terms. Several aspects caused particular resentment.

- Germany had to accept the blame for starting the war (the War Guilt Clause). The Germans thought this was unfair as they believed the start of the war was due to the actions of a range of countries, not just Germany.
- The reparations figure was about 2 per cent of Germany's annual output. Germany feared it would be unable to repay this money and rebuild the country. The loss of territory including the industrial areas of the Saar and Upper Silesia made it more difficult to pay the reparations.
- Limiting the army to 100 000 men increased unemployment in a country already suffering serious economic problems.

Key term

The Ruhr—the heavily industrialised area of western Germany named after the river that flows through the region. It was a huge centre for the coal, iron, and steel industry.

Stage 1 The first instalment of reparations was paid by Germany in 1921.

↓

Stage 2 In 1922 Germany couldn't pay the amount due and asked for more time. The British agreed, the French did not.

↓

Stage 3 The French, together with the Belgians, occupied the Ruhr to seize coal and iron as reparations. In January 1923, the occupation of the centre of German industry began.

↓

Stage 4 German workers used "passive resistance"; that is, German workers would not work in the mines or accept orders from the occupiers. The result was that there would be nothing to take away.

↓

Stage 5 The French reacted harshly, killing over 100 workers and expelling over 100 000 old-age pensioners. The halt in production caused the collapse of the German currency.

↓

Stage 6 The government's response was to print money. This caused prices to rise out of control and resulted in hyperinflation.The German currency was virtually worthless. People's savings became valueless and old-age pensioners suffered as they were on fixed incomes. Prices rose faster than incomes. Prices in the shops were increasing almost every hour. People could not afford food and heating. The Weimar government was in danger of collapse.

↓

Stage 7 In August 1923 Gustav Stresemann became Chancellor. He introduced a rescue plan that:

- ended passive resistance in the Ruhr
- stopped the printing of money in November 1923 and stabilised the currency by introducing the temporary Rentenmark
- resumed reparation payments to the Allies
- resumed production in the Ruhr.

▲ **Fig. 9.2** *Stages of the crisis in the Ruhr*

To what extent did the Republic recover after 1923 under Stresemann?

The next six years were characterised by economic recovery and some have called them the "Golden Years" of the Republic. There were certainly some positives, as outlined below.

Area	Positive developments	Remaining issues
The economy	• Stresemann introduced a temporary currency, the Rentenmark, and the Ruhr industries restarted production. In 1924 this temporary currency was replaced by the permanent Reichmark. • In 1924 Stresemann agreed the Dawes Plan with the United States. This linked Germany's reparations payments to economic performance. In addition, American loans of 800 million gold marks helped to kick-start the German economy. German industry benefited from this investment: inflation and unemployment fell, industry expanded, and exports increased. By 1928 German industrial production was greater than pre-war levels. • The Young Plan of 1929, which reduced reparations, further helped Germany's economic recovery.	• Some groups, including shopkeepers, farmers, and small businessmen still struggled. • Unemployment still remained too high. • The economic recovery was based on American loans.
Foreign policy	• Germany signed a wider European agreement called the Locarno Treaties of 1925. Germany agreed to accept the terms of the Treaty of Versailles. The Locarno Treaties placed Germany on an equal level with signatories, providing guarantees for the frontiers of Germany, France, and Belgium. • France left the Ruhr by 1925. • In 1926 Germany was admitted to the League of Nations as a responsible member of the international community.	• Some felt that by accepting the Treaty of Versailles and not seeking to change the terms, Streseman was further betraying Germany.
Cultural aspects	• The 1920s was a decade of cultural revival in Germany, especially Berlin. • The new democratic republic was committed to civil liberties. It lifted censorship, encouraged artists, writers, film and theatre directors, and designers. The rejection of traditional approaches resulted in the favouring of expressionism. • At a popular level, night clubs, dance halls, cafés, and restaurants increased, allowing opportunities for cabaret artists, singers, and dance bands.	Many of these developments were regarded with shock and disgust by the right-wing of German politics. Artistic development was seen a sign of decadence, corruption and moral decay.

The Golden Age of the Weimar Republic was not to last though. The Great Depression that followed the Wall Street Crash had a devastating effect on Germany.

Renewed economic crisis

- Following the Wall Street Crash of October 1929 the American economy went into recession and many of the loans offered to Germany since 1924 were recalled.
- The German economy suffered a double blow. The Germans had to cope with a world depression and the consequent reduction in export orders, but had to repay substantial amounts of money to the United States. Unemployment rose to alarming levels. By 1932 the German unemployment figure stood at 6 million—one-third of the workforce.

Key term

Wall Street Crash—the collapse of the New York Stock Exchange on 29 October 1929. The crash started the Great Depression and stock prices did not return to a similar level until late 1954.

Political instability

- Support for the moderate parties that made up the coalitions of the Weimar governments began to decline.
- As the German people searched for alternatives and saw governments fail, support for the two extreme parties, the Nazis and the communists, rose from 13 per cent in 1928 to 52 per cent in 1932.

Recap

- The Weimar Republic recovered in the years 1924–8 and solved many of the problems of the immediate post-war period.
- The work of Stresemann was crucial to this.
- The improvements were temporary though, and depended largely on foreign investment, particularly from the United States.
- The years 1924–8 can only be considered "The Golden Years" of the Republic if you compare to them to the years before and after.

Why was Hitler able to dominate Germany by 1934?

What did the Nazi Party stand for in the 1920s?

Key points from the Nazi Party objectives published in 1920 included:

- the union of all Germans in a Greater Germany
- the destruction of the Treaties of Versailles and St Germain (which would then allow the union of Germany and Austria)
- German citizenship exclusive to those of German blood (thereby excluding Jews)
- no more immigration of non-Germans
- a strong central government in Germany
- generous provision for old-age pensioners.

The German Workers' Party (DAP, the forerunner of the Nazi Party) was established by Anton Drexler in January 1919. It was an extremist national party. At the end of the war Hitler had stayed in the army working for the intelligence services. Sent to spy on the DAP, Hitler was impressed by its political views and joined the party. Soon he was taking responsibility for publicity, propaganda, and public speaking.

In 1920 the Party published its 25-Point Programme and renamed itself the National Socialist German Workers' Party (known as Nazis). The Programme showed strong nationalist and anti-Semitic features. The swastika was used as the party badge.

In July 1921 Hitler replaced Drexler as leader. In August 1921 he founded the SA (Storm Troopers), who were noted for their violence against any opposition.

The Munich Putsch, 1923

Hitler wanted to achieve the violent overthrow of the unpopular Weimar Republic and replace it with a Nazi government. He viewed the current government as weak due to the Ruhr Crisis and its handling of hyperinflation. Supported by wartime leader General Ludendorff, he attempted to seize power.

- 8 November: Storm Troopers forced their way into a political meeting in a Munich beer hall. They planned to take over Munich and march into Berlin. Kahr, the Prime Minister of Bavaria, was forced at gunpoint to give support to the revolution.
- 9 November: Kahr went back on his promise. Hitler marched through the streets of Munich to gain support. Armed police opened fire, killing 16 Nazis.
- 26 February: Hitler was placed on trial for treason. He used his trial as a propaganda exercise, generating publicity for his views and media attention. He was leniently sentenced to five years in prison, and served only nine months. Ludendorff was acquitted.

Was the Munich Putsch a failure for Hitler?

Yes	No
The army remained loyal to the Weimar government. Hitler and Ludendorff were arrested and charged with high treason. The loyalty of Bavarian politicians had been underestimated. Hitler miscalculated the mood of the German people. They did not rise to support him. Hitler was branded a criminal and imprisoned. The Nazi Party was banned.	The trial gave Hitler the opportunity to gain publicity for his ideas. Hitler used his time in prison to write *Mein Kampf* (*My Struggle*). The trial showed that Hitler had sympathisers within the judiciary. Hitler only served nine months and this was in great comfort at Landsberg Castle.

By the end of the 1920s the Nazis were a minority party. In the general election of May 1928 they won 12 seats in the Reichstag, polling 2.6 per cent of the votes.

Key fact

Mein Kampf is an autobiographical book by Adolf Hitler. It outlines his political ideology and future plans for Germany. It heavily emphasises the superiority of the German (Aryan) race, especially in comparison with Jews and Slavs; the dangers of communism; the need for "lebensraum" or living space; and ambition for Germany to become the dominant state in Europe.

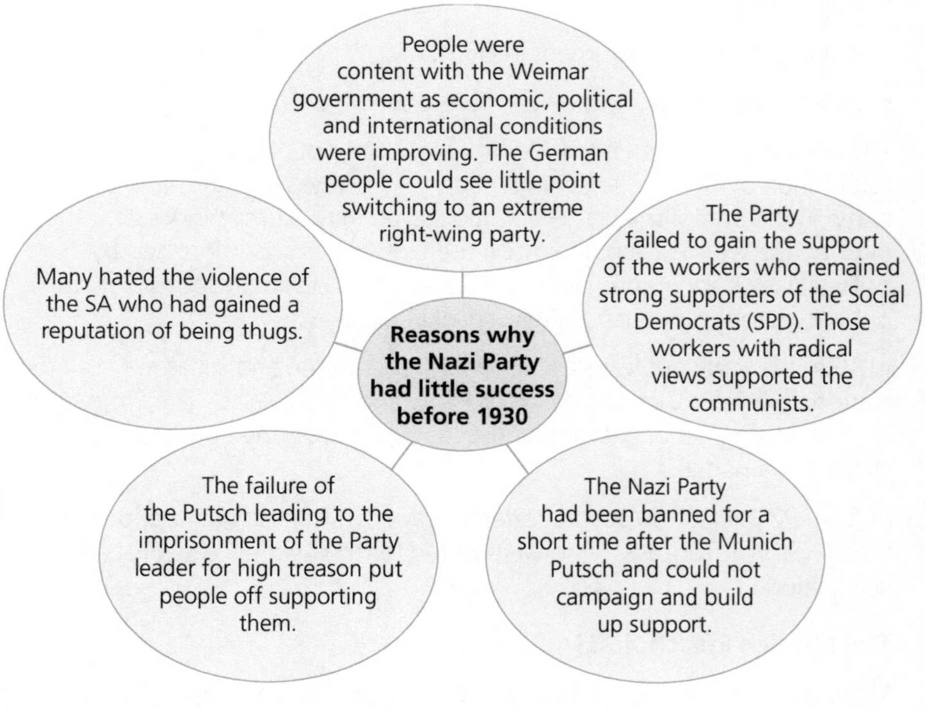

Reasons why the Nazi Party had little success before 1930

- People were content with the Weimar government as economic, political and international conditions were improving. The German people could see little point switching to an extreme right-wing party.
- The Party failed to gain the support of the workers who remained strong supporters of the Social Democrats (SPD). Those workers with radical views supported the communists.
- The Nazi Party had been banned for a short time after the Munich Putsch and could not campaign and build up support.
- The failure of the Putsch leading to the imprisonment of the Party leader for high treason put people off supporting them.
- Many hated the violence of the SA who had gained a reputation of being thugs.

▲ **Fig. 9.3** *Reasons why the Nazi Party had little success before 1930*

Why was Hitler able to become Chancellor by 1933?

In October 1929 Stresemann died. The economy he had built up was fragile, being dependent on American loans. In the same month disaster struck as the Wall Street Crash occurred.

As unemployment increased, many Germans felt let down by the Weimar Republic and turned to extremist parties. Support for the Nazis and communists increased. In the 1930 elections the communists (KPD) gained 77 seats, the Nazis 107. There are several reasons why Hitler was elected Chancellor in 1933.

The impact of the Great Depression	The Wall Street Crash in the United States started the Great Depression. As a result, many American banks recalled their loans. German businesses began to close. Millions became unemployed. By 1930 unemployment had reached 4 million. It was at 6 million by 1932.
The appeal of the Nazis	Hitler and the Nazis promised to get people back to work and to provide food. They gained support from all areas of German society, including powerful industrialists. They also offered a strong response to the rising communists and a promise to return Germany to its pre-war standing and power.
The fear of communism	In the 1930 elections the communists (KPD) gained 77 seats. There was fear of a communist revolution. This worried many industrialists and farmers. They turned to the Nazis, who opposed the communists. The SA and SS gave an impression of discipline and order.
Political unrest	Germany was thrown into economic chaos and no government could solve the problems. President Hindenburg ruled by decree. There were five governments in the period 1929–32, each in power for only a few months. As mainstream politicians failed to address the problems Germany faced, people began to look to alternatives such as the Nazis, who offered radical solutions.
Long-term issues	The reliance on money from the United States came about as a result of the treaties signed in the 1920s. For some this showed the long-term damage of the Treaty of Versailles, and resentment grew once more. The Nazis offered a return to traditional values, away from the cultural experimentation of the 1920s and back to uniting behind one leader.

The Nazi appeal was broad and offered something to many disgruntled voters. At a time when other politicians looked uncertain and weak, the Nazis appeared to be a party of action—promising jobs, a more nationalistic foreign policy, and strength against communism.

Exam tip

General tip: in questions on how the Nazis gained popularity, it is important to note the skilled tactics they used.

Key fact

President Hindenburg was a former war hero who had commanded the German military during the second half of the First World War. He became president in 1925. He was old fashioned in his views and strongly supported the right wing.

Goebbels introduced new campaigning methods to increase the Nazi share of the vote, including the following.

- The Nazis relied on generalised slogans rather than detailed policies.
- They repeatedly accused the Jews, the communists, and the Weimar politicians of causing the current difficulties.
- Posters and pamphlets were widely distributed and displayed.
- Large rallies were held.
- The Nazis provided soup kitchens and hostels for the unemployed.
- Hitler was a powerful speaker. He travelled by plane to rallies all over Germany.
- Film, radio, and records brought the Nazi message to everybody.

	March 1932	**Presidential election 1932: Hitler opposed the elderly President Hindenburg and campaigned under a promise to build a better Germany and overturn Versailles. This was not enough to get him the support he needed and despite going to a second vote, Hitler was unsuccessful.**
Elections for the Reichstag: the NSDAP won 230 seats and was the largest party in the Reichstag, although it lacked an overall majority. The election campaign had been a violent one with street battles between Nazis and communists. Nearly 100 people were killed.	**July 1932**	
	November 1932	**Elections for the Reichstag. A government formed under von Papen lacked support and was forced to call another election. The support for the Nazis dropped to 192 seats but theirs remained the largest party.**
Elections for the Reichstag. Another government, this time led by von Schleicher, found it impossible to govern. In the resulting election the Nazis won 288 seats and theirs was by far the biggest party, although it still lacked a majority.	**March 1933**	

▲ **Fig. 9.4** *Timeline of the elections of 1932–3*

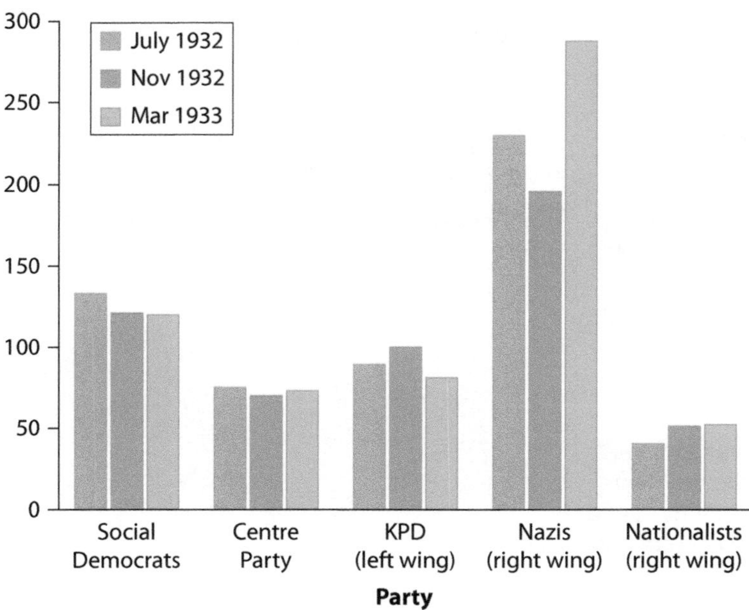

▲ **Fig. 9.5** *Results of the elections of 1932–3*

How did Hitler become Chancellor in January 1933?

Faced with the continued rise of the NSDAP, and the popularity of Hitler, von Papen managed to persuade Hindenburg to agree a political deal. Hitler would become Chancellor with von Papen Vice-Chancellor. With only a few Nazis in the Cabinet, von Papen was confident that Hitler could be controlled. On 30 January 1933 Hitler was named Chancellor.

How did Hitler consolidate his power in 1933–4?

Why Hitler was not a dictator	Events that occurred	Consequences
Other parties could oppose him	**The Reichstag Fire, 27 February 1933** On the evening of 27 February 1933 the Reichstag building burnt down. A Dutch communist, van der Lubbe, was arrested and charged with starting the fire. Hitler claimed it was proof of a communist plot against the state. Hitler took the opportunity to whip up public fear against the supposed communist threat. There were many theories as to how the fire started including that the Nazis might have started it themselves.	President Hindenburg was persuaded by Hitler to issue an emergency decree. The decree gave Hitler wide-ranging powers, including the power to deal with the "state of emergency" that had arisen following the Reichstag Fire. The decree curbed freedom of speech and the right of assembly. It gave the police an excuse to arrest communists. In Prussia over 4000 were arrested in the days immediately after the fire. Hitler was now out of control.
He did not have total political control	**The Enabling Act, 23 March 1933** Hitler still did not have enough elected support to have complete control of Germany. He wanted to pass any laws he chose without the use of the Reichstag, but to change the constitution in this way he required two-thirds of the votes of the Reichstag members. To gain this level of votes he expelled the 81 communist members from the Reichstag and ordered the SA to continue their intimidation of the opposition. Only the Social Democrats dared oppose the measure. The Act was passed by 441 votes to 94.	Hitler was now dictator of all Germany. He could now pass laws for four years without consulting the Reichstag. He was able to ban all other political parties. Germany was now a one-party state. In May 1933 the trade unions were abolished, their leaders arrested and funds confiscated. Strike action was made illegal. All workers had to belong to the German Labour Front. The civil service was purged of all Jews. The democratic Weimar Republic had been destroyed.

Why Hitler was not a dictator	Events that occurred	Consequences
Elements of his party were a threat to him	**The Night of the Long Knives, June 1934** Hitler was worried about the growing independence of Ernst Röhm, the leader of the SA. He decided to take action at the end of June. There were rumours that Röhm was in favour of merging the army with the SA under his leadership, and Röhm was open in his view that he favoured a "second revolution" and more extreme nationalistic policies. Hitler felt he needed to reassure the army and show the SA leaders who was in control. On the night of 30 June 1934 Röhm and other SA leaders were arrested and shot. During the next two weeks several hundred senior SA men, other rivals and potential enemies, including von Schleicher, were also murdered by the SS.	The army could no longer be in any doubt that Hitler favoured its members in preference to the SA. The SA was brought firmly under the control of Hitler's leadership.
President Hindenburg could remove him	When President Hindenburg died on 2 August 1934 Hitler proclaimed himself Chancellor and Reich Führer.	As such he was Head of State and Commander-in-Chief of the Army. Every soldier was required to swear an oath of personal loyalty to Adolf Hitler. Hitler's dictatorship was now a matter of fact as well as a matter of law. Hitler had achieved total power.

Recap

- In a period of 18 months Hitler established himself as a dictator.
- The Enabling Act gave him total political power over the Reichstag and other parties.
- The Night of the Long Knives meant that potential threats in his own party were eliminated.
- The death of Hindenburg meant that Hitler could combine the role of President with the role of Chancellor. The position of Führer was established.

How effectively did the Nazis control Germany, 1933–45?

Control through terror

The SS: led by Heinrich Himmler, the SS had extensive powers to arrest, detain without charge, interrogate, search, and confiscate property. They were responsible for running the concentration camps and implementing Nazi racial policies, including the Final Solution.

The Gestapo: the German secret police, the Gestapo, were feared by the ordinary citizens as they had sweeping powers. They spied on Germans by tapping telephones, intercepting mail, and accessing information through a network of informers, which made it unsafe for anyone to express anti-Nazi views.

The courts and judges: judges had to take an oath of loyalty to Hitler. Jewish judges and lawyers were sacked. Capital offences were increased to make, for example, telling anti-Nazi jokes and listening to a foreign radio station punishable by the death sentence.

Concentration camps: enemies of the Nazis were sent to the camps as well as gypsies, beggars, and tramps. Discipline was harsh and there were many deaths from beatings and torture. During the Final Solution these camps were used for the extermination of the Jewish population. The first camp was opened at Dachau, Germany in 1933.

▲ **Fig. 9.6** *Control through terror*

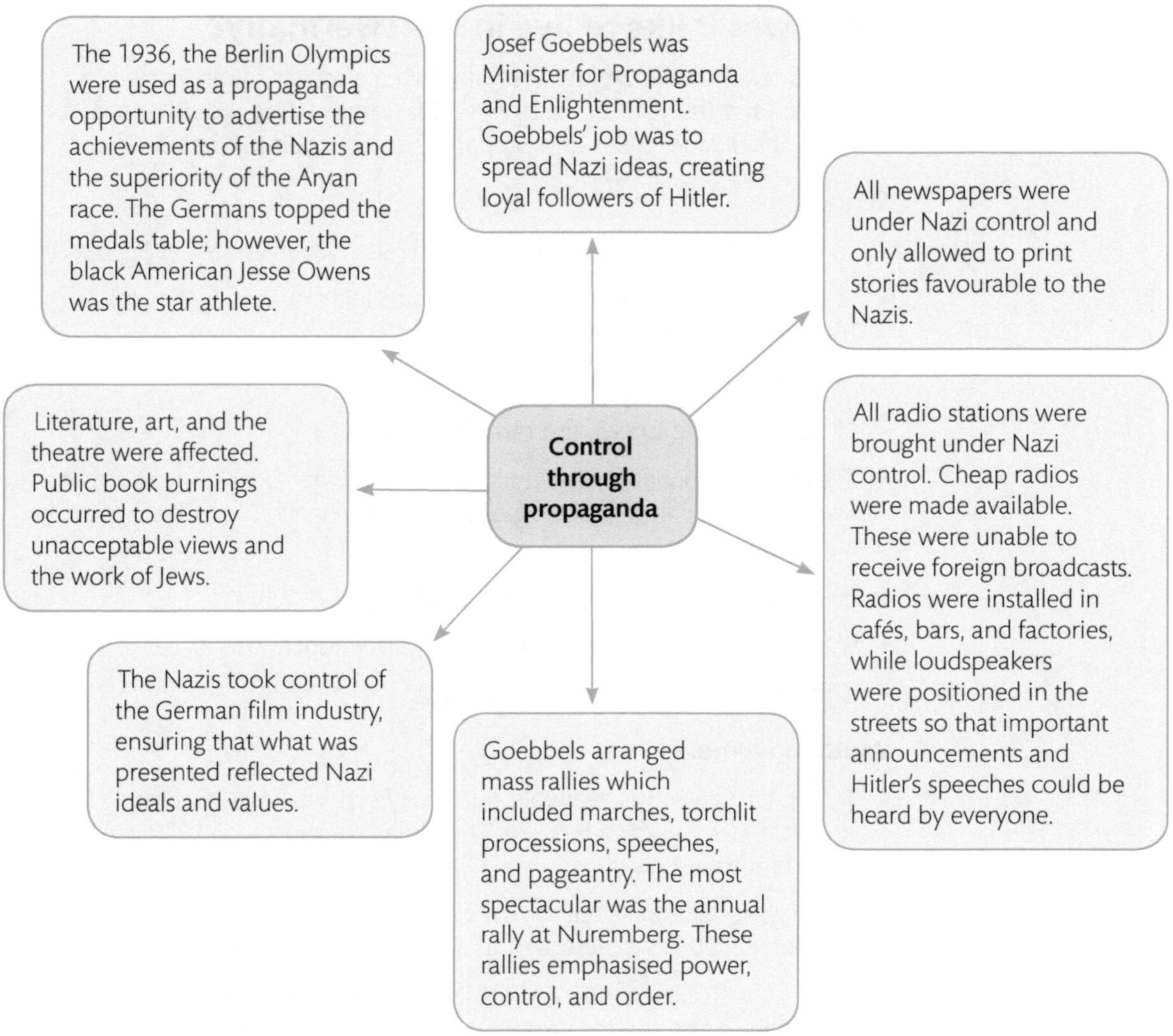

Control through propaganda

Josef Goebbels was Minister for Propaganda and Enlightenment. Goebbels' job was to spread Nazi ideas, creating loyal followers of Hitler.

All newspapers were under Nazi control and only allowed to print stories favourable to the Nazis.

All radio stations were brought under Nazi control. Cheap radios were made available. These were unable to receive foreign broadcasts. Radios were installed in cafés, bars, and factories, while loudspeakers were positioned in the streets so that important announcements and Hitler's speeches could be heard by everyone.

Goebbels arranged mass rallies which included marches, torchlit processions, speeches, and pageantry. The most spectacular was the annual rally at Nuremberg. These rallies emphasised power, control, and order.

The Nazis took control of the German film industry, ensuring that what was presented reflected Nazi ideals and values.

Literature, art, and the theatre were affected. Public book burnings occurred to destroy unacceptable views and the work of Jews.

The 1936, the Berlin Olympics were used as a propaganda opportunity to advertise the achievements of the Nazis and the superiority of the Aryan race. The Germans topped the medals table; however, the black American Jesse Owens was the star athlete.

▲ **Fig. 9.7** *Control through propaganda*

Worked example

Who were the Gestapo? (4)

The Gestapo acted as Nazi Germany's secret police force. Under the control of Himmler, the head of the SS, the Gestapo were responsible for the monitoring of German people and their activities. Using informants and observation they targeted those considered a threat to Nazi Germany. The Gestapo acted outside of the normal judicial process and had their own courts with the power to send people to concentration camps or to be killed. During the war the Gestapo targeted resistance movements who sought to oppose the German war effort.

Exam tip

To answer this question think about what the Gestapo did as well as who its members were. Aim to write two well-developed points.

What was it like to live in Nazi Germany?

The Nazi regime affected the lives of young people through formal education and the youth movement. This combination would ensure future generations of loyal Nazis and prepare them for their future role in society.

Schools

- Schools in Germany were controlled by the Nazi Ministry of Education.
- Teachers had to take an oath of loyalty to Hitler and join the Nazi Teachers' League.
- Jewish teachers were sacked.
- All schools were to give the same message.
- The curriculum was changed to ensure that Nazi ideas and racial beliefs were reflected in the teaching of subjects such as biology, history, and mathematics.
- Religious education was removed from the curriculum.
- Emphasis was placed on sport and physical education.
- Girls were taught "home-making" skills.

Youth movements

- The Hitler Youth was available outside of school. It was founded as a voluntary organisation in 1926. The Hitler Youth Law of 1936 made attendance virtually compulsory. Other youth groups were banned.
- There were separate sections for boys (The Hitler Youth) and girls (The German League of Maidens) and for different age groups.
- Children were indoctrinated with Nazi ideas, including extreme prejudice against Jews and the idea that the peace settlement was an injustice.
- Boys were given basic military training and discipline including drill, campcraft, map reading, and looking after a rifle. Running, hiking, and tracking enhanced physical fitness.
- Girls were prepared for motherhood, learning domestic skills such as cooking, sewing, and managing the household budget.

How did young people react to the Nazi regime?

Not all young Germans enjoyed the opportunities offered by the Hitler Youth. Some expressed themselves through the "Swing" movement and the Edelweiss Pirates. These groups believed in freedom of expression and values that often conflicted with those of the Nazis.

Worked example

"Nazi policies towards young people were effective in controlling them." How far do you agree with this statement? Explain your answer. (10)

It can be argued that the Nazi state was successful in its policies towards young people. The Youth movements set up, with the Hitler Youth for boys and the League of German Maidens for girls, proved successful in that by 1939 they had over 7 million members. They were used to prepare boys and girls for their roles in life and offered opportunities to participate in camps, hikes, and parades, for example. The Nazis' policies in schools were also effective at controlling young people. Tight control over the curriculum and teaching within schools meant that the education system reflected what the Nazis wanted their young people to learn.

However, it can be argued that the policies directed towards young people were not effective as the Nazi state failed to achieve total obedience. Opposition groups from young people emerged such as the White Rose Group and the Edelweiss Pirates. These groups refused to conform with the Nazi state, and instead promoted activities that directly opposed Nazi ideals such as smoking and listening to jazz music. As the war developed, these groups distributed leaflets encouraging others to challenge the Nazi state.

Overall, the Nazis achieved largely what they wanted in terms of young people—those growing up in the regime were mainly obedient and prepared for later life. As the regime developed though, so did disengagement as the young fought against the need to conform and found ways to express themselves.

Exam tip

This question needs a balanced answer that considers the two sides of the question. Think about how the Nazis were effective in controlling young people, and the successes of organisations such as the Hitler Youth before evaluating them with evidence about alternative organisations, for example the White Rose Group.

How successful were Nazi policies towards women and the family?

The Nazis believed in traditional Aryan family values including women's role as wives and mothers—partly because this gave stability but more importantly to raise the birth rate. Nazi ideals were encouraged through specific measures.

- In 1933 marriage loans were introduced for Ayran couples. Couples could receive up to 1000 Reichsmarks if the woman gave up her work. Goods rather than cash were given to stimulate the economy. For each child the couple had, 25 per cent was taken off the loan amount.
- Enrolment for women at university was severely restricted.
- Divorce was made easier so that women could remarry and have more children.

- Women were forced out of work. They were expected to remain at home, to look after their husband and children. After 1937 there was a reversal in this policy as women were needed to work in the armaments factories.

What was the impact of these policies?

- The birth rate had increased by 1939.
- Marriages increased from 516 000 in 1932 to 772 000 in 1939.
- The number of women working increased between 1933 and 1939. The number of women working in agriculture increased from 4.6 million to 4.9 million; in industry the figure increased from 2.7 million to 3.3 million.
- The number of women studying at university drastically fell.

Did most people in Germany benefit from Nazi rule?

When Hitler came to power, unemployment was at almost 6 million. By 1938 there was almost no unemployment. The Nazis introduced public works schemes: building autobahns, schools, hospitals, and houses. Rearmament created jobs, as did the introduction of conscription to the armed forces. Increased opportunities came from an attempt at introducing self-sufficiency to reduce the need for imports of raw materials and food. The key change for workers was the creation of the Nazi Labour Front after trade unions were abolished—membership was optional but without it workers struggled to find a job. The Nazis also introduced other measures for workers.

- The "Strength Through Joy" programme gave workers cheap theatre and cinema tickets.
- The "Beauty of Labour" movement improved working conditions by introducing washing facilities and low-cost canteens.
- The "Reich Labour Service" was set up to tackle unemployment. All 18–25-year-olds had to serve for six months. They provided cheap labour for state projects.
- Workers were offered cut-price cruises on the latest luxury liners.
- Workers saved in a state scheme to buy a Volkswagen Beetle, although no worker ever received a car.

However, all this came at a cost. Wages were low while working hours increased. The availability of consumer goods was also limited and worsened as the war began.

Why did the Nazis persecute many groups in German society?

In Hitler's view the German people constituted the Aryan race. They were the master race, superior in terms of intelligence, physique, and work ethic. To preserve the purity of the Aryan race, it was essential to maintain its separateness. Hitler also believed that Germany was overburdened with "undesirables" (people he did not want in German society). He regarded these as a drain on the resources of the state. Hitler's views had been evident in his book, *Mein Kampf*, in the 1920s but now in power he introduced legislation to persecute the half a million Jews living in Germany.

Anti-Semitism

Key term

Anti-Semitism—hostility to, prejudice, or discrimination against Jews, Judaism, and Jewishness.

	March 1933	Jews were banned from the professions and government employment.
Aryan and non-Aryan children were forbidden from playing together.	**April 1933**	
	September 1933	Race Studies becomes a part of the school examination syllabus.
The Nuremberg Laws removed German citizenship from Jews and forbade marriage between Jews and non-Jews.	**September 1935**	
	January 1936	Jews had all electrical equipment, bicycles, typewriters, and records confiscated.
The Nazis organised Kristallnacht (Night of Broken Glass) as a reprisal for the shooting of a German diplomat by a Jew. Nazi mobs attacked and burnt Jewish shops, homes, businesses, and synagogues. Over 100 Jews were murdered.	**November 1938**	
	February 1939	Jews had all jewellery, gold and silver confiscated.
Jews could be evicted from their homes without a reason being given.	**April 1939**	

▲ **Fig. 9.8** *Timeline of anti-Semitic measures*

Persecution of other groups

The Nazis persecuted many other groups they thought to be inferior.

Gypsies violated the Nazis' racial and efficiency requirements and were sent to concentration camps. Other undesirable groups suffered the same fate.

Following the Sterilisation Law of 1933, mentally ill people were compulsorily sterilised. In 1939 such people were killed in euthanasia programmes.

How much opposition was there to the Nazi regime?

Group	Actions taken
Religious opposition	At first the Catholic Church agreed not to interfere with Nazi policies (Concordat of 1933), in return for protection of the rights of the Catholic Church in Germany. However, Hitler broke the agreement and the Nazis were denounced as anti-Christian by the Pope. Many churchmen spoke out against the Nazis, including Pastor Niemöller, who spent eight years in a concentration camp for forming a rival church to the Nazi Reich Church. Bishop Galen spoke out strongly against euthanasia, forced sterilisation, and concentration camps. He was kept under house arrest until the end of the war.
Opposition among the young	Although many young people joined the Hitler Youth, there were some who rejected this influence. Members of the "Swing" movement were condemned by the Nazis because they were interested in British and American popular music and dance, including banned jazz music. They also accepted Jews into their groups. The Edelweiss Pirates mocked the Nazis through song, attacked members of the Hitler Youth, distributed broadsheets, and scrawled graffiti on walls. During the war they spread anti-Nazi propaganda and, in 1944, took part in an attack on the Gestapo during which an officer was killed. Twelve Pirates were publicly hanged in November 1944. The White Rose Group formed by university students in Munich was another group of young opponents. The leaders, Hans and Sophie Scholl, were executed in 1943 for anti-Nazi activities.
Military opposition	In 1944 a group of senior army officers planned to assassinate Hitler. They placed a bomb in a suitcase under a table at a meeting Hitler attended. The bomb went off, but Hitler was unharmed. The "July Bomb Plot" had failed and it led to 5000 executions.

Why was there not more opposition? The harsh punishments suffered by those who opposed the regime, coupled with the fear of the Gestapo and SS, meant that most Germans conformed with the Nazi State. The effective measures taken by the Nazis to establish control meant that there was very little opportunity to organise meaningful opposition.

How did the coming of war change life in Nazi Germany?

- Food rationing began in September 1939. Clothes rationing followed in November 1939.
- Propaganda encouraged support of the war effort. The Gestapo watched for people who did not give their support.
- The gamble of invading the Soviet Union in 1941 resulted in civilians facing cutbacks, shortages, and longer working hours. Labour shortages saw increasing numbers of women in the factories.
- From 1942 Albert Speer began to direct the war economy, focusing on the armaments industry.
- In 1944 Germany directed all its resources in a "Total War".
- The cinemas remained open and were the only entertainment on offer. They showed propaganda films.
- There were massive bombing raids on German cities, undermining morale. One of the most significant was the bombing of Dresden.
- By the end of the war, 3 million civilians had died. The survivors experienced food shortages.

The Final Solution

- As the German army captured huge areas of Eastern Europe, millions of Jews came under Nazi control. The SS shot around 800 000 Jews.
- At the Wansee Conference in January 1942 it was decided to eliminate all European Jews. Captured Jews were taken to remote death camps in Poland equipped with gas chambers and crematoria.

The Nazis killed around 6 million Jews through gassing, shooting, working them to death, and starvation. They tried to cover up their murderous acts.

Review

1. What problems faced Germany immediately following the end of the war in 1918? **[4]**
2. What was the Reichstag Fire? **[4]**
3. Describe the occupation of the Ruhr in 1923. **[4]**
4. Describe the Munich Putsch of 1923. **[4]**
5. Why were the people of Germany unhappy with the Treaty of Versailles? **[6]**
6. Why were the achievements of the Nazi Party limited before 1929? **[6]**
7. Why did the Nazis attempt to control young people? **[6]**
8. Why was the Enabling Act important? **[6]**
9. Why did Hitler arrange the Night of the Long Knives? **[6]**
10. Why was the death of Hindenburg important? **[6]**
11. Why were there so many uprisings in Germany in the years 1919–22? **[6]**
12. Why was there an economic crisis in 1923? **[6]**
13. How important was the Reichstag Fire as a reason for Hitler being able to establish a dictatorship? **[10]**
14. "Most people benefited from Nazi control of Germany." How far do you agree with this statement? Explain your answer. **[10]**

For further information review this section in the Student Book.

1. What was the Night of the Long Knives? **[4]**

Analysis

- ✓ In the answer aim to make two well-explained points about the event that consider actions, details, and motive.
- ✓ The question focuses on the events between 30 June and 2 July 1934 when Hitler targeted his political opponents and potential threats.
- ✓ Leading members of the SA, including the leader Ernst Röhm, were killed.
- ✓ Members of the SA, former political rivals such as von Schleicher, and others were also killed.
- ✓ Hitler's motives were to ensure that those who remained were loyal to him and the state, and that the threat posed by the SA was eliminated.

Mark scheme

1 mark for each relevant point, additional mark for supporting detail, maximum 2 marks per point made.

Student answer

The Night of the Long Knives occurred in June 1934 and was an attempt by Hitler to brutally crush those he thought might be capable of plotting to replace him. The main targets were members of the SA, including their leader Ernst Röhm. Röhm and hundreds of others were killed over several nights of violence. Hitler had feared that the SA was increasingly out of control, and there seemed to be a disagreement about what policies Germany should be following. With the action taken Hitler ensured that the threat posed by the SA was eliminated and his control of Germany was secure.

Examiner feedback

This is an excellent thorough answer: it offers good explanation of the events, some detail of what occurred, and motives and outcomes for Hitler. 4 marks awarded.

2. Why has the period 1923–9 been described as the "Golden Years"? **[6]**

Analysis

- ✓ In the answer aim to make two well-explained reasons that focus on the improvements Germany made.
- ✓ The work of Stresemann in this period is the focus in the question.
- ✓ Germany made great improvements in the areas of politics, the economy, and also in terms of foreign policy.
- ✓ A more stable economy followed after agreement with the Dawes Plan and Young Plan regarding debt repayments and loans from the United States.
- ✓ In terms of foreign policy, Germany benefited from better relations with other European countries after the Locarno treaties.

Mark scheme

Level 1:	general answer lacking specific contextual knowledge (1 mark)
Level 2:	identifies AND/OR describes reasons (2–3 marks)
Level 3:	explains ONE reason (4–5 marks)
Level 4:	explains TWO reasons (6 marks)

Student answer

The period in question is often referred to as the "Golden Years" of Weimar Germany as it was a time of relative improvement. The credit for this work goes in large part to Gustav Stresemann who acted as Chancellor and Foreign Minister in this period. There is no doubt his work was important, as he helped rebuild Germany both with regard to the economy, which had suffered severely in the years of hyper-inflation that followed the Ruhr crisis, and also with its poor relations with other European countries after the war and the Treaty of Versailles.

Examiner feedback

The answer starts well and correctly identifies several reasons. However, there isn't enough explanation and the reasons need to be expanded in order to achieve higher marks. 3 marks awarded.

3. "The Night of the Long Knives was the most important step in Hitler's consolidation of power in the period 1933–4." How far do you agree with this statement? Explain your answer. **[10]**

Analysis

✓ The answer needs to cover the importance of the Night of the Long Knives, but balanced against other factors that consolidated Hitler's power.

✓ Hitler's consolidation of power centred on ensuring that the threats to his position were eliminated.

✓ The Night of the Long Knives focused on the threat posed by members of the SA. This action ensured that they could no longer challenge him.

✓ However, there are other issues to consider—the Enabling Act gave Hitler political power which meant that a dictatorship was all but established; furthermore, the death of Hindenburg meant that there was no longer a person with the authority to remove Hitler's power.

Mark scheme

Level 1:	general answer lacking specific contextual knowledge (1 mark)
Level 2:	identifies AND/OR describes reasons (2–3 marks)
Level 3:	gives a one-sided explanation (4–5 marks) or one explanation of both sides (4–6 marks)
Level 4:	explains both sides (7–9 marks)
Level 5:	explains with evaluation (10 marks)

Student answer

The murderous events of the Night of the Long Knives were clearly important in the consolidation of power in the period 1933–4 for Hitler, as they meant that the threat that political rivals posed to him was dealt with and Hitler had firmly established power over his party.

However, while the Night of the Long Knives was important, it came quite late in the period of consolidation and by this point Hitler had largely established a political dictatorship. The Enabling Act of 1933 was crucial in this, as it meant that Hitler could now pass laws for four years without consulting the Reichstag. Using this power he was able to ban all other political parties, abolish trade unions, and centralise Nazi power. This helped consolidate his power as he was able to ensure he had political dominance.

An even earlier event had also helped consolidate his power. The Reichstag Fire of February 1933 helped eliminate the communist threat and ensure that communists were seen as a public enemy. When the Reichstag building burnt down, a Dutch communist, van der Lubbe, was arrested and charged with starting the fire. Hitler claimed it was proof of a communist plot and used it to create fear of the supposed communist threat. This allowed him to pass further laws restricting people's liberties.

Examiner feedback

The answer is very strong on the opposing factors, and does well to explain political issues and also the importance of the Reichstag Fire. However, there could be more detail on the Night of the Long Knives, as it is the factor raised in the question. 7 marks awarded.

You need to know:

- how far the American economy boomed in the 1920s
- how far American society changed in the 1920s
- how widespread intolerance was in American society
- why Prohibition was introduced and later repealed
- how far the roles of women changed during the 1920s
- the causes and consequences of the Wall Street Crash
- what Hoover did to try to combat the Great Depression
- why Roosevelt won the election of 1932
- what the New Deal, introduced in 1933 was; how successful it was
- how far the character of the New Deal changed after 1933
- why the New Deal encountered opposition
- why unemployment persisted despite the New Deal

Background: the build-up to the 1920s boom

Industry in the United States, based on huge natural resources of coal, timber, iron, and oil, as well as farming, had grown steadily since the mid-19th century.

Although only involved in fighting towards the end of the First World War, American businesses made money supplying arms and equipment as well as loaning money.

The 1920s became the boom years in the United States. However, not everyone shared in the boom with many, notably black, Americans continuing to suffer poverty.

How far did the American economy boom in the 1920s?

Factors on which the economic boom was based	
Invention and innovation	Advances in chemicals and synthetics brought rayon, Bakelite (a form of plastic), and cellophane into common use. Electricity meant consumer goods, including radios, washing machines, vacuum cleaners, and refrigerators, became widely available.
Republican policies	The Republican governments of the 1920s followed financial policies favourable to industry. The approach taken was known as laissez-faire, where the government favoured non-intervention. Taxation was kept low and high import tariffs were introduced.
Mass production	Assembly-line production was used by Henry Ford in the manufacture of cars. This method of production was copied for other goods and led to a fall in their prices.

▲ **Fig. 10.1** *Model T Ford car coming off the production line*

Factors on which the economic boom was based	
The car industry	The car industry was central to economic success in the United States. With the cost of a car reducing in price, one in five Americans owned one by 1929. The car industry boosted a wide range of associated industries including producers of glass, rubber, steel, and leather. The number of roads increased, as did roadside filling stations, hotels, and restaurants.
Mass marketing	Advertising for radio and the cinema was developed, while giant billboards displayed posters alongside highways. New merchandise was advertised in magazines, newspapers, and mail order catalogues.

Why was there a boom?

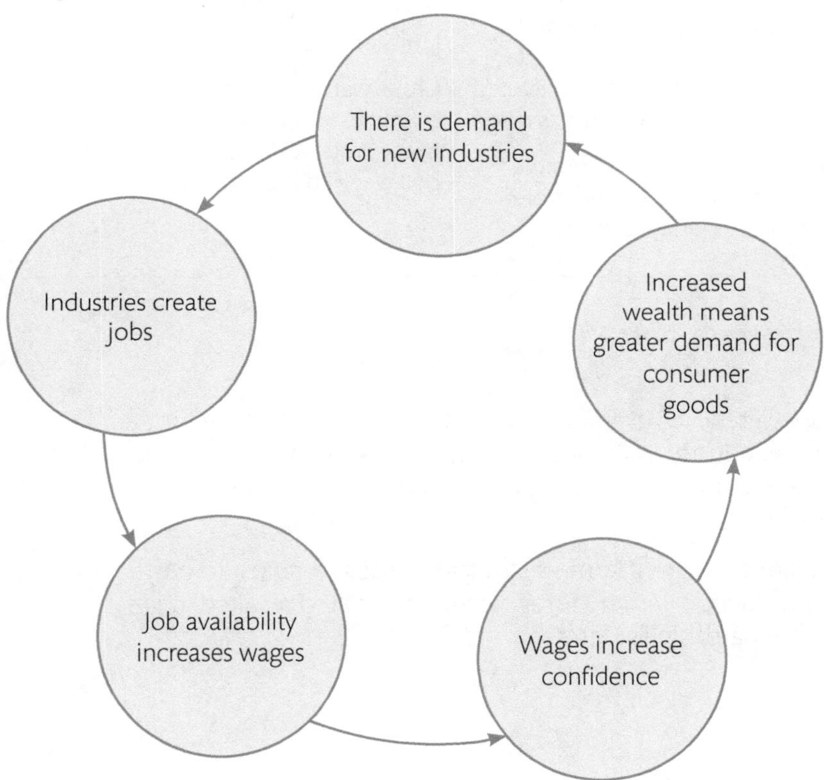

▲ **Fig. 10.2** *Factors leading to a boom*

Recap

Production-line manufacturing meant reduced prices and quicker production of goods. Cars, household items, and radios were mass-produced at a cheap price.

Low taxation and a "laissez-faire" approach from the government were also prevalent.

As jobs became more available, wages rose—and so did personal spending.

Why did some industries prosper while others did not?

Industry grew	Agriculture did not share in the prosperity
The 1920s were a golden age for the construction industry. New businesses required offices and showrooms and they had to be connected by new roads. Many public buildings, including schools, were constructed, as were skyscrapers. Steel production, which was an established industry, gained significant new business from the construction sector. The steel industry was also boosted by car manufacture, as were the industries producing glass, rubber, and leather. While there was an increased demand for clothes, there was less demand for cotton and woollen textiles. The demand was for clothes manufactured using synthetic materials such as rayon. The coal industry suffered from the increased use of cleaner, and more efficient, oil, gas, and electricity alternatives.	During the First World War, agriculture had boomed with exports to Europe. These exports were no longer needed once the war had ended. One of the problems was overproduction. The United States could not eat all the food that was produced; neither could the surplus be exported. As a result, prices fell. American agriculture was facing competition from Canada and Argentina. Many European countries would not take American farm products because the United States had placed high tariffs on imports. Crops were also lost to pests. For example, in cotton-growing areas many crops were devastated by the boll weevil during the 1920s.

Industry grew: for example, the 1920s were a golden age for the building industry, with dazzling new skyscrapers and many public buildings constructed during this period. The car industry also prospered.

Agriculture suffered: farmers struggled, crops were lost to pests, and overproduction with no foreign market to sell to resulted in great financial hardship for farmers.

Which Americans didn't benefit from the boom?

- Families: by 1929, around 60 per cent of families lived below the poverty line.
- Black Americans: with the agricultural slump many moved north to work in the lowest paid sectors such as domestic service. They were segregated into slum areas such as Harlem in New York.
- Native Americans: they mainly lived in reservations where agricultural land was poor quality. Those who remained in the reservations suffered from poverty, poor education, and ill health.
- Immigrants: often only the lowest-paid jobs were available to immigrants. Many suffered religious discrimination and lacked education.

Worked example

How far did all Americans benefit from the boom? (4)

It can be seen that for some American the boom in the 1920s wasn't really a boom. Minority groups suffered.

Black Americans still suffered from segregation and from living in slum areas. The roles they took in society were often the lowest paid, such as jobs in domestic service.

Native Americans suffered, as many still lived in reservations and suffered from poverty, poor education, and ill health. The land they were given was poor in quality, making it difficult to grow crops.

Exam tip

While many Americans benefited greatly from the boom, certain groups didn't. To answer this question choose two groups who suffered rather than benefiting and explain briefly why they suffered.

How far did American society change in the 1920s?

What were the "Roaring Twenties"?

Following the end of the First World War, Americans benefited from increased prosperity. Some spent their new wealth on entertainment.

For some young women life was much freer. For example, this was the decade of less-restrictive clothing than previously: skirts and dresses were shorter, made from lightweight material. Other aspects of a freer life for some young women were wearing make-up, going out without a chaperone, going to night clubs, and dancing to jazz music.

The car gave Americans the freedom of movement to visit clubs, cinemas, and restaurants.

For the majority of the population, however, the "Roaring Twenties" were more an image than a reality.

Entertainment opportunities	
The cinema	Cinema provided an opportunity to escape from the mundane parts of everyday life. Cinema audiences more than doubled, reaching 95 million in 1929. Many new stars were created by Hollywood, including Charlie Chaplin, Mary Pickford, and Rudolph Valentino. "Talkies" arrived in 1927 with the release of the film *The Jazz Singer* starring Al Jolson. Some Americans expressed concern that movies corrupted public morals.
Jazz	Jazz music originated in the African-American community of the south. Jazz was linked to dance music and led to the formation of many night clubs. One well-known jazz performer was Duke Ellington. Jazz appealed to young whites who found it exciting, dynamic, and modern. A new dance, the Charleston, became popular.
Radio	Radio broadcast light musical entertainment to a mass audience, producing the age of the great dance bands. As variety theatres declined, radio provided a fresh start for many artists.
Sport	Sport became a form of mass entertainment. For example, huge crowds attended baseball games.

How widespread was intolerance in American society?

- Many established Americans wanted to maintain traditions and were fearful of those who threatened the American way of life.
- Many saw a threat coming from new immigrants: communists, anarchists, blacks, Jews, and Catholics.
- It was the ambition of many Americans to maintain the supremacy of the white, Anglo-Saxon, Protestant community (WASPs).

Cause	Details	Examples of behaviour
The Red Scare	This was caused by the large number of immigrants arriving from southern and eastern Europe. It was thought that they would attempt to spread communist and anarchist ideas following the Bolshevik Revolution in Russia in 1917.	Suspected agitators were arrested and deported. A series of bomb blasts in 1919 offered evidence of a supposed conspiracy against the state. The case of Italian immigrants Vanzetti and Sacco, who were executed for murder despite evidence being flawed, illustrates the widespread fear of immigrants from southern and eastern Europe.
Religious intolerance	Fundamentalist Christians in rural areas of the south believed in a literal interpretation of the Bible rather than accepting Darwin's theory of evolution.	The fundamentalists succeeded in outlawing the teaching of evolution in six states. In Tennessee, biology teacher John Scopes deliberately broke the law by teaching evolution. The so-called "monkey trial" of 1925 was a national sensation. Scopes was found guilty.
The Jim Crow laws	In the south, black people suffered from segregation under the Jim Crow laws. Most lived in poverty and permanent fear of lynch mobs.	Laws covered everything from marriages to hospital treatment and included the education of children: "[The County Board of Education] shall provide schools of two kinds; those for white children and those for colored children." (Texas law)
Immigration policy	This law restricted entry to the United States of certain national groups.	This affected immigrants from southern and eastern Europe. Immigrants from China and Japan were completely barred. The law resulted in 85 per cent of immigrants to the United States coming from northern Europe.
The Ku Klux Klan	The Ku Klux Klan (also known as simply "the Klan") was the most extreme example of intolerance and racism during the 1920s.	The Klan claimed to have a membership of 5 million in 1925. Membership included high-ranking politicians and government officials. The Klan's hatred went wider than their hatred of black people. Catholics, Jews, foreigners, liberals, and homosexuals were also targets. The most extreme forms of persecution included beating, mutilation, and lynching.

Apply

Write a fact file about three types of intolerance in American society in the 1920s and 1930s.

Why was Prohibition introduced and later repealed?

The 18th Amendment to the American Constitution was passed through Congress in 1919. This prohibited the manufacture, transport, and sale of alcohol.

Why was Prohibition introduced?

- It was claimed that alcohol caused social problems such as poverty, crime, violence, and ill health. The Anti-Saloon League and the Women's Temperance Union were strong campaigners for abolition, suggesting the United States would become a better place.
- The Protestant Church supported the cause, believing that alcohol brought a decline in moral standards and family life in the big cities.
- Some believed that grain used for alcohol could be better used for making bread.
- Some politicians saw it as an opportunity to gain votes.
- Some industrialists, including Nelson Rockefeller, argued that Prohibition would be good for the economy as it would reduce workers' absenteeism and increase efficiency.

Why was Prohibition repealed?

- Consumption of alcohol increased as illegal bars, called "speakeasies", became common. It is believed that by 1929 New York had 32 000 illegal drinking bars.
- Some people tried to make their own alcohol. This was called "moonshine". Drinking moonshine could cause death.
- It was impossible to prevent alcohol being smuggled into the United States. Many of those involved in this illegal trade made large amounts of money. "Bootleg" rum was smuggled from the West Indies and whisky from Canada.
- Prohibition boosted crime. Organised gangs controlled the manufacture and sale of alcohol. There was much feuding between the gangs, leading to incidents such as the Valentine's Day Massacre of 1929 when rival gang members were murdered by Al Capone's gang.
- State officials, judges, senior police officers, and jury members were often given bribes to overlook evidence of consumption of alcohol, or to make a lenient judgment.

Why did Prohibition end?

Practicality	The policy proved unworkable. It was clear by the early 1930s that Prohibition had failed.
Context	At the time of the Depression it seemed illogical to spend public money trying to enforce the law. This money would be better used in creating jobs for the unemployed.
Cost	Money could be made from imposing taxes and duties on alcohol.

Recap

Prohibition was meant to address some of the ills in American society, but it proved unworkable as a policy—it did not have public support.

Americans used "speakeasies" (illegal bars) and "moonshine" (home-made alcohol) as ways to get around the ban.

The illegal alcohol trade also caused wider issues, with rival gangs battling each other for control of this lucrative market, and bribing policemen and government officials to overlook illegal business activity.

When Roosevelt came to power he supported the proposal to repeal Prohibition. This was done under the 18th Amendment. Prohibition ended in December 1933.

Worked example

Why was Prohibition repealed? (6)

Prohibition was ended as it seemed to have been a failed policy. Despite attempts to stop the sale of alcohol, consumption of alcohol actually increased as illegal bars, called "speakeasies", became common. It has been claimed that New York had 32 000 illegal drinking bars by 1929. Some people even tried to make their own alcohol called moonshine.

Prohibition also boosted crime. Gangs controlled an illegal trade in alcohol despite some police efforts to prevent this.

Clashes between gangs led to violence such as the Valentine's Day Massacre of 1929 when rival gang members were murdered by Al Capone's gang. As the police struggled to control the trade in illegal alcohol, violence increased.

Some argued that at the time of the Depression it seemed illogical to spend public money trying to enforce the law of Prohibition and instead the money should be used to create jobs and support the economy.

Exam tip

Prohibition was a failure for many reasons, including the lack of public cooperation, the rise of gang clashes, and the corruption of the police. To answer this question, choose two reasons and explain them.

How far did the roles of women change during the 1920s?

The 1920s brought a revolution in the role of some women. Some became known as "flappers". These were often young, wealthy, middle- and upper-class women from the larger towns and cities. These women were the "showy and noisy" minority.

Politics	In 1920 women got the vote in all states. They now made up 50 per cent or more of the electorate.
Work	The number of women in employment increased by 25 per cent to 10 million by 1929, although women continued to be paid less than men for precisely the same work. Office work and manufacturing accounted for much of the increase of employment for women. In some new industries, such as electronics, women workers were preferred to men.
Dress	Corsets were abandoned and women began wearing shorter, more lightweight skirts and dresses, and the dresses were often sleeveless. The new fashions and materials, such as rayon, permitted greater movement and self-expression.
Lifestyle	Women began smoking, drinking, and kissing in public. Chaperones were no longer required. Women also drove cars. It has been suggested that Henry Ford introduced coloured cars in 1925 as a response to the female market. Previously all Ford cars had been black. Short hair and make-up became symbols of the new freedom. Women were acting with more independence. The divorce rate increased from 100 000 in 1914 to 205 000 in 1929. Labour-saving devices affected the lives of a minority: only 30 per cent of households owned a vacuum cleaner and 24 per cent owned a washing machine.

Did the changes affect all women?

Not all women were affected by the changes. Compared to women in towns and cities, women from rural areas were less affected, continuing their traditional roles and restricted lives. Many of these women actually opposed the changes.

What were the causes and consequences of the Wall Street Crash?

How far was speculation responsible for the Wall Street Crash?

On the stock market everything depended on confidence in the share prices rising. By the end of the 1920s the American economy was slowing down. On "Black Thursday", 24 October 1929, the fall in share prices turned into panic. Prices plunged and desperate investors sold their shares to try to cut their losses.

Thousands were bankrupted as the stock market went into free fall.

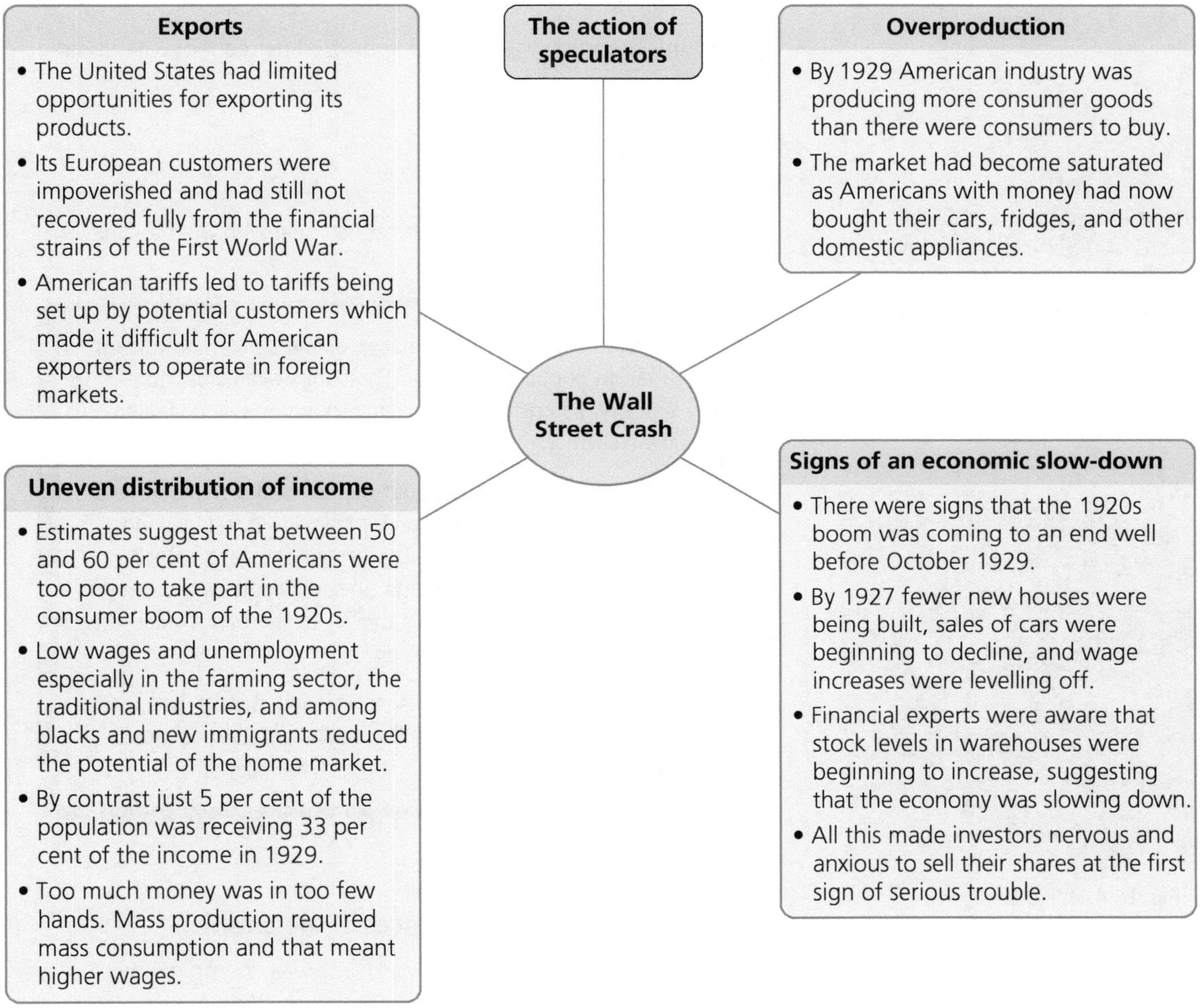

The Wall Street Crash

Exports

- The United States had limited opportunities for exporting its products.
- Its European customers were impoverished and had still not recovered fully from the financial strains of the First World War.
- American tariffs led to tariffs being set up by potential customers which made it difficult for American exporters to operate in foreign markets.

The action of speculators

Overproduction

- By 1929 American industry was producing more consumer goods than there were consumers to buy.
- The market had become saturated as Americans with money had now bought their cars, fridges, and other domestic appliances.

Uneven distribution of income

- Estimates suggest that between 50 and 60 per cent of Americans were too poor to take part in the consumer boom of the 1920s.
- Low wages and unemployment especially in the farming sector, the traditional industries, and among blacks and new immigrants reduced the potential of the home market.
- By contrast just 5 per cent of the population was receiving 33 per cent of the income in 1929.
- Too much money was in too few hands. Mass production required mass consumption and that meant higher wages.

Signs of an economic slow-down

- There were signs that the 1920s boom was coming to an end well before October 1929.
- By 1927 fewer new houses were being built, sales of cars were beginning to decline, and wage increases were levelling off.
- Financial experts were aware that stock levels in warehouses were beginning to increase, suggesting that the economy was slowing down.
- All this made investors nervous and anxious to sell their shares at the first sign of serious trouble.

▲ **Fig. 10.3** *Causes of the Wall Street Crash*

What impact did the Wall Street Crash have on the economy?

- The stock market crash was an economic disaster. The share prices did not stop falling for three years.
- Businesses and banks went bust. Around 11 000 banks stopped trading.
- The economy had to adjust to a general reduction in trade and demand for American goods both at home and abroad.
- Businesses had to reduce their operations by cutting production.
- Workers were dismissed or had their wages reduced.
- Less money in the economy meant that people could not afford to buy goods, and business confidence collapsed. Any thought of expansion had to be abandoned.
- By 1933 the economy was producing only 20 per cent of what it had produced in 1929.

Exam tip

In the answer try to explain the reason behind Roosevelt's actions, but also add some specific detail to support your point.

Worked example

Why did Roosevelt feel it was important to deal with the banking crisis? (6)

Roosevelt felt that the collapse of the banks would mean a fall in public confidence. The banks were close to collapse as customers were panicking and withdrawing their savings.

With such uncertainty Roosevelt ordered a national bank holiday to pass his Emergency Banking Act. Unsound banks were closed down. The remainder were helped with government grants and advice. People with savings were asked to return their money to the banks when the banks reopened.

Through these measures Roosevelt felt that he had addressed concern about the banks' possible collapse, and that he had helped to support the economy.

▲ **Fig. 10.4** *A "Hooverville" in Seattle, 1934*

What were the social consequences of the crash?

- By 1933 nearly one in four of the workforce was unemployed.
- There were no welfare benefits for those without an income (but rents and mortgages still had to be paid).
- Many faced eviction from their home, often being reduced to begging, scavenging in rubbish dumps for food scraps, and sleeping on park benches.
- Shanty towns of tents and makeshift huts, constructed from scrap metal and cardboard boxes, grew up on the edges of towns and cities. These "towns" became known as "Hoovervilles" after the President.

- The unemployed queuing for food from charities or soup kitchens became a common sight.
- In 1932 the government lost support as a result of the way it dealt with the "Bonus Marchers", a group of thousands of destitute army veterans. Their peaceful protest ended in tragedy as the government used the army to disperse them, resulting in 2 veterans being killed and nearly 1000 injured.

The Wall Street Crash had a devastating effect.

- A cycle of suffering was caused—as businesses were forced to close, jobs were lost so people had less money. This forced more businesses to close and tax revenue to fall.
- By 1933 one in four workers was unemployed.
- There was visible unemployment—it was common to see unemployed workers queuing in the streets for food at soup kitchens or for help from other charity organisations.
- Many people were forced to live in shanty towns.

What did Hoover do to try to combat the Great Depression?

- In 1930 taxes were cut by $130 million to inject more purchasing power into the economy.
- Tariffs were increased by the Hawley-Smoot Act (1930) to protect American-produced food and goods.
- Money was provided to finance a building programme to create more jobs. The most famous project was the Hoover Dam on the Colorado River.
- Employers were encouraged to make voluntary agreements with their employees to maintain wages and production.
- The Reconstruction Finance Corporation (1932) was set up to provide loans, amounting to $1500 million, to businesses facing hard times.
- The Federal Farm Board was set up to buy surplus produce in an attempt to stabilise prices.

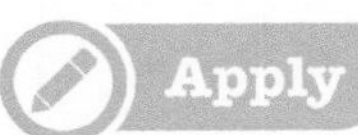

Write a fact file that explains the economic and social consequences of the Wall Street Crash.

Why did Roosevelt win the election of 1932?

	President Herbert Hoover	Franklin D Roosevelt
Approach to the crisis	Hoover's approach to the crisis was to "sit it out" until prosperity returned. When he took action it was regarded as too little, too late.	Roosevelt's election campaign was about giving Americans a "new deal".
Social policies	He was against the government providing welfare support as he thought it would undermine the United States' individualism. This gave the impression of being unsympathetic. This was confirmed by his actions against the Bonus Marchers.	He had a reputation for helping those in need when, as Governor of New York, he set up schemes to help the elderly and the unemployed.
Personality	He failed to project himself as a man of vision, giving an impression of being grim-faced and conservative in his approach.	He had an upbeat personality and appeared warm, charming, and optimistic when on the campaign trail. This approach gave confidence to Americans that they would be helped. He had suffered from polio and many Americans admired the way he had coped with this.

How successful was the New Deal?

What was the New Deal as introduced in 1933?

- The term "New Deal" was applied to various measures introduced by Roosevelt between 1933 and 1938 to rescue the United States from the Great Depression.
- The first phase, introduced between March and June 1933, is referred to as Roosevelt's "First Hundred Days".
- Roosevelt spoke to the public via radio broadcasts, explaining his policies in an informal and friendly manner.

His first action was to deal with the banking crisis. A main feature of this first phase was the creation of "alphabet agencies".

Exam tip

The answer to this question should start with a definition of what the New Deal was, and include specific issues that Roosevelt was trying to address.

Worked example

What was Roosevelt's New Deal of 1933? (4)

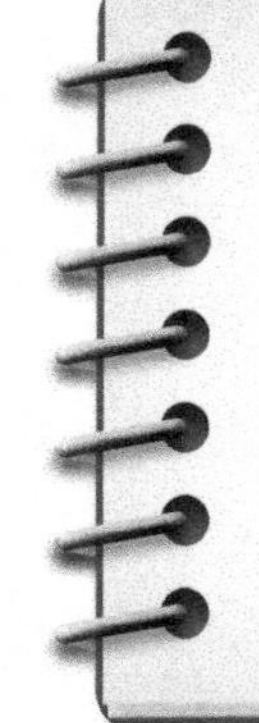

The "New Deal" was the term used for specific measures taken by Roosevelt between 1933 and 1938. Following the Wall Street Crash, the New Deal was devised in an attempt to rescue the United States from the Great Depression.

Between March and June 1933 Roosevelt's "First Hundred Days" saw him try to deal with the banking crisis through his creation of "alphabet agencies" and the passing of the Emergency Banking Act.

The First Hundred Days

Area for reform	Situation	Government action	Effect
Banks	Banks were close to collapse as customers were panicking and withdrawing their savings.	Roosevelt ordered a four-day national bank holiday while the Emergency Banking Act was passed through Congress. Unsound banks, around 5 per cent of the total, were then closed down while the remainder were helped with government grants and advice.	Those with savings were asked to return their money to the banks when they reopened. Public confidence was restored and the banking system survived.
The unemployed	Unemployment stood at nearly 13 million in 1933, approximately 25 per cent of the workforce.	The Civilian Conservation Corps (CCC) was set up to provide voluntary employment for young men aged 18 to 25. They carried out conservation work, such as planting new forests. The Public Works Administration (PWA) provided jobs by initiating major construction projects such as dams, bridges, railways, schools, hospitals, and houses.	Wages were low but the scheme provided work for over 2 million men during the nine years of its existence. The PWA spent $7 billion between 1933 and 1939 creating millions of jobs for skilled workers.
Farmers	The collapse of food prices after 1929 had left the farming industry in crisis.	The Agricultural Adjustment Agency (AAA) paid farmers to take part of their land out of cultivation and reduce their livestock. Millions of acres of sown land were ploughed up and 6 million piglets were slaughtered.	Prices rose, and between 1933 and 1939 farmers' incomes doubled. Farm labourers were not helped by this measure, however, and many found themselves unemployed.
Industry	Wages and production remained low.	The National Industrial Recovery Act set up the National Recovery Administration (NRA) aiming to stabilise production and prices, and to improve working conditions and pay. Voluntary codes were drawn up to regulate prices, output, hours, and wages. Businesses that adopted these codes displayed the NRA badge. The public were encouraged to buy from these companies.	The scheme led to an improvement in working and ended price-cutting wars, but it favoured large firms. When the scheme was declared unconstitutional by the Supreme Court in 1935 Roosevelt made no attempt to revive the idea.
The poor	Relief for the poor had been drastically cut, meaning that the employed were also often homeless too.	The Federal Emergency Relief Administration (FERA) had a budget of $500 million to assist those in desperate need.	The money was used to fund soup kitchens, provide clothing and bedding, and set up work schemes and nursery schools.

How far did the character of the New Deal change after 1933?

During 1935, Roosevelt introduced a new phase of reforms that became known as the "Second New Deal".

- **The Wagner Act, 1935** confirmed the right of workers to join a trade union and replaced the unconstitional National Industrial Recovery Act.
- **The Social Security Act, 1935** provided old-age pensions, unemployment benefit and help for the sick and disabled. It was based on a national insurance scheme.
- **The Works Progress Administration (WPA), 1935** supported efforts to find jobs for the unemployed through a broad range of projects and work programmes.
- **The Resettlement Administration (RA), 1935** aimed to move 500 000 families to areas of better land. While some families benefited, many farm workers remained in poverty.

Apply

Prepare a table of information relating to life for various groups in the United States in the mid-1930s. Complete columns for workers in industry, workers in agriculture, and the unemployed. Include the problems each group faced and what help was available.

Why did the New Deal encounter opposition?

There were people who thought that Roosevelt did not go far enough in his reforms, while others thought he was too radical.

Radical opposition came from critics such as the following individuals.

- Father Coughlin became disillusioned as he felt Roosevelt was failing to tackle the problems of the poor. Coughlin broadcast his ideas on radio every Sunday evening to an enormous national audience.
- Dr Francis Townsend campaigned for pension reform through his "Townsend Clubs". He claimed that Roosevelt was more interested in preserving society than changing it.
- Huey Long planned a major redistribution of wealth to stimulate the economy. He planned to take money from the very rich and redistribute it among the less affluent.

Conservative opposition came from the following groups.

- Republicans believed that there should be minimal government intervention and low taxation. The New Deal was seen to undermine what were regarded as core American values. They thought that Roosevelt was becoming too powerful and was acting like a dictator.
- Businessmen resented the level of government interference. They thought it was a form of socialism and un-American. They were unhappy with Roosevelt's support for trade unions.
- The rich thought that it was unfair that they had to pay to help the less fortunate. Many felt that Americans had always believed in self-help. They said that the policy would encourage people to be lazy.
- Some state governors argued that aspects of the New Deal conflicted with the rights of state governments to manage their own affairs.

There was also opposition from the Supreme Court.

- The main role of the Supreme Court was to ensure that any measures introduced were consistent with the American Constitution.
- The nine Republican judges at the Supreme Court disliked the political policies on which the New Deal was based.

- They declared the National Recovery Administration (NRA) and the Agricultural Adjustment Act (AAA) unconstitutional.
- Following his re-election in 1936, Roosevelt wanted to appoint six additional judges sympathetic to his policies.
- He was accused of trying to overthrow the Constitution and acting like a dictator.
- He withdrew his plan to appoint new judges who would support the New Deal.

Worked example

"The New Deal was a failure." How far do you agree with this statement? Explain your answer. (10)

It can be argued that the New Deal failed in many ways despite the high acclaim and praise it earned. There were some who thought that the New Deal, and Roosevelt in particular, didn't go far enough in what was achieved. Individuals such as the outspoken Father Coughlin thought Roosevelt failed to tackle the problems of the poor and voiced this view on his weekly radio broadcast. Similarly, Dr Francis Townsend thought that the New Deal didn't reform the situation for the elderly and campaigned for pension reform through his "Townsend Clubs".

Roosevelt also faced political opposition from Republicans who believed that there should be minimal government intervention and low taxation—the New Deal seemed to undermine this through increased government intervention in people's lives. Republicans saw Roosevelt as building his own power base, and acting like a dictator.

However, the New Deal can be judged a success in many ways. Roosevelt's policies gave many Americans new hope, new confidence, and a sense of purpose. He also managed to address several of the key problems facing the country. Unemployment fell by over 30 per cent between 1933 and 1939, and the introduction of welfare payments and other emergency benefits such as food, clothing, and shelter helped millions who needed it most. Ordinary workers benefited from the support of trade unions, and farmers saw an increase in prices.

Overall. although the New Deal was far from perfect, and certain groups felt it didn't go far enough, it managed to address several grave problems facing the United States at a time of severe crisis.

Exam tip

When answering 10-mark questions remember to examine both sides of the question as well as offering a summative conclusion to the argument.

Why did unemployment persist despite the New Deal?

In 1933 Roosevelt became President and the unemployment figure was 12.8 million. In 1941 this figure was 5.6 million. During the years of the New Deal, unemployment never fell below 5 million. What were the reasons for this?

- The New Deal found work for millions of people but it was in jobs that were not secure.
- Incomes for many Americans remained low, reducing the money available to spend on American goods.
- There was a worldwide depression so the foreign market was not purchasing American goods. Import tariffs were common practice in Europe as well as the United States.
- Changes in manufacturing required fewer labourers.

Did the fact that the New Deal failed to solve unemployment mean that it was a failure?

	The New Deal as a success	The New Deal as a failure
Unemployment	Unemployment fell by over 30 per cent between 1933 and 1939.	Unemployment never fell below 14 per cent of the workforce between 1933 and 1939.
Industry	Industrial development and prosperity were stimulated by the construction of schools, roads, and hydro-electric dams.	Imposed rules and regulations, the increases in taxation, and the encouragement given to trade unions held back industrial development.
Trade unions	Trade union membership increased to over 7 million. Many strikes were settled in the workers' favour. Working conditions generally improved, as did workers' pay.	Businessmen and industrialists strongly disliked the encouragement given to unions under the Wagner Act. Some companies were prepared to use violence to break up strikes and sit-ins.
Particular groups	Large-scale farmers benefited from the reductions in acreage and livestock, and the increase in prices. The introduction of welfare payments and other emergency benefits such as food, clothing, and shelter helped millions who needed it most.	Tenant farmers, labourers, and sharecroppers were forced off the land by government plans to reduce agricultural production. Although some black people made gains in employment and housing they did not benefit as much as white people—Roosevelt needed the support of Democrats in the south and this prevented him from introducing civil rights laws the southern Democrats would have opposed.

	The New Deal as a success	The New Deal as a failure
The impact of the New Deal	The impact was **huge**– Roosevelt's policies gave many Americans new hope, new confidence, and a sense of purpose.	The impact was **limited**– it was pre-war defence spending and the supplying of armaments to Britain and France that stimulated the economy. Rearmament rather than the New Deal was primarily responsible for the economic revival of 1939 and 1941.

Review

1. What was the main development in the car industry during the 1920s? **[4]**
2. What problems did farmers face in the 1920s? **[4]**
3. How significant were Republican policies in causing the boom in the United States in the 1920s? **[4]**
4. How significant was the impact of the economic boom on the people of America? **[4]**
5. Describe the activities of the Ku Klux Klan. **[4]**
6. Describe a Hooverville. **[4]**
7. Why was the American economy showing signs of weakness by 1929? **[6]**
8. Why did the government deal harshly with the Bonus Marchers? **[6]**
9. Why did some industries prosper more than others during the boom in the 1920s? **[6]**
10. To what extent was intolerance a feature of American society in the 1920s? **[10]**
11. "The significance of the impact of the Ku Klux Klan on American society was greater than that of Prohibition." How far do you agree with this statement? Explain your answer. **[10]**
12. "Hoover could only blame himself for losing the presidential election of 1932." How far do you agree with this statement? Explain your answer. **[10]**
13. How significant was speculation as a cause of the Wall Street Crash? **[10]**
14. How important was Roosevelt's promise of a "new deal" in him being elected President in 1932? **[10]**
15. How significant was the opposition of the Supreme Court in limiting the impact of Roosevelt's New Deal? **[10]**

For further information review this section in the Student Book.

1. What was Prohibition? **[4]**

Analysis

- In the answer aim to write two well-explained points setting out what prohibition was and why it was introduced.
- Prohibition meant that the manufacture, transport, and sale of alcohol was illegal.
- It was introduced in the United States in an attempt to address social issues which many believed were caused by alcohol such as poverty, crime, violence, and ill health.
- Various campaigners wanted prohibition introduced, including the Anti-Saloon League, and the Women's Temperance Union.
- Others saw the benefit as improving the work ethic of ordinary Americans who thought a sober society would be a harder-working one.

Mark scheme

1 mark for each relevant point, additional mark for supporting detail, maximum 2 marks per point made.

Student answer

Prohibition was the prohibiting of the manufacture, transport, and sale of alcohol in the United States in 1919. It was the 18th Amendment to the American Constitution and lasted 13 years.

Examiner feedback

The answer correctly explains the facts of prohibition, in terms of what it was and how long it lasted. This is one developed point, and another is needed to secure full marks. 2 marks awarded.

2. Why was the New Deal criticised? **[64]**

Analysis

✓ In the answer aim to make two well-developed points explaining different reasons why the New Deal was criticised.

✓ The New Deal faced political opposition from the Republicans, who thought that it represented too much interference in people's lives and gave Roosevelt too much power.

✓ It was also opposed by the Supreme Court, who ruled that the National Recovery Administration (NRA) and the Agricultural Adjustment Act (AAA) were unconstitutional.

✓ Additionally, different elements of society disliked it—some of the rich thought that it was unfair that they had to pay to help the less fortunate, while others such as Father Coughlin felt that Roosevelt was failing to tackle the problems of the poor.

Mark scheme

Level 1:	general answer lacking specific contextual knowledge (1 mark)
Level 2:	identifies AND/OR describes reasons (2–3 marks)
Level 3:	explains ONE reason (4–5 marks)
Level 4:	explains TWO reasons (6 marks)

Student answer

The New Deal was criticised as it was seen to be too interfering in people's lives and there were groups who resented this. Republicans believed that there should be low taxation, and the New Deal was seen to undermine this. Businessmen also resented the level of government interference, as they felt that Roosevelt's support for trade unions undermined their own abilities to run their businesses. The wealthier people in American society also felt it was too much—it was their taxes that were used to support the unemployed and they felt that this government help would encourage people to be lazy.

Examiner feedback

This is a strong explanation of one reason why some Americans disliked the New Deal. There are different groups covered, and it is a well-developed point. To gain the additional mark another reason needs to be covered. 5 marks awarded.

3. "The roles of women changed little during the 1920s."
How far do you agree with this statement? **[10]**

Analysis

- ✓ You need to evaluate the argument in the question by considering the evidence that the roles of women changed very little in the 1920s. Then you need to present evidence that supports the opposite view.
- ✓ Women continued to be paid less for work.
- ✓ The much heralded labour-saving devices were only used in a minority of homes.
- ✓ It is worth noting that women from rural areas were less affected by the changes. They continued in their traditional roles and were less influenced by the changes in the larger towns and cities.
- ✓ However, there were significant developments—women could now vote, many more jobs were created and society for them developed through a more relaxed attitude to fashions and lifestyles.

Mark scheme

Level 1:	general answer lacking specific contextual knowledge (1 mark)
Level 2:	identifies AND/OR describes reasons (2–3 marks)
Level 3:	gives a one-sided explanation (4–5 marks) or one explanation of both sides (4–6 marks)
Level 4:	explains both sides (7–9 marks)
Level 5:	explains with evaluation (10 marks)

Student answer

Evidence seems to suggest that for women roles changed a great deal during the 1920s. In 1920 women got the vote in all states. The opportunity for employment also increased and the number of women working increased by 25 per cent to 10 million by 1929.

Their roles in the home also changed, as labour-saving devices such as vacuum cleaners and washing machines came onto the market.

Women also drove cars and their appearance started to change, as short hair and make-up became symbols of the new freedom. This new independence saw an increase in the divorce rate from 100 000 in 1914 to 205 000 in 1929.

Examiner feedback

Many reasons for why women's roles changed are identified here, covering a range of areas. However, what the student doesn't do is explain the points made, or offer a counter argument. 3 marks awarded.

You need to know:

- how the Jewish state of Israel was established
- how Israel was able to survive despite the hostility of its Arab neighbours
- what the impact of the Palestinian refugee issue was
- why it has proved impossible to resolve the Arab-Israeli issue

Background: history of the conflict between the Israelis and Palestinians

Conflict between Israelis and Palestinians arises from the fact that both can lay a historical claim on land in the Middle East. The Jews can trace their occupation of Palestine back at least until 1000 BCE and they lived there until being expelled by their Roman rulers around 135 CE. The Jews settled in almost every part of the Roman Empire until the Middle Ages when they were expelled, settling in Russia and Poland. In the 19th century, facing persecution, many Jews fled to Western Europe and the United States.

For many centuries, the Arabs lived in the lands we now call the Middle East. The Arabs all spoke Arabic and were converted to Islam, becoming Muslims. By the end of the 19th century the Arab Empire, which from the 7th century had spread across the Middle East and North Africa, was in gradual decline under the control of the Turks. With the persecution of Jews in Europe increasing, both groups developed plans to create a homeland in Palestine. A form of Jewish nationalism, Zionism, gained support with 60 000 Zionists settling in Palestine by 1914.

How was the Jewish state of Israel established?

What were the causes of conflict between Jews and Arabs in Palestine?

The First World War was a turning point in the Arab struggle for independence as well as the Jewish struggle for a homeland.

- The British offered to create an Arab homeland in return for assistance in the war against the Turks. At the same time they offered to create a Jewish homeland in Palestine. This appealed to the United States (where many Jews had settled) and encouraged the United States to enter the war against Germany.
- What this did was to create further potential for conflict.
- At the end of the war, control over the region was passed to Britain under the terms of a League of Nations mandate. For the next 30 years the British government ruled Palestine.
- The Arabs were resentful of the British betrayal and were even more angered by increasing Jewish immigration. The Zionists, meanwhile, feared the British were aiming for the creation of an Arab state in Palestine.

The fact that the British were unable to satisfy either Arabs or Jews resulted in violence throughout the 1920s and early 1930s. Further complications arose due to several events.

- 1933 onwards—Nazi anti-Semitism drove many Jews to flee to Palestine. If the British restricted immigration they were accused of not helping Jews avoid Nazi persecution. If they allowed unrestricted immigration, the Arabs' fears of losing their country would increase.

- 1937—the Peel Commission, a British enquiry, recommended the partition of Palestine into two separate states. The Arabs rejected this and continued fighting.
- 1939—a British White paper was published that made no reference to partition, and so outraged the Jews. With war in Europe looming, the British government attempted to pacify the Arabs so that oil supplies from the Middle East would continue.

Both the Jews and the Arabs felt they had a legitimate claim on Palestine. The British were attempting to find a solution that pleased both sides, but the reality of doing this was very difficult.

Recap

The Jews and the Arabs were both important to Britain: Arab support in the Middle East was vital for trade and oil supplies, while there were strong ties to the Jewish community in both Britain and the United States.

What was the significance of the end of the Second World War for Palestine?

After the war ended, the newly elected British Labour Government was unsympathetic towards Zionism. The British government wanted an independent Palestine in which Arabs and Jews would share power. Britain began blocking the mass immigration of Jews to Palestine. The refusal by the British to allow the entry of survivors of the Holocaust was widely criticised.

- In October 1945 the Haganah, militant Zionists, joined forces with Irgun and Lehi in a guerrilla war against the British authorities. Acts of terrorism against the British increased. Two British soldiers were hanged by members of Irgun. This was in revenge for the execution of three Irgun members.
- On 22 July 1946 the most notorious act against the British occurred. The Irgun bombed the King David Hotel, a base for the British authorities, killing over 90 people.
- In July 1947 a ship carrying 4000 Holocaust survivors, the Exodus, was sent back to Europe.
- By 1948, 220 British soldiers had been killed by Jewish terrorists under the banner of the Hebrew Resistance Movement in an attempt to force the British out.

US President Truman began to put pressure on Britain to allow Jewish refugees to enter Palestine. Many Americans now supported a state of Israel.

Facing extreme political pressure from the United States, as well as being aware of the problems at home to deal with, Britain gave up control of Palestine.

The UN and Palestine

In February 1947 the British announced that it would hand Palestine over to the UN and that its mandate would end on 15 May 1948.

In November 1947 the UN decided that Palestine would be divided into two states, one Jewish and one Arab.

- The Arab territories would consist of three geographically separate areas.
- The Jews were to be given over half of the land, but only formed one-third of the population.
- Jerusalem would be governed by an international trusteeship.
- The two new states would form one economic union, with a single currency and customs area.

On 10 October 1947 the United States announced support for partition as President Truman was anxious not to lose access to oil supplies.

Three days later the Soviet Union also announced its support.

However, the plan was rejected by both the Arabs and Jews.

Why the Jews didn't like the plan	Why the Arabs didn't like the plan
• Some Jews were unhappy that many Jewish settlements were included within the Arab state. • The Jews did not like the idea of the city of Jerusalem being controlled by an international force.	• The Jews were given a larger area of Arab land, which the Arabs did not want to relinquish. • The Arabs thought the western powers should find a home for the Jews elsewhere. • The Arab state would be divided into three zones. It would have no direct access to the sea as Jaffa, the main Arab port, would be cut off from the rest of the Arab land. This land was mostly desert country, making it difficult to farm.

Responsibility for implementation of the plan was given to a new body, the UN Palestine Commission. Britain refused access to Palestine for the new body.

With the British setting 1 May 1948 as the date of their withdrawal, Jews and Arabs prepared themselves for a military solution to the future of Palestine.

Why did the British hand Palestine over to the United Nations? (6)

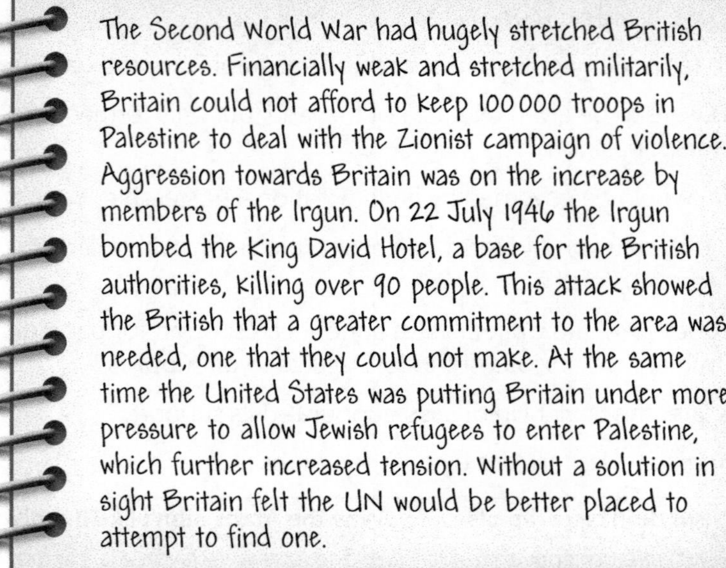
The Second World War had hugely stretched British resources. Financially weak and stretched militarily, Britain could not afford to keep 100 000 troops in Palestine to deal with the Zionist campaign of violence. Aggression towards Britain was on the increase by members of the Irgun. On 22 July 1946 the Irgun bombed the King David Hotel, a base for the British authorities, killing over 90 people. This attack showed the British that a greater commitment to the area was needed, one that they could not make. At the same time the United States was putting Britain under more pressure to allow Jewish refugees to enter Palestine, which further increased tension. Without a solution in sight Britain felt the UN would be better placed to attempt to find one.

Exam tip

The level of specific detail in an answer is always important, and this answer provides a good model: it presents relevant factual information that backs up the point being made.

Why was Israel able to win the war of 1948–9?

Civil war in Palestine

- In December 1947, following the publication of the Partition Plan, violence between Jews and Arabs intensified. This violence included a fierce struggle to control the roads leading to Jerusalem.
- Soldiers from Iraq and Syria came to Palestine to aid the Arabs. In the meantime, Haganah, using its experience of fighting the British in the Second World War, organised Jewish defence forces. Immediately before the British withdrawal some of the bloodiest fighting took place in and around Jerusalem.
- The actions of the Irgun and Lehi fighters helped to create terror in the minds of Arab villagers. In one incident on 10 April 1948 the village of Deir Yassin was attacked by Irgun fighters who claimed it was an Arab headquarters. Over 250 of the men, women, and children from the village were killed.
- By May 1948, when the British withdrew, 300 000 Arabs had fled from what was to become the new Jewish state. Their departure demoralised those Palestinians who remained.
- In April 1948 the Jews captured the city of Haifa and attacked Jaffa. Over 100 000 Palestinians fled from these two towns. Neighbouring Arab governments were unhappy about the news of large numbers of Palestinian refugees, fearing they would have to support them.

The war of independence

On 14 May 1948 the new state of Israel was proclaimed by David Ben-Gurion, the new leader of the Israeli government. On the following day armies from five Arab states (Egypt, Syria, Jordan, Lebanon, and Iraq) invaded Israel.

1. The first ceasefire was in June. By this time the Arabs, ordered by the UN, had occupied approximately one-third of Israel's territory, including the Jewish quarter of Jerusalem.
2. The second phase proved more successful for the Israelis. They were able to recapture the parts of Jerusalem previously lost, push the Syrians back and completely remove the Egyptian forces from Israeli land.
3. In the third phase of fighting, Israel consolidated its earlier gains and even crossed into southern Lebanon.

An armistice was agreed between Israel and Egypt on 24 February 1949 and with other Arab combatants between March and July.

Israeli strengths and Arab weaknesses

Israeli strengths	Weaknesses of the Arab forces
The determination of the Israeli people—the Israelis: • were fighting for their survival and were determined to win • had a desire to protect what they had been fighting for since 1945 • were helped by morale-boosting support from the United States • received financial help from Jews in Europe and the United States. The Israeli armed forces: • used the experience gained in the Second World War and the guerrilla campaign against the British • were better equipped than the Arab forces • had total air superiority • had strong military leadership.	The weaknesses of the Arab forces included: • inexperienced military forces with weak military leadership • unreliable communications that impacted on medical supplies • their numbers—the Arabs had 7000 fewer fighters than the 30 000 Israelis.

Significance for Israel

- Israel was able to increase its territory by 21 per cent. Britain, France, and the United States agreed to protect Israel against future incursions.
- Israel suffered heavy losses, with 4000 soldiers and 2000 civilians losing their lives.

Significance for the Arabs

- The Arab states failed in their bid to destroy Israel. Any, hope the Palestinians had of creating their own state had been destroyed.
- For the Palestinian Arabs it was "the catastrophe". The entire population was now divided between the five Arab nations and two areas of Palestine not taken over by Israel; the West Bank and Gaza.
- Around 700 000 Arabs had fled their homes and many were now living in refugee camps.
- There was now a reason for future Palestinian freedom fighters to join the conflict.

Apply

Read from the beginning of this chapter again. Produce a mind map to show the issues that exist over Palestine and have brought Israelis and Palestinian Arabs to a state of conflict.

How was Israel able to survive despite the hostility of its Arab neighbours?

The Suez Crisis, 1956

By 1956 the Arab–Israeli conflict was to raise its head again as Arab nations refused to accept the new nation of Israel.

Events leading to war

The United States and Britain wanted to maintain an ally in the Middle East. They offered to help the President of Egypt, Nasser, to build the Aswan Dam. They thought this would help to control him. Nasser requested weapons to defend Egypt from Israeli reprisal raids but, because he recognised the new communist government in China, funding was withdrawn.

- In September 1955, Nasser shocked the West by agreeing to buy Russian arms from Czechoslovakia, a communist ally of the Russians.
- On 26 July 1956 Nasser announced the nationalisation of the Suez Canal and the blockading of the Straits of Tiran, at the entrance to Gulf of Aqaba. This latter action would prevent Israeli ships from reaching the Port of Eilat.
- Between 22 and 24 October 1956 the British and French Foreign Ministers met with Israeli Prime Minister David Ben-Gurion in France for secret talks. They agreed:
  - to teach Nasser a lesson
  - to destroy the Fedayeen
  - to break the blockade of the Tiran Straits.

They assumed that Israel would invade the Sinai Peninsula. Britain and France would then call on Israeli and Egyptian forces to withdraw. Britain and France, acting as peacemakers, would then invade Suez to stop the fighting and remove Nasser.

Events of the war

- Israel invaded Egypt on 29 October 1956, advancing deep into Sinai.
- The next day France and Britain ordered both Israel and Egypt to withdraw.
- Egypt refused. Britain and France responded with military action. There were worldwide protests at this action.
- The UN voted for an immediate ceasefire and the United States refused to support the invasion.
- The Arab countries stopped supplying oil to Britain. The Russians threatened to use military force.
- The Americans refused to supply oil to Britain and France so these two countries had no choice but to agree to a humiliating ceasefire.

The British and French believed that a show of force would make Nasser withdraw.

The reaction of the United States to the use of military action against Nasser was a shock to Britain

Results of the war for Israel

- The war demonstrated that Israel was able to inflict heavy military defeats on its Arab rivals.
- The bases of the Fedayeen had been destroyed.
- All of Sinai had been occupied. (Israel withdrew in 1957.)

- The blockade of the Tiran Straits had been removed.
- Israel was able to secure its relationship with the United States.

Results of the war for the Arab world

- The war was a heavy defeat.
- Nasser became the hero of the Arab world for defying Britain and France.
- Nasser had gained complete control of the Suez Canal.
- Many Arab states became more anti-Western and willing to seek Russian aid.
- They were united in opposition to the state of Israel.
- Arab states acquired funding for the Aswan Dam and supplies of weapons from the Soviet Union.

Results of the war for Britain and France

- In the eyes of the international community the credibility of the two countries was severely damaged.
- They had not achieved any of their aims.
- Nasser remained in power in Egypt.
- The Suez Canal was closed.
- The governments in Britain and France had to introduce petrol rationing.

The Six-Day War, 1967

After the Suez Crisis, Israel continued to modernise its army, aided by the United States, Britain, France, and West Germany. The Arabs continued to receive military support from the Soviet Union.

Events leading to war

Tensions in the Middle East continued to develop as several countries took aggressive actions.

- Border skirmishes continued between the Israelis and Palestinian guerrilla groups such as Fatah. This was a constant problem for those living in border settlements.
- At the 1964 Cairo Conference, the Palestine Liberation Organisation (PLO) was created.

Apply

Israel had to withdraw from land it had conquered. Does this mean that Israel gained little from the Suez–Sinai War? In a table with columns "Yes" and "No", list points supporting each view.

Recap

For Britain: the Suez Crisis did not end well. The British damaged relations with the United States and the Arab nations.

For Israel: the crisis showed the military might the Israelis possessed, and they were also able to secure key territorial gains.

The Suez Crisis strengthened the position of Nasser as a powerful figure in the region.

- Following the overthrow of its government, Syria became more violently anti-Israeli and border raids continued.
- On 11 May 1967 Israel's Prime Minister warned that Israel would strike back against Syria if the attacks continued.

The following day a false account began to spread throughout the Arab countries. According to the information passed by the Soviet Union to Syria and Egypt, Israel was massing its armed forces on the Syrian border, ready to attack.

Nasser put 100 000 troops on alert. On 16 May he increased tension by ordering the UN force that had been patrolling the Israeli–Egyptian border since 1956 to leave Egyptian territory.

On 23 May Nasser closed the Gulf of Aqaba to Israeli ships. Israel regarded this as an act of aggression.

By 28 May Egypt, Jordan, Syria, Iraq and Lebanon were among the eight Arab states ready to attack.

On 5 June the Israeli air force took off and the conflict began.

Events of the war

Monday 5 June	Israeli air force bombed and destroyed almost all Egyptian planes while they were still on the ground. Both the Jordanian and Syrian air forces were virtually crippled.
Tuesday 6 June	Israeli troops entered Sinai and the West Bank. In a race to the Suez Canal, the Israelis decimated the Egyptian military capability. There was heavy fighting between Israelis and Jordanians for control of the West Bank of the River Jordan and Jerusalem.
Wednesday 7 June	The Israelis won control of Sinai and Jerusalem. A UN demand for a ceasefire with Egypt was accepted by Israel. Jordan accepted the proposed ceasefire.
Thursday 8 June	Israel won control of the West Bank. Egypt accepted the UN demand of a ceasefire after suffering a heavy defeat in Sinai.
Friday 9 June	Israel attacked Syria, taking the Golan Heights.
Saturday 10 June	Syria accepted the UN proposal of a ceasefire.

Results of the war for Israel

- The Israelis were fighting for their nation's survival and achieved an exceptional victory against Arabs armed with modern Soviet weaponry. The speed of attack and the pre-emptive air strike planned by Moshe Dayan had been crucial.

- The speed of dealing with Egyptian and Jordanian forces brought an early ceasefire. This allowed Israel to divert all its attention to Syria and the Golan Heights.
- In six days, Israel had managed to triple its size and increase its security.
- The eastern part of Jerusalem was captured. The holy city was now under Israeli control for the first time in nearly 2000 years.

Results of the war for the Arab world

- The conflict created the issue of the plight of over 1 million Palestinian Arabs living in Gaza, the West Bank, East Jerusalem and the Golan Heights. The UN started to explore ways to achieve a lasting peace.
- The Arabs were more hostile than ever, still refusing to recognise Israel.

Exam tip

It is a good idea to set out the results of the war for two different groups affected by the war—Israeli leaders and also those suffering the human cost of the war through the refugee crisis. This answer could further develop to include impact on Arabic nations if a broader scale was needed.

Worked example

What were the results of the Six-Day War? (4)

For Israel the war meant that it gained huge amounts of territory in a short time. In less than a week the country had tripled its size and crucially it had captured the eastern part of Jerusalem, a hugely important religious site for Israel.

Another significant impact of the war was the refugee situation it created. One million Palestinian Arabs living in Gaza, the West Bank, East Jerusalem, and the Golan Heights were displaced and became refugees.

The Yom Kippur War, 1973

Events leading to war

The Arabs had been humiliated in the Six-Day War and wanted to regain their pride. Nasser died in 1970 to be replaced by Anwar Sadat. The new ruler was keen to bring change.

- Sadat wanted to regain Sinai.
- In return Sadat was willing to recognise the state of Israel.
- The Israelis had no wish to open discussions. Sadat had hoped the United States would use its influence but this did not happen.
- Support for Sadat came from Saudi Arabia and Syria for a further war, especially as the Israelis were increasing their control over Sinai and the Golan Heights.
- For Sadat, the building of new Jewish settlements in the occupied territories was extreme provocation.

Events of the war

On 6 October 1973, Egyptian and Syrian forces launched an attack. It was the Jewish holiday of Yom Kippur. Large numbers of Israeli forces were on holiday and the Israelis were caught by surprise.

Part of Sinai was taken back, Israeli forces were defeated at the Golan Heights and Soviet-supplied surface-to-air missiles were effective against the Israeli air force.

It took the Israelis three days to mobilise fully. Once mobilised (on 9 October) the Israelis:

- recaptured the Golan Heights within two days
- pushed the Egyptians back across the Suez Canal, cutting off their Third Army
- were aided by US President Nixon, who refused to broker a ceasefire until Israel regained all its lost territory.

Oil was also a factor in this war.

- Arab oil-producing states decided to reduce oil production until the Israelis withdrew from lands they had occupied since 1967.
- Saudi Arabia banned oil exports to the United States. Supplies to Europe were reduced significantly.
- Over 12 months, prices of oil in the United States increased 387 per cent, triggering a rise in unemployment and an economic crisis. The embargo was removed in March 1974.

A joint United States–Soviet initiative arranged through the UN brought fighting to an end on 24 October.

The Yom Kippur attack was another military success for the Israelis. However, the Arab world realised that significant power could result from using oil as a factor of control over Western involvement in the Middle East.

Results of the war for Israel

- The war showed again the military superiority of the Israelis and their ability to inflict huge casualties on their opponents despite the vulnerabilities highlighted by the surprise attack.
- Israel realised that lasting security could only be achieved by diplomacy.

Results of the war for the Arab world

- By using the oil embargo the Arab states had found an effective way to limit foreign support and bring a conclusion to the conflict.
- Egypt and the United States developed closer relations. This was a change in American policy.

In 1973 President Nixon stated, "Oil without a market does not do a country much good." What do you think he meant? How does this quote impact on American support for Israel in conflicts at this time? Write two short paragraphs, one to answer each of these questions.

Results of the war for other nations

- The oil embargo was a powerful economic weapon resulting in rising prices in the West and damage to economies of a number of nations. There was a view that a solution to the problems in the Middle East should be found.
- The embargo illustrated the vulnerability of the West to changes in oil cost and supply, resulting in the United States starting a programme to become self-sufficient in oil by 1980.

How significant was superpower involvement in Arab–Israeli conflicts?

The involvement of the United States

- Support to Israel started with the creation of the state of Israel.
- In the early years, Israel relied more on France than the United States for economic and military support. Indeed, the United States tried to limit arms sales to Israel and its Arab neighbours.

- Under Eisenhower, American policy moved towards finding a lasting peace.
- The Israeli invasion of Egypt in 1956 shocked and concerned the United States who insisted Israel withdraw from its position in the Sinai desert.
- In 1957 American support for non-communist regimes in the Middle East gave more positive support to Israel's security.
- Driven by the fear of communist expansion in the region, military loans had reached record levels by the end of the 1960s.
- President Johnson adopted a strongly pro-Israel policy, with major arms deals and the protection of Israel's gains following the 1967 war.
- The most significant military contribution was in the Yom Kippur War, where the United States responded quickly to replace large numbers of tanks destroyed in the surprise attack.
- The United States played a key role in the ending of the war of 1973, driven by the oil issue and a need to maintain good relations with the Soviet Union. President Nixon and his National Security Advisor, Henry Kissinger, organised settlements between Egypt and Israel, and Syria and Israel in the early months of 1974.

American support for Israel can be seen to support the United States' own objectives too, such as protecting oil supplies and funding non-communist regimes.

The involvement of the Soviet Union

- During the early years of Israel's existence, Stalin saw the possibility of an ally in the Middle East. He was also keen to reduce British influence in the region.
- By 1955, within the context of the Cold War, the United States' refusal to supply arms to Egypt opened the way for Czechoslovakia, a Soviet ally.
- The Soviets' links with Nasser and Egypt were strengthened, with financial aid given for the Aswan Dam project and diplomatic support during the Suez Crisis of 1956. The Soviets exploited this to the full, deflecting attention away from the invasion of Hungary.
- In 1967 the Soviet Union passed intelligence to Egypt about the build-up of Israeli forces on the Syrian border. This information proved to be false. Did the Soviet Union intend to provoke a war in the Middle East at a time when the United States was distracted by Vietnam?
- The Soviet Union supported Egypt before the Yom Kippur War, providing surface-to-air missiles and anti-tank weapons. This enabled the Egyptians to prevent Israel using its air superiority to the full.
- The Soviet Union was involved in brokering a ceasefire, after which relations between the two countries deteriorated.

By the 1990s how far had problems that existed between Israel and her neighbours been resolved?

Israeli–Palestinian attempts at peacemaking in the 1970s

- After the Yom Kippur War of 1973 Egypt was the first of the Arab states to appear willing to recognise the state of Israel. Similarly, Palestinian political leader Yasser Arafat and some PLO leaders were less determined to remove the state of Israel.
- In 1974 Arafat was invited to speak at the UN. Although some Israelis were encouraged by this, many were extremely dissatisfied with the UN. The main issues still remained.

- In 1977 Sadat surprised the world by going to Israel to discuss peace. A month later Israel's Prime Minister Begin went to Egypt and peace talks were started. In September 1978, following a slowdown in the talks, Sadat and Begin went to Camp David, the retreat of the US President, to meet President Carter.
- A framework for peace was drawn up. The main points were that:
  - Israeli forces were to be withdrawn from Sinai
  - Egypt was to regain all of Sinai within three years
  - Israeli shipping was to have free passage through the Suez Canal and the Straits of Tiran.

In March 1979 a peace treaty was signed confirming the points agreed at Camp David. Both sides recognised the other's right to have secure, recognised boundaries.

Israeli–Palestinian attempts at peacemaking in the 1990s

By the end of 1991 the prospect of peace for the region still seemed far off. The resistance group Hezbollah inflicted heavy casualties on the Israelis.

In 1991 the PLO broke away from the rest of the Arab world to support Iraqi dictator Saddam Hussein against a American-led coalition.

In October 1991 Israel met with delegations from Arab countries to renew the peace process. Secret talks in Oslo, away from the glare of the media, were started.

From these talks "The Declaration of Principles" was signed. It included:

- Israel recognising the PLO as the "representative of the Palestinian people"
- a phased withdrawal of Israeli troops from Gaza and the West Bank
- elections to be held for the new Palestinian Authority.

In May 1994 the new Authority was given control of Gaza and Jericho, and later the Palestinian area of the West Bank. This was perceived in Israel as a triumph in diplomacy for Foreign Minister Shimon Peres, as he relinquished less than was demanded.

Also in 1994 Jordan signed a peace treaty with Israel, settling disputes over their borders.

Israel's relations with Syria remained bitter. Opposition continued to be shown through violence on both sides. Despite this the Middle East Peace Accord was signed which stated that:

- Israel would withdraw from many West Bank towns
- talks on the status of Jerusalem, the West Bank and Gaza would start the following year
- Israel would maintain control of its civilian settlements
- the status of Hebron would be decided at a later date.

Fundamental differences still remained, including the status of Jerusalem.

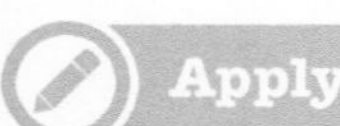

Make a timeline from 1973 to 1990. Mark on it the different attempts at finding a peaceful solution to the crisis.

How did the issue of Lebanon add to tensions?

- Fleeing from Egypt, 100 000 Palestinian refugees moved to Lebanon.
- From 1968 the PLO based itself in Lebanon, launching daily cross-border attacks on Israel. The Israelis carried out reprisal raids, the most spectacular in 1968 when Israeli troops landed at Beirut airport in helicopters, blowing up 13 Lebanese aircraft.
- The attacks, and reprisals, continued. After the Munich Olympics, Israel killed 118 suspected PLO guerrillas in a raid.
- In 1978 there was an invasion of 26 000 Israeli troops with the aim of taking control of southern Lebanon. This was in response to the PLO killing Israeli civilians in a bus hijack. In an attempt to restore peace, the UN sent a peacekeeping force.
- Following continued attacks the UN organised a ceasefire in July 1981.
- In June 1982 a large Israeli military force carried out a full-scale invasion with the aim of removing the PLO. Civilian casualties were high. The invasion saw the dispersal of the PLO.
- Public opinion condemned Israel for a massacre within the refugee camps.
- By 1985 the last of the Israeli forces had left Lebanon.

What was the impact of the Palestinian refugee issue?

Why were there so many Palestinian refugees?

- The events of 1947 and 1948 created a huge refugee crisis. Around 700 000 Arabs left their homes, going mostly to the West Bank, Gaza Strip, Jordan, Syria, or Lebanon. Most refugees were forced to live in camps in atrocious conditions
- Some argued that the Israelis carried out a deliberate policy of expulsion in order to occupy as much of Palestine as possible.
- Others believed that Arab leaders encouraged a mass exodus in order to gain public support for their cause.
- The refugee crisis worsened as a result of the 1967 war, as refugees fled from Sinai, Gaza, and the West Bank.
- Jewish settlers moved in so the refugees could not return.

Out of the bitterness and frustration arose the PLO (Palestine Liberation Organisation).

- The influx of Palestinian refugees into Lebanon created a new issue for Israel.
- The PLO used Lebanon as a staging post for attacks against Israel.
- The refugee problem was not confined to Lebanon: over 700 000 Arabs moved in the period—mostly to the West Bank, the Gaza Strip, Jordan, Syria, or Lebanon—and often lived in appalling conditions.

How effective was the PLO in promoting the Palestinian cause?

From its beginnings until 1976

- In 1959 Al-Fatah was formed, launching guerrilla raids into Israel.
- In 1964 Fatah and other resistance groups combined to form the PLO. The PLO was dedicated to using force to gain the return of the Palestinian homeland.
- After the defeat of the Arab states in the 1967 war the PLO increasingly deployed terrorist methods against Israel and Western companies.

At the same time Egypt and Syria were more concerned about lands they had lost and less concerned about the Palestinian refugees. This convinced many Palestinians that they were on their own in fighting for their homeland.

Following the war most refugees went to Jordan. Fatah began to recruit volunteers from the refugee camps. Raids into Israel increased, followed by full-scale Israeli reprisal attacks. At this stage thousands were joining the resistance fighters.

In 1968 Arafat became leader of the PLO. He wanted to limit raids to Israeli territory. Extremist Palestinians were unhappy with this and carried out attacks on other parts of the world.

Attacks carried out by the PLO and their results		
	Palestinian terrorism	**Outcome**
December 1968	An Israeli passenger plane attacked at Athens airport. One person was killed.	The Israelis attacked and destroyed 13 aircraft at Beirut airport.
September 1970	Four planes hijacked by Palestinian extremists. Three were flown to Dawson Field, Jordan. While passengers were set free, the planes were blown up.	Jordan feared international intervention. King Hussein decided to rid Jordan of the PLO. During Palestinian resistance 10 000 of them were killed. The PLO moved to Syria and Lebanon.
November 1971		In revenge for their expulsion, the Jordanian Prime Minister was murdered by Black September terrorists.
September 1972	Black September kidnapped 11 Israeli athletes taking part in the Olympic Games. All the athletes were killed.	The Palestinians got massive publicity for their cause. They failed to gain the release of 200 of their comrades who were in prison in Israel. The Israelis gained their revenge by carrying out reprisal raids, killing 200 refugees. The PLO became terrorists in the eyes of the Western press.
October 1972	Black September hijacked a Lufthansa plane, demanding the release of those jailed for their part in the Munich Olympics attack.	
1974		The Arab League declared the PLO to be the "sole legitimate representative of the Palestine people". Arafat was invited to speak at the UN.
July 1976	An Air France Flight was hijacked by PFLP (Popular Front for the Liberation of Palestine) terrorists and flown to Entebbe, Uganda. The 104 Jewish passengers were threatened with death unless Palestinian prisoners around the world were released. An Israeli special-forces unit killed the hijackers and rescued all but three of the hostages.	Again much publicity was gained but not the release of prisoners. People in Europe began to ask if the guerrillas were in fact terrorists or freedom fighters.

In the 1980s

- Following their expulsion from Jordan in 1970, most of the PLO forces moved to Lebanon and from there continued to launch attacks on Israel.
- In March 1978, following a PLO attack on a bus carrying Israelis that killed 34, Israel invaded south Lebanon.
- In June 1982 Israel again invaded Lebanon with the goal of destroying the PLO. By August the PLO had moved to Tunisia.

Although the PLO had been accepted as the voice of the Palestinians, the use of force against the Israelis had brought little success. Arafat turned to diplomacy, attempting to build better relations with the United States and Jordan.

Negotiations for a homeland came to nothing. In late 1987 a group of young Palestinians started an uprising against the Israelis. This was known as the Intifada. The Israeli forces faced demonstrations and stone throwing, which provoked a violent backlash from Israel. The Palestinian Intifada lasted until 1990, signalling there would be no peace in the region without a solution to the Palestinian problem. Israel responded with an "iron fist" policy. Over 500 Palestinians were killed and well-documented stories of Israeli brutality appeared in the national press. Foreign governments and the UN were publicly critical.

Israel and Arafat

After leaving Lebanon, Arafat changed his approach. He wanted a compromise with Israel but had to avoid appearing to be a traitor to the cause.

In December 1988 Arafat publicly accepted the existence of Israel and rejected the use of terrorism. The Americans, welcoming this change, invited the PLO for talks.

Some Israelis, including many in the Labor Party, welcomed the PLO change of policy. Others, including the Likud Party, were distrustful, claiming it was a trick and that the PLO had not really changed.

The Intifada was a violent uprising carried out over a period of years by Palestinians frustrated at their failure to secure a homeland for themselves. Israel responded with extreme violence and many hundreds were killed.

Why did Arab states not always support the Palestinian cause?

Jordan expelled the PLO in 1970. At the time the PLO were carrying out terrorist violence and King Hussein feared Israeli reprisals. He also thought the PLO was acting as though it ruled most of Jordan.

Lebanon: when the PLO attacked Israel, the Israelis responded with their own strikes. The Maronites of the government condemned them, refusing to accept the power of the PLO. The Muslims in the government gave their support to the PLO. This division led to a full-scale civil war in which 40 000 people were killed and large areas of Beirut destroyed. The war came to an end when the Syrians invaded to defeat and expel the PLO.

Egypt abandoned the PLO completely after making peace with Israel in 1979.

Why else did countries withdraw support?

- The financial costs involved in funding the PLO were a factor. An annual figure of $250 million was agreed in 1978 but only Saudi Arabia paid its share.
- The PLO caused problems for the governments of Arab states, including Jordan and Lebanon.
- Arafat's change of strategy towards a diplomatic route cost him the support of Syria.
- Arafat's decision to support Saddam Hussein in Kuwait was disastrous as it placed the PLO in opposition to a coalition of the United States and Arab states.
- The rise of extremists after 1991 led to several Arab states negotiating individually with Israel.

How did international perceptions of the Palestinian cause change over time?

The UN's view

The UN responded quickly to the initial problem, providing basic amenities. The policies of Israel and the conflicting demands of the Arab states made the work almost impossible. By the middle of the 1950s the operation effectively ceased as an acceptable solution could not be found.

The United States' view

By the end of the 1980s it was clear to the US administration that there could be no lasting peace in the Middle East without a resolution to the Palestinian issue. In 1993 negotiations started in Oslo between Palestinian and Israeli representatives.

Perceptions of the PLO

The upsurge of violence by the PLO led to widespread condemnation. Arafat was criticised for allowing the attacks. Fortunes improved when the PLO was recognised by the Arab League in 1974 and Arafat was allowed to address the UN. Backing from African and Asian states at the UN strengthened its position. The following years saw the PLO return to international isolationism as support from Arab states was lost.

Why has it proved impossible to resolve the Arab-Israeli issue?

Why has the UN been unable to secure a lasting peace?

The UN has made many attempts to resolve the situation.

- The UN tried to redraw the original partition plan, but again this was not accepted. A UN mediator was assassinated following this rejection.
- Between 1956 (the Suez War) and 1982 (the Israeli invasion of Lebanon) the UN acted as peacemaker, for example in ordering the British and French forces to leave Suez. More often the UN was ineffective as the United States held the position of power in the region. The UN's vulnerability was highlighted when prior to the Six-Day War it allowed Nasser to dictate that it withdraw from Egypt.
- After the Six-Day War the UN introduced Resolution 242. Unfortunately the issue of Israel's newly captured territories remained a stumbling block to negotiation. This resolution remains the basis of all attempts at peace.
- In 1973 the UN went to Egypt in a peacekeeping capacity.
- In 1978 the UN oversaw the withdrawal of Israel from Lebanon. This happened again in 1982 when protection and humanitarian aid was offered to the civilian population. However, the intervention of the United States gradually reduced the UN's role.
- The UN has been accused of having an anti-Israeli bias. This can be exemplified by Arafat's address in 1974 and a UN Resolution, passed in 1975, which equated Zionism with racism. This Resolution was revoked in 1991.
- Since the end of the Cold War the UN has failed to make a significant contribution to peace in the region. One reason for this is the increasing

American intervention in peacekeeping and the decline in Soviet influence.

- In addition, the nature of the conflict has changed from a conflict between nations to one between ethnic groups such as Fatah and Hamas (Islamic Resistance Movement). The second change has come with radicalisation of the conflict, with extremists on both sides showing a willingness to use violence.

How far have international diplomatic negotiations improved Israel's relations with Arab states and the Palestinians?

Attempt at peace	Details
1978 Camp David Accords	A framework for peace was agreed. Six months later Egyptian and Israeli leaders signed a peace treaty (the Camp David Accords) recognising the right of each other to live in peace within recognised, secure boundaries. The Accords were bitterly opposed by some Arab countries, including Libya and Syria. The agreement was a great breakthrough, but the Palestinian issue remained.
1991 Madrid Conference	The United States persuaded the Israelis and Palestinians to hold face-to-face talks. Progress was limited and disrupted by extremist violence.
1993 Oslo Peace Agreement	This paved the way for self-government for the Palestinians. The agreement was intended to build trust and confidence between Palestinians and the Israelis. Main issues to resolve in the next five years were: • the future of Jerusalem, as both wanted it as their capital • what would happen to the Jewish settlements in the occupied territories • whether Palestinian refugees would have a right to return to their homes from Lebanon, Jordan, Syria, and other Arab countries • the formation of an independent Palestinian state– not only was the idea of "independence" a significant issue but decisions were needed about what area it would cover: whether it should be be all, or part, of Palestine. If the state covered all of Palestine this would mean the end of Israel.
2000 attempt by President Clinton	Clinton attempted to revive the peace process but the talks ended with no significant progress over the issues outstanding from 1998.
2004 attempt by President George W Bush	Bush presented his "road map" for peace. This depended on an end to violence but the Palestinian bombings and Israeli assassinations continued.

Why do you think recent attempts to find peace have been attempted by the United States, rather than the UN? Write a bullet list giving your ideas.

How have divisions within Israel affected the peace process?

Political obstacles

- During 1948–67 the Labor Party dominated Israeli politics. The focus at that time was ensuring survival and building a democratic state.
- The election of Likud in 1977 gave greater prominence to religion.

- Both parties have maintained the hard-line stance in relation to denying the right of Palestinians to self-determination and the rejection of the notion of an independent Palestinian state.
- For much of the period neither party would negotiate directly with the PLO. This only changed in 1994.
- The aims of the two parties differ. Likud has consistently pursued a goal of creating a "Greater Israel", thus denying any claims over the West Bank, while the Labor Party believes Israel's security would be best served by achieving a peaceful resolution. The hard-line stance of Likud was highlighted by Menachem Begin during the Camp David agreement discussions, while Yitzhak Rabin's Labor Party brought a different approach to the discussion following the election of 1992.
- In 1996 the newly elected government opposed any further negotiations with Arafat and the Palestinian Authority.

Other obstacles to peace

- Ethnic groups came to Israel from Arab countries and Europe, many of whom did not speak Hebrew, and found it difficult to find work or to achieve senior positions. This discrimination was resented and they turned against Labor and towards Likud.
- There is a difference between religious and non-religious Jews and the link to the Orthodox Jews' belief in relation to the establishment of Israel being part of God's plans.
- In November 1995, following an Israeli peace rally in Tel Aviv, Prime Minister Rabin was shot dead. The assassin was a member of an Israeli group opposed to any peace with Palestinians. After a series of suicide bombings on crowded buses the hardliners gained more support.
- A second Intifada started in September 2000. The underlying cause was the frustration and anger of Palestinians in the occupied West Bank and Gaza. Limited progress had been made towards peace, and violent Israeli reprisals to Palestinian suicide bombings continued.
- In March 2002 Ariel Sharon launched "Operation Defensive Shield" in response to Hamas killing 29 Israelis in a suicide bombing. Raids were carried out inside Palestinian towns and refugee camps on the West Bank and Gaza. Targeted assassinations were introduced.

Produce a mind map to illustrate the difficulties faced in reaching a solution to the Arab–Israeli issue.

How have rivalries among Palestinians affected progress towards a settlement?

- The PLO was created in 1964. Its dominant group was Fatah. The aim of the organisation was to achieve a homeland for Palestinian people. Following early use of violence, Arafat turned to a more peaceful approach after leaving Lebanon.
- Hamas was formed in 1987, emerging as the most prominent rival to the PLO, pledging violence to achieve its declared aim—the destruction of Israel. Following the murder of 29 Palestinians in a mosque in Hebron, Hamas launched a campaign of violence against Israel, using mainly suicide bombers. They carried out bus bombings in early 1996, killing nearly 60 Israelis. Arafat was blamed for not controlling the militants and Israel moved troops back into Gaza and the West Bank. Curfews were imposed and border crossings closed between Israel and the occupied territories. This was to prevent suicide bombers but it prevented many Palestinians going to work.

- Hezbollah ("the Party of God") was formed in 1982. One of its aims was to turn Lebanon into an Islamic state.

Abbas replaced Arafat, who died in 2004, and in February 2005 he persuaded Palestinian militants to call a halt to their bombings. Israeli and Palestinian leaders met in Egypt and called a halt to violence. In the summer, Jewish settlers and troops withdrew from Gaza. The Jewish settlements on the West Bank still remained as a barrier to peace.

In the Palestinian elections of 2006, Hamas won a majority of seats but refused to recognise the state of Israel. As a result, Israel and the United States, together with many European governments, refused to have any dealings with Hamas.

In July 2006 Lebanese Hezbollah militants crossed into Israel and captured two Israeli soldiers. They demanded the release of hundreds of freedom fighters and Palestinians held in Israeli jails, but were refused. Israeli air attacks followed with the militants hitting back by launching missiles.

Almost 1000 Lebanese civilians were killed. In August the UN arranged a ceasefire and deployed a peacekeeping border force.

Prospects for peace

The main issue, the Palestinian problem, still remains at the centre of the conflict.

Peace will be difficult unless leaders of both sides control their extremists who are opposed to compromise. The Israeli extremists believe they must retain the West Bank while extremist Palestinians believe that all of Palestine should be returned, even if this means the destruction of Israel.

Unlike Egypt and Jordan, Syria has never made a peace treaty with Israel.

The Golan Heights, captured in 1967, remain in Israeli hands.

Full American support would be required to reach a resolution. The United States is the one country that is able to exert enough pressure and, as a giver of aid to Israel, would have a huge influence.

A settlement to the issue remains elusive. Violence continues between the two sides, with Palestine heavily supported by other foreign nations and Israel relying on American backing.

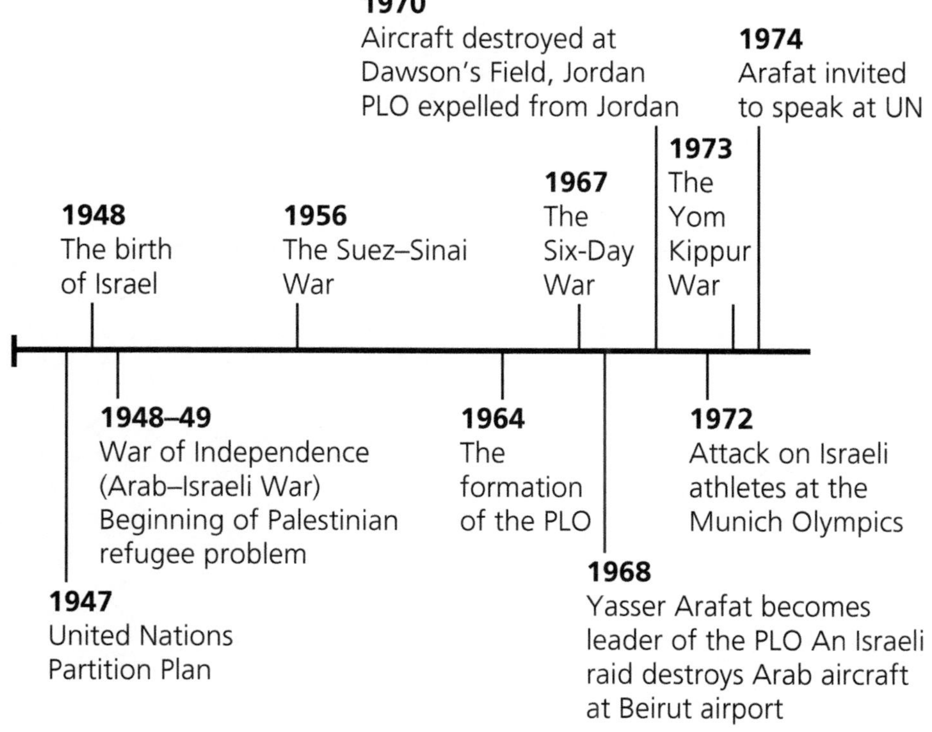

Review

1. What is the reason for the conflict between the Jews and the Arabs in Palestine? [4]
2. Describe events in 1956 that contributed to the Suez Crisis. [4]
3. What were the results of the Yom Kippur War of 1973? [4]
4. What political divisions within Israel have affected the peace process? [4]
5. Why was the Second World War significant for Palestine? [6]
6. Why did the Arabs reject the UN plans to partition Palestine? [6]
7. Why was Israel able to win the war of 1948–9? [6]
8. Why did the Six-Day War take place? [6]
9. Why were towns on the West Bank a source of tension between Israeli and Palestinians? [6]
10. Why were discussions at Camp David in 1978 important? [6]
11. Why was the PLO formed? [6]
12. How far was the 1948–9 war between the Jews and Arabs avoidable? Explain your answer. [10]
13. "The actions of the Palestinian Arabs in response to British actions were justifiable." To what extent do you agree with this statement? Explain your answer. [10]
14. How far, by the 1990s, had problems that existed between Israel and her neighbours been resolved? [10]
15. How significant was the role of the United States compared to that of the Soviet Union in Arab–Israeli conflicts? [10]
16. "It is impossible to resolve the Arab–Israeli issue." To what extent do you agree with the statement? Explain your answer. [10]

For further information review this section in the Student Book.

1. What was the Suez–Sinai war? **[4]**

Analysis

✓ Two well-developed points will secure the maximum marks here.

✓ The two points might relate to the causes of the conflict, such as tensions between Israel and Egypt. Alternatively, the points could focus on the conflict itself and how events played out.

✓ The role of other countries such as the United States or Britain is also credit-worthy, but needs tying to the Arab–Israeli issue.

Mark scheme

1 mark for each relevant point, additional mark for supporting detail, maximum 2 marks per point made.

Student answer

The Suez–Sinai War in 1956 was when the Soviet Union first helped the Arabs by providing them with military arms and equipment. Through other Warsaw Pact countries the Soviets supplied fighter planes, warships, bombers, and other armaments. It was seen as though the Soviet Union was directly providing help for the Arabs.

Examiner feedback

The student clearly knows a lot about the support provided by the Soviet Union for the Arab nations. However, the answer doesn't really address the question. It doesn't focus on the war or relate information well to the question asked. While knowledge is important, keeping the focus on the question is the crucial part of answering it well.
1 mark awarded.

2. Why was the Suez Canal important in the Israel–Palestine conflict? **[6]**

Analysis

✓ This answer needs to include well-explained reasons such as the following.

✓ The Suez Canal was important economically to Israel due to trade.

✓ It also was important because it provided the shortest ocean link between the Mediterranean and the Indian Ocean.

✓ This route was crucial for transporting oil-over 1 million barrels of oil moved along the canal every day to Western Europe and the United States. The canal was therefore important to the British, French, and Americans.

Mark scheme

Level 1:	general answer lacking specific contextual knowledge (1 mark)
Level 2:	identifies AND/OR describes reasons (2–3 marks)
Level 3:	explains ONE reason (4–5 marks)
Level 4:	explains TWO reasons (6 marks)

Student answer

The canal was important to Israel as it was the route used by the Israelis to reach the Port of Eilat, a crucial trade route. The canal was also important as it represented a wider clash between the Arab world and the West, which supported Israel. Egypt, an Arab nation, controlled the canal and regularly clashed with Israel over border disputes.

Examiner feedback

The student has correctly identified two reasons why the Suez Canal was important. However, these reasons need greater explanation to warrant a higher mark. 3 marks awarded.

3. "Oil played a major role in changing the nature of the Arab-Israeli conflict." To what extent do you agree with this statement? Explain your answer. **[10]**

Analysis

- ✓ When a factor is stated in the question it is important to explore that factor first. The stated factor then needs to be evaluated against other factors.
- ✓ Oil was definitely important in changing the way that the United States offered support to Israel, particularly after the Yom Kippur War.
- ✓ There are other reasons to explore though—the role of the UN, Israel's strength, the Arab nations working together, the refugee crisis, and also other countries' changing perception of Israel.

Mark scheme

Level 1:	general answer lacking specific contextual knowledge (1 mark)
Level 2:	identifies AND/OR describes reasons (2–3 marks)
Level 3:	gives a one-sided explanation (4–5 marks) or one explanation of both sides (4–6 marks)
Level 4:	explains both sides (7–9 marks)
Level 5:	explains with evaluation (10 marks)

Student answer

It can be argued that oil was definitely important in having an impact on the changing the nature of the Arab–Israeli conflict. Oil is a precious commodity throughout the world but the United States, as one of the key oil consumers, had a vested interest in keeping the supply routes open. When the United States supported Israel during the Yom Kippur war of 1973, Arab oil-producing states decided to reduce oil production and some went further—Saudi Arabia banned all oil exports to the United States. This had a significant impact on American policy and the Americans then pursued a peaceful end to the conflict with a joint United States–Soviet initiative arranged through the UN.

However, perhaps oil was less significant in the changing nature of the Arab–Israeli conflict. It doesn't feature as in issue in the conflicts of 1956 and 1967 and as the United States became more self-sufficient in oil production in the 1980s this was less of an issue.

Examiner feedback

The idea of oil as a factor is explored well. The answer offers good concrete evidence for this in citing the conflict in 1973. However, the answer is not well-balanced: the statement that oil is less significant needs to be followed by an exploration of other factors that played a major role in changing the nature of the conflict. 5 marks awarded.

Anschluss The term given to the unification of Germany with its neighbour, Austria.

Anti-Semitism Hostility to, prejudice, or discrimination against Jews, Judaism, and Jewishness.

The British Expeditionary Force (BEF) The British Army sent to fight in the Low Countries alongside France against Germany prior to the First Battle of Ypres on 22 November 1914. Unlike the conscripted forces of Germany and France, the BEF consisted of volunteer troops, who were renowned for their shooting skills.

Coalition government A government formed by multiple political parties promising to cooperate for the common good, reducing the dominance of an absolute party within that coalition. The usual reason for this arrangement is that no single party can achieve a majority in the parliament.

COMECON The Council for Mutual Economic Assistance – an economic organisation that comprised of the countries of the Eastern Bloc under the leadership of the Soviet Union between 1949–91, along with a number of communist states elsewhere in the world.

Containment The United States' government policy under Truman, based on the principle that communist governments would eventually collapse provided they were prevented from expanding their influence.

Enfilade fire First World War tactic of firing across the longest line of soldiers to create a "beaten zone" of fire which would entrap enemy troops as they attempted to progress forward.

Lebensraum The territory which a group, state, or nation believes is needed for its natural development – particularly relating to the post-First World War German concept of settler colonialism into eastern Europe.

Mandated territories The former colonies of defeated countries of the Ottoman Empire, such as Palestine, Syria and Mesopotamia, which were taken over by the League of Nations and legally transferred to other countries in the aftermath of the First World War.

"Morning hate" All sides in the First World War would attempt to prevent a surprise dawn raid by firing rifles and throwing grenades in the direction of the enemy; this was frequently repeated at dusk.

Mustard gas Chemical weapon used by the Germans for the first time at Ypres in 1917, its sulphuric compound created blisters, burning the eyes, skin, and lungs.

NATO The North Atlantic Treaty Organization – a military alliance of countries founded on 4 April 1949 to strengthen international ties between member states, especially the United States and Europe, and to serve as a collective defence against an external attack. It remains in existence today.

Operation Michael The German offensive launched in 1918 to push troops into France; also referred to as the Ludendorff Offensive or Spring Offensive.

"Race to the sea" The attempt by both sides to capture the Channel ports and outflank each other from the middle of September until the middle of October 1914.

The Ruhr The heavily industrialised area of western Germany named after the river that flows through the region. It was a huge centre for the coal, iron and steel industry.

Unrestricted submarine warfare A German naval strategy in the First World War which declared the waters around Great Britain to be a war zone; all shipping in that zone could be targeted, without warning.

Vietminh A communist-dominated nationalist movement, formed in 1941, that fought for Vietnamese independence from French rule.

Vietnamisation Support given by the United States to strengthen the South Vietnamese army to allow the gradual withdrawal of American combat troops from the Vietnam War.

Wall Street Crash The collapse of the New York Stock Exchange on 29 October 1929. The crash started the Great Depression and stock prices did not return to a similar level until late 1954.

The Warsaw Pact A collective defence treaty signed between the Soviet Union and seven Soviet satellite states of central and eastern Europe in Warsaw, Poland in May 1955, during the Cold War. Its members were the Soviet Union, Albania, Poland, Romania, Hungary, East Germany, Czechoslovakia and Bulgaria.